The Voice of Tomorrow

Harper Sato's Media Reforms

Sam Wang

ISBN: 9783100005540
Imprint: Telephasic Workshop
Copyright © 2024 Sam Wang.
All Rights Reserved.

Contents

The Rise of Harper Sato   **1**
A Star is Born   1

Bibliography   **11**
The Birth of "The Voice of Tomorrow"   14
Harper's Influence on Media Culture   26
Transforming the News Landscape   40
Overcoming Adversity   52

Harper Takes on Political Corruption   **65**
Unveiling the Truth   65
The Fallout from Harper's Investigations   78

Bibliography   **91**
Harper's Advocacy for Government Transparency   91
The Grassroots Movement Inspired by Harper   104
Harper's Enduring Influence on Politics   116

Bibliography   **121**

Harper's Quest for Climate Justice   **131**
Awakening to the Climate Crisis   131

Bibliography   **137**

Bibliography   **143**
Building a Coalition for Change   145
Challenging the Fossil Fuel Industry   158
A Global Movement for Climate Action   171

The Legacy of Harper's Climate Activism   182

Harper's Lasting Contribution to Society   195
The Evolution of Media in Harper's Wake   195
Political Transparency and Accountability   207
The Fight for Environmental Justice   220
Inspiring Future Innovators   231

Bibliography   237

Bibliography   243
Harper's Lasting Impact on Society   246

Index   255

The Rise of Harper Sato

A Star is Born

Early Life and Dreams

Harper Sato was born in a small town that was a microcosm of the larger societal issues that would later shape her worldview. From an early age, Harper exhibited an insatiable curiosity about the world around her. Growing up in a family that emphasized the importance of education and critical thinking, she was encouraged to ask questions and seek out answers. Her parents, both educators, instilled in her a love for learning and a belief in the transformative power of knowledge.

As a child, Harper often found herself captivated by stories told through various media—books, television, and radio. This fascination laid the groundwork for her future career in media. She would spend countless hours watching news programs, absorbing the way stories were framed and presented. It was during these formative years that she began to dream of becoming a journalist, envisioning herself as a voice for the voiceless and a champion for truth.

In her teenage years, Harper faced the harsh realities of societal inequities. Growing up in a diverse community, she witnessed firsthand the disparities in access to information and representation in the media. This exposure ignited a passion for social justice within her. She began to realize that the media played a crucial role in shaping public perception and influencing societal norms. The more she learned, the more determined she became to challenge the status quo.

One pivotal moment in her early life occurred during a high school journalism class. Tasked with reporting on local issues, Harper chose to cover the lack of resources at her school, which disproportionately affected students from lower-income families. Her article, which highlighted the struggles of her peers, garnered significant attention and sparked discussions among students, teachers, and administrators. This experience solidified her belief in the power of storytelling and the responsibility that came with it.

Theoretical frameworks surrounding media representation and social justice began to resonate with Harper as she delved deeper into her studies. The critical theory of media, particularly the work of scholars like Stuart Hall, illuminated the ways in which media can perpetuate stereotypes and reinforce power dynamics. Harper became acutely aware of the implications of media narratives on marginalized communities, further fueling her desire to pursue a career in journalism.

However, the path to her dreams was not without obstacles. Harper encountered skepticism from those who believed that a young woman of color could not succeed in the male-dominated field of media. These challenges only served to strengthen her resolve. She became involved in various extracurricular activities, including the school newspaper and debate team, honing her skills and building her confidence.

As she approached graduation, Harper faced a critical decision: where to pursue her higher education. She applied to several prestigious universities, ultimately choosing a school known for its strong journalism program. This decision was not merely about academic prestige; it was about positioning herself in an environment that would challenge her and allow her to grow as an aspiring journalist.

In her first year of college, Harper was introduced to the concept of media reform—an idea that would become central to her life's work. She learned about the importance of ethical journalism and the role of the media in democracy. Courses on media ethics and the impact of digital technology on journalism opened her eyes to the complexities of the industry. She became increasingly aware of the challenges posed by misinformation and the need for transparency in reporting.

Throughout her college years, Harper continued to cultivate her dreams. She sought internships at local news stations and online media outlets, where she gained practical experience and built a network of mentors and peers who shared her passion for reforming the media landscape. Each experience reinforced her belief that journalism could be a powerful tool for change, capable of holding those in power accountable and amplifying the voices of those often overlooked.

In summary, Harper Sato's early life was marked by a series of formative experiences that shaped her dreams and aspirations. Her childhood curiosity, combined with her exposure to societal inequities and the transformative power of storytelling, laid the foundation for her future endeavors in media reform. As she navigated the challenges of pursuing her dreams, Harper remained steadfast in her commitment to ethical journalism and social justice, setting the stage for her eventual rise as a leading voice in the media landscape.

Discovering Her Passion for Media

Harper Sato's journey into the world of media began not as a mere career choice but as a profound calling that emerged from her unique experiences and environment. Growing up in a multicultural neighborhood, Harper was exposed to a diverse array of voices and stories, each contributing to her understanding of the world. This rich tapestry of experiences ignited her curiosity about the power of media to shape narratives and influence public perception.

The Influence of Early Experiences

From a young age, Harper was captivated by the stories that unfolded around her. Whether it was the local news covering community events or her family's conversations about current affairs, she realized that media played a pivotal role in connecting people to their realities. The importance of representation became evident to her as she noticed the lack of diverse perspectives in mainstream media. This realization sparked her desire to enter the field, aiming to amplify voices that were often marginalized or overlooked.

Academic Pursuits and Critical Thinking

Harper's passion for media was further fueled by her academic pursuits. In high school, she excelled in subjects like journalism, sociology, and media studies. These disciplines not only honed her writing skills but also equipped her with critical thinking tools necessary to analyze media content. She became particularly interested in the concept of *media literacy*, which emphasizes the ability to access, analyze, evaluate, and create media in various forms. According to the National Association for Media Literacy Education (NAMLE), media literacy is essential for fostering informed and engaged citizens in a democratic society.

$$\text{Media Literacy} = \frac{\text{Access} + \text{Analyze} + \text{Evaluate} + \text{Create}}{4} \qquad (1)$$

This equation illustrates the multifaceted nature of media literacy, highlighting the skills necessary for effective engagement with media. Harper's commitment to understanding these components laid the groundwork for her future endeavors in media reform.

Internships and Real-World Experience

To gain practical experience, Harper sought internships at local media outlets. During her time at a community radio station, she learned the intricacies of broadcasting and the importance of ethical journalism. One particularly impactful experience involved covering a local protest advocating for environmental justice. This event not only solidified her belief in the power of media to effect change but also exposed her to the challenges faced by journalists in reporting on contentious issues.

Confronting Challenges in the Media Landscape

As Harper delved deeper into the media landscape, she encountered the harsh realities of the industry, including the prevalence of sensationalism and the pressure to conform to corporate interests. She was particularly disheartened by the phenomenon of *clickbait journalism*, where headlines were crafted to attract clicks rather than convey meaningful information. This realization fueled her determination to pursue a different path—one that prioritized integrity and authenticity in storytelling.

The Role of Mentorship

Recognizing the importance of mentorship, Harper sought guidance from established journalists and media professionals. One such mentor was a seasoned investigative journalist who had dedicated her career to exposing corruption and advocating for transparency. Through their discussions, Harper learned about the ethical dilemmas journalists often face and the critical role of accountability in media. This mentorship not only provided her with practical insights but also inspired her to envision a media landscape that could challenge the status quo.

A Defining Moment

The defining moment in Harper's journey came when she attended a media conference focused on the future of journalism. Listening to panel discussions about the impact of technology on media consumption and the rise of independent journalism, she felt a surge of inspiration. It became clear to her that the future of media was not just about reporting the news but about fostering dialogue, promoting social justice, and empowering communities. This revelation solidified her passion for media reform and set her on a path to becoming a leading voice for change.

Conclusion

In conclusion, Harper Sato's discovery of her passion for media was a multifaceted journey shaped by her early experiences, academic pursuits, and real-world challenges. Her commitment to ethical journalism and media reform became the foundation for her future endeavors, as she sought to create a platform that would amplify marginalized voices and challenge the dominant narratives in society. As she embarked on this path, Harper understood that the media's power could be harnessed not just to inform but to inspire and mobilize communities toward meaningful change.

Harper's Unique Perspective

Harper Sato's unique perspective on media reform is rooted in her diverse background, personal experiences, and a keen understanding of the socio-political landscape. This perspective not only sets her apart as a media innovator but also shapes her approach to addressing critical issues within the industry. In this section, we will explore the theoretical frameworks that inform Harper's vision, the problems she identifies within traditional media, and the concrete examples that illustrate her distinctive approach.

Theoretical Frameworks

At the core of Harper's perspective is the concept of *critical media literacy*, which emphasizes the importance of analyzing and evaluating media content rather than passively consuming it. This theory posits that media consumers must be equipped with the skills to discern bias, recognize misinformation, and understand the socio-economic contexts that shape media narratives. Harper's education in communications and her early exposure to media criticism instilled in her a deep appreciation for this framework.

Moreover, Harper draws from the *social constructivist theory*, which suggests that individuals construct knowledge and meaning through their interactions with others and their environment. This perspective informs her belief that media should not only reflect reality but also actively engage communities in shaping narratives that affect their lives. By prioritizing the voices of marginalized communities, Harper aims to create a media landscape that is inclusive and representative.

Identifying Problems in Traditional Media

Harper's unique perspective is also characterized by her critical examination of the problems inherent in traditional media structures. She identifies several key issues:

- **Consolidation of Media Ownership:** The concentration of media ownership in the hands of a few corporations limits diversity of thought and restricts the range of narratives available to the public. Harper argues that this consolidation leads to a homogenization of content, where sensationalism often trumps substantive journalism.

- **Misinformation and Fake News:** In an age of rapid information dissemination, the spread of misinformation poses a significant threat to informed public discourse. Harper is acutely aware of the challenges posed by social media platforms that prioritize engagement over accuracy, leading to the viral spread of false narratives.

- **Lack of Representation:** Traditional media often fails to represent the diverse voices and experiences of society. Harper highlights the underrepresentation of women, people of color, and other marginalized groups in media narratives, which perpetuates stereotypes and reinforces systemic inequalities.

Concrete Examples of Harper's Approach

Harper's unique perspective translates into actionable strategies that challenge the status quo. Here are some concrete examples that illustrate her innovative approach:

1. **The Launch of "The Voice of Tomorrow":** Harper's flagship program exemplifies her commitment to redefining media narratives. By featuring stories from individuals who have traditionally been silenced, she provides a platform for underrepresented voices. The show incorporates interactive segments where viewers can engage directly with the content, fostering a sense of community and shared experience.

2. **Collaborations with Grassroots Organizations:** Recognizing the power of grassroots movements, Harper actively collaborates with local organizations to amplify their messages. For instance, her partnership with environmental activists not only raises awareness about climate issues but also empowers communities to take action. This collaboration is rooted in her belief that media should serve as a tool for social change.

3. **Educational Initiatives:** Harper's commitment to critical media literacy extends beyond her programs. She spearheads educational initiatives aimed at equipping young people with the skills to navigate the media landscape. Workshops and online courses focus on analyzing news sources, understanding bias, and developing media production skills, thereby fostering a generation of informed media consumers and creators.

Conclusion

In conclusion, Harper Sato's unique perspective is a synthesis of critical media literacy, social constructivism, and a deep awareness of the challenges facing traditional media. Her identification of key issues such as media consolidation, misinformation, and lack of representation informs her innovative strategies for reform. Through her groundbreaking work, Harper not only challenges existing media paradigms but also inspires a new generation of journalists and media consumers to engage critically with the world around them. As she continues to navigate the complexities of the media landscape, Harper remains steadfast in her belief that a more equitable and inclusive media is not only possible but essential for a thriving democracy.

Navigating the Competitive Industry

The media industry is notoriously competitive, characterized by rapid changes in technology, audience preferences, and the emergence of new platforms. For Harper Sato, navigating this landscape was akin to trying to dance on a tightrope while juggling flaming torches—exciting, but also perilous. This section explores the challenges Harper faced in her ascent through the media ranks, the strategies she employed to overcome them, and the broader implications for future media professionals.

The Competitive Landscape

The media industry is defined by a few key characteristics that contribute to its competitive nature:

- **Market Saturation:** With the advent of the internet, the number of media outlets has exploded. This saturation creates a fierce battle for audience attention, as consumers are bombarded with content from traditional television, online news platforms, social media, and streaming services. According to a report by the Pew Research Center, as of 2021, nearly 86%

of U.S. adults get news from digital devices, a significant increase from just 59% in 2016 [1].

- **Technological Advancements:** The rapid evolution of technology has transformed how news is produced and consumed. From artificial intelligence (AI) in news curation to virtual reality (VR) in storytelling, media professionals must continuously adapt to stay relevant. A study by the Reuters Institute for the Study of Journalism indicates that 70% of journalists believe technology will significantly change their job in the next five years [2].

- **Economic Pressures:** Many traditional media organizations struggle with declining revenue from advertising and subscriptions, compelling them to cut costs, often at the expense of quality journalism. The Media Insight Project found that 65% of Americans believe that news organizations prioritize profits over journalistic integrity [3].

Harper's Strategies for Success

Faced with these daunting challenges, Harper Sato employed several strategies that not only helped her navigate the competitive media landscape but also positioned her as a leader in media reform.

1. **Embracing Digital Innovation:** Understanding the importance of digital platforms, Harper was an early adopter of social media to engage with her audience. By leveraging platforms like Twitter and Instagram, she could disseminate information quickly and interactively, thus building a loyal following. This approach aligns with the theory of *media convergence*, which posits that different media forms and channels are increasingly interconnected [4].

2. **Fostering Collaborative Networks:** Harper recognized that collaboration could amplify her impact. She built alliances with independent journalists, activists, and academic institutions, creating a network that shared resources and expertise. This cooperative approach is supported by the *network theory*, which emphasizes the significance of social connections in achieving collective goals [5].

3. **Prioritizing Ethical Journalism:** In an era of misinformation, Harper distinguished herself by adhering to high ethical standards. She championed transparency and accountability in her reporting, which not only garnered

public trust but also set a benchmark for others in the industry. The *social responsibility theory* of the press underscores the necessity for media to serve the public good, reinforcing Harper's commitment to ethical journalism [6].

4. **Adapting to Audience Needs:** Harper's keen understanding of audience preferences allowed her to tailor her content effectively. By utilizing data analytics to assess viewer engagement, she could produce content that resonated with her audience's interests, thus enhancing viewer loyalty. This strategy is rooted in the *uses and gratifications theory*, which suggests that audiences actively seek out media that fulfills their specific needs [7].

Challenges Faced

Despite her innovative strategies, Harper encountered numerous obstacles that tested her resolve:

- **Resistance from Established Media:** As a newcomer, Harper faced skepticism from traditional media outlets, which often viewed her progressive ideas as a threat. She experienced pushback from colleagues who were entrenched in conventional practices, leading to conflicts that required her to demonstrate resilience and assertiveness.

- **Financial Constraints:** Establishing a new media platform often comes with significant financial challenges. Harper had to navigate funding issues, seeking grants and sponsorships while maintaining editorial independence. This balancing act is crucial, as the *advertising paradox* suggests that reliance on advertising can compromise journalistic integrity [8].

- **Navigating Misinformation:** The proliferation of fake news and misinformation presented a formidable challenge. Harper found herself in a constant battle to verify facts and combat false narratives, a task that required both diligence and creativity. The *information overload theory* posits that an excess of information can hinder decision-making, making it vital for journalists to curate content effectively [9].

Conclusion

Navigating the competitive media industry is no small feat, especially for innovators like Harper Sato. Through her strategic use of digital platforms, collaborative networks, and commitment to ethical journalism, she not only overcame significant obstacles but also redefined the standards of media engagement. Her journey exemplifies the challenges and triumphs faced by future media professionals, highlighting the importance of adaptability, resilience, and integrity in a rapidly evolving landscape.

Bibliography

[1] Pew Research Center. (2021). *The Future of News*. Retrieved from `https://www.pewresearch.org`

[2] Reuters Institute for the Study of Journalism. (2021). *Journalism, Media, and Technology Trends*. Retrieved from `https://www.reutersinstitute.politics.ox.ac.uk`

[3] Media Insight Project. (2020). *The Role of News in American Life*. Retrieved from `https://www.mediainsight.org`

[4] Jenkins, H. (2006). *Convergence Culture: Where Old and New Media Collide*. New York: NYU Press.

[5] Wasserman, S., & Faust, K. (1994). *Social Network Analysis: Methods and Applications*. Cambridge: Cambridge University Press.

[6] McQuail, D. (2005). *McQuail's Mass Communication Theory*. London: Sage Publications.

[7] Katz, E., Blumler, J. G., & Gurevitch, M. (1973). Uses and Gratifications Research. *Public Opinion Quarterly*, 37(4), 509-523.

[8] McChesney, R. W. (2000). *Rich Media, Poor Democracy: Communication Politics in Dubious Times*. New York: New Press.

[9] Bawden, D. (2008). *Information Overload: A Review*. Progress in Information Science, 5(1), 1-16.

Breaking Through the Glass Ceiling

In the media industry, the phrase "glass ceiling" refers to the invisible barriers that prevent women and other marginalized groups from advancing to the highest levels of leadership and influence. Harper Sato's journey exemplifies the struggle against these barriers and her determination to break through them, not only for herself but also for future generations of women in media.

The Concept of the Glass Ceiling

The glass ceiling is often described as an unacknowledged barrier that limits the advancement of women and minorities in the workplace. According to [?], this term was first popularized in the 1980s, highlighting the challenges women face in climbing the corporate ladder despite their qualifications and capabilities.

$$\text{Advancement} = \text{Competence} + \text{Opportunity} + \text{Support} \qquad (2)$$

Where: - **Advancement** refers to the career progression within an organization. - **Competence** is the individual's skill set and qualifications. - **Opportunity** denotes the chances provided by the organization to rise through the ranks. - **Support** encompasses mentorship, sponsorship, and organizational culture that encourages diversity.

Harper's early career was marked by the persistent presence of this glass ceiling. Despite her remarkable talents and innovative ideas, she faced skepticism and bias from industry gatekeepers. The media landscape was predominantly male-dominated, with few women in positions of power, leading to a culture that often undervalued female perspectives.

Challenges Faced by Harper

Throughout her journey, Harper encountered various challenges that illustrated the systemic issues contributing to the glass ceiling:

- **Stereotypes and Bias:** Harper often faced gender-based stereotypes that questioned her capabilities as a leader. These biases manifested in both overt and subtle ways, such as being interrupted in meetings or having her ideas attributed to male colleagues.

- **Limited Representation:** The lack of female role models in senior positions made it difficult for Harper to envision her future in the industry. Research by [?] shows that the absence of representation can hinder women's ambition and confidence in pursuing leadership roles.

- **Work-Life Balance:** As a young woman aspiring to climb the ranks, Harper struggled with the societal expectations of balancing work and personal life.

The pressure to conform to traditional gender roles often conflicted with her professional aspirations, leading to feelings of inadequacy.

Strategies for Breaking the Glass Ceiling

Despite these challenges, Harper employed several strategies to break through the glass ceiling:

- **Building a Support Network:** Harper actively sought mentorship from established female leaders in media. This network provided her with guidance, encouragement, and invaluable insights into navigating the industry. Studies indicate that mentorship is crucial for women to advance in male-dominated fields [?].

- **Advocating for Diversity:** Harper became an outspoken advocate for diversity and inclusion within her organization. She pushed for initiatives that aimed to recruit and retain women and underrepresented minorities, emphasizing the importance of diverse perspectives in media.

- **Embracing Authenticity:** By embracing her unique voice and experiences, Harper was able to differentiate herself in a crowded field. Her authenticity resonated with audiences and helped her gain recognition as a thought leader. Research shows that authenticity can enhance leadership effectiveness, particularly for women [?].

Examples of Success

Harper's efforts to break through the glass ceiling culminated in several significant achievements:

- **Leadership Positions:** Harper eventually ascended to a senior leadership role, where she implemented policies that promoted gender equity and diversity within her organization. Her appointment served as a powerful example for aspiring female leaders.

- **Recognition and Awards:** Harper's groundbreaking work in media reform earned her numerous accolades, including recognition from industry organizations for her contributions to promoting diversity and ethical journalism.

- **Inspiring Others:** Through her platform, Harper inspired countless young women to pursue careers in media. Her story became a beacon of hope, demonstrating that it is possible to shatter the glass ceiling with determination and resilience.

Conclusion

Harper Sato's journey through the media landscape serves as a testament to the challenges and triumphs associated with breaking through the glass ceiling. By confronting biases, advocating for change, and embracing her authenticity, Harper not only advanced her own career but also paved the way for future generations of women in media. Her legacy is a powerful reminder that while the glass ceiling may be formidable, it is not impenetrable. With collective effort and unwavering determination, it can be shattered, allowing for a more equitable and inclusive media landscape.

The Birth of "The Voice of Tomorrow"

Harper's Vision for a Better Media

In an era where misinformation spreads faster than a cat video can go viral, Harper Sato emerged with a vision for a media landscape that not only informs but empowers. Her approach was grounded in the belief that journalism should serve as a beacon of truth, illuminating the darkest corners of society and holding power to account. This vision was not merely aspirational; it was a calculated response to the systemic failures of traditional media, which often prioritized sensationalism over substance.

Theoretical Framework

Harper's vision can be understood through the lens of the *Public Sphere Theory*, as articulated by Jürgen Habermas. Habermas posits that the public sphere is a space for critical debate and discourse, essential for a functioning democracy. Harper sought to reclaim this space by ensuring that media outlets operate as forums for diverse voices, fostering dialogue rather than division.

$$P = \frac{C}{D} \tag{3}$$

Where:

- P = Public engagement
- C = Quality of content
- D = Distrust in media

Harper recognized that increasing the quality of content (C) could enhance public engagement (P), thereby reducing the overall distrust in media (D). This formula encapsulated her belief that a commitment to integrity and ethical journalism could restore faith in the media.

Identifying the Problems

Harper's vision was also a response to several pervasive problems within the media landscape:

- **Misinformation and Fake News:** The rise of social media platforms has led to the rapid dissemination of false information, often outpacing fact-checking efforts. Harper understood that without intervention, this trend could undermine public trust in legitimate news sources.

- **Corporate Influence:** Many media organizations have become beholden to corporate interests, leading to biased reporting that favors profitability over journalistic integrity. Harper aimed to dismantle these structures by promoting independent media that prioritize truth-telling.

- **Lack of Diversity:** The media landscape has historically marginalized voices from underrepresented communities. Harper envisioned a media ecosystem that amplifies these voices, ensuring that stories from all walks of life are told and heard.

Concrete Steps Towards Change

To actualize her vision, Harper implemented several strategic initiatives:

- **Ethical Journalism Standards:** Harper established a set of ethical guidelines that prioritize accuracy, fairness, and accountability. These standards were designed to combat the sensationalism that had become rampant in mainstream media.

- **Community Engagement:** Understanding that journalism should be a two-way street, Harper initiated programs that encouraged community members to participate in the news-gathering process. This not only enriched the content but also fostered a sense of ownership among the audience.

- **Training Future Journalists:** Harper launched educational initiatives aimed at equipping young journalists with the tools they need to navigate the complexities of modern media. By emphasizing critical thinking and ethical reporting, she aimed to cultivate a new generation of media professionals committed to her vision.

Examples of Success

One of the first major projects under Harper's vision was the launch of "*The Voice of Tomorrow*." This platform was designed to be a model of transparent and responsible journalism. It featured segments dedicated to fact-checking, investigative reporting, and storytelling that highlighted marginalized communities.

For instance, during a critical election cycle, "*The Voice of Tomorrow*" produced a series of investigative reports uncovering the influence of dark money in political campaigns. These reports not only informed the public but also sparked discussions across social media platforms, leading to increased awareness and activism around campaign finance reform.

Furthermore, Harper's commitment to diversity was exemplified in her collaboration with various community organizations. Through partnerships, she ensured that stories from indigenous populations, people of color, and other marginalized groups were prominently featured, challenging the status quo of media representation.

Conclusion

Harper Sato's vision for a better media was not merely about improving journalistic practices; it was about redefining the role of media in society. By prioritizing truth, transparency, and diversity, she aimed to create a media landscape that empowers individuals and fosters informed citizenship. As she often stated, "A well-informed public is the cornerstone of democracy." Through her unwavering commitment to this vision, Harper not only transformed media practices but also ignited a movement that continues to inspire future innovators in the field.

Assembling a Dynamic Team

In the competitive landscape of media reform, Harper Sato understood that her vision for "The Voice of Tomorrow" could only be realized through the collaboration of a dynamic team. The assembly of this team was not merely a matter of filling positions; it was an intricate process that required careful consideration of skills, diversity, and shared values. This section explores the strategic approach Harper took to build her team, the challenges faced, and the theoretical frameworks that informed her decisions.

Theoretical Frameworks for Team Assembly

To effectively assemble her team, Harper drew upon several theories of team dynamics and organizational behavior. One such theory is *Belbin's Team Roles*, which identifies nine distinct roles that individuals can play within a team, such as the Coordinator, Shaper, and Completer-Finisher. By understanding these roles, Harper aimed to create a balanced team where each member could contribute their unique strengths while mitigating weaknesses.

Another relevant framework was *Tuckman's Stages of Group Development*, which outlines the phases that teams typically go through: Forming, Storming, Norming, Performing, and Adjourning. Harper anticipated these stages and prepared her team to navigate the inevitable conflicts and challenges that would arise, fostering an environment of trust and collaboration.

Identifying Core Values and Skills

Harper began by defining the core values that her team would embody. These values included integrity, creativity, and a commitment to social justice. She believed that a shared sense of purpose would not only motivate her team but also align their efforts towards the common goal of media reform.

In terms of skills, Harper prioritized a diverse set of competencies. She sought individuals with expertise in investigative journalism, digital media, data analysis, and community engagement. This multidisciplinary approach was crucial for addressing the multifaceted challenges of modern media landscapes, such as misinformation and corporate influence.

Recruitment Strategies

To attract top talent, Harper employed innovative recruitment strategies. She utilized social media platforms to reach potential candidates, leveraging her own growing influence to promote the vision of "The Voice of Tomorrow." Harper also collaborated with universities and media organizations to host workshops and seminars, creating a pipeline for emerging journalists and media reform advocates.

Furthermore, she emphasized the importance of inclusivity in her hiring practices. By actively seeking candidates from underrepresented backgrounds, Harper aimed to amplify diverse perspectives within the team. This commitment to diversity was not just a moral imperative; research has shown that diverse teams are more innovative and effective at problem-solving.

Building Team Cohesion

Once the team was assembled, Harper focused on building cohesion among its members. She organized team-building activities that encouraged open communication and collaboration. These activities ranged from brainstorming sessions to informal gatherings, fostering a sense of camaraderie and trust.

To facilitate ongoing development, Harper implemented regular feedback mechanisms. Utilizing *360-degree feedback* allowed team members to provide and receive constructive criticism, promoting continuous improvement and adaptability. This approach aligned with the principles of *Agile methodology*, which emphasizes iterative progress and responsiveness to change.

Challenges Encountered

Despite her strategic planning, Harper faced several challenges in assembling her team. One significant obstacle was the pervasive culture of skepticism towards media reform initiatives. Many potential candidates were hesitant to join a project that could expose them to backlash from established media institutions.

Additionally, Harper encountered difficulties in balancing the diverse perspectives within her team. While diversity was a strength, it also led to disagreements and differing priorities. To address this, Harper employed conflict resolution strategies, such as mediation and active listening, to ensure that all voices were heard and valued.

Examples of Success

The culmination of Harper's efforts in assembling a dynamic team was evident in the successful launch of "The Voice of Tomorrow." The show quickly gained traction, attracting a wide audience and sparking conversations about media ethics and accountability. The diverse backgrounds of the team members contributed to a rich tapestry of ideas and approaches, enabling the show to tackle complex issues with nuance and depth.

One notable example was the episode addressing misinformation during a major political event. The team collaborated to investigate the spread of false narratives, utilizing data journalism techniques to present factual information in an engaging manner. This episode not only resonated with viewers but also garnered praise from media critics, solidifying the team's reputation as a credible source of information.

Conclusion

Assembling a dynamic team was a pivotal step in Harper Sato's journey to reform the media landscape. Through a thoughtful approach grounded in theory, values, and innovative recruitment strategies, she created an environment where creativity and collaboration flourished. While challenges were inevitable, the team's resilience and commitment to their mission ultimately paved the way for impactful media reform. Harper's experience highlights the importance of strategic team assembly in driving meaningful change, serving as a model for future innovators in various fields.

The Launch of the Revolutionary Show

In the bustling media landscape of the early 21st century, where sensationalism often overshadowed substance, Harper Sato emerged as a beacon of hope with her groundbreaking show, *The Voice of Tomorrow*. The launch of this revolutionary program marked a pivotal moment not only in Harper's career but also in the evolution of media itself.

Conceptual Framework

The foundation of *The Voice of Tomorrow* rested on several theoretical pillars, including the *Public Sphere Theory* posited by Jürgen Habermas. According to Habermas, the public sphere is a space where individuals can come together to discuss societal issues, free from the constraints of government and commercial interests. Harper's vision was to create a platform that embodied this ideal, fostering informed discourse and empowering marginalized voices.

Challenges in Development

However, the journey to launch was fraught with challenges. The traditional media institutions were resistant to change, often viewing Harper's innovative approach as a threat to their established norms. The initial concept faced skepticism from executives who were more concerned with ratings than with fostering genuine dialogue. Harper's team encountered significant hurdles, including:

- **Funding Issues:** Securing financial backing for a show that prioritized ethics over sensationalism proved difficult. Many investors were hesitant to support a project that deviated from the formulaic approach of mainstream media.

- **Audience Expectations:** The challenge of attracting a viewership accustomed to clickbait headlines and superficial content loomed large. Harper understood that changing audience expectations would require innovative marketing strategies and compelling content.

- **Technical Limitations:** The production team faced technological constraints, including outdated equipment and limited access to advanced broadcasting tools. Overcoming these obstacles necessitated creative problem-solving and resourcefulness.

The Launch Event

The launch event for *The Voice of Tomorrow* was meticulously planned to generate excitement and anticipation. It took place in a vibrant urban setting, with a live audience composed of activists, journalists, and community leaders. The event featured:

- **A Panel Discussion:** Harper moderated a panel that included experts from various fields, discussing the role of media in shaping public opinion and the importance of ethical journalism.

- **Interactive Components:** Attendees were encouraged to participate through live polling and social media interactions, allowing them to voice their opinions on pressing issues.

- **A Launch Video:** A powerful video showcasing the show's mission and vision was presented, highlighting stories of individuals whose voices had been marginalized in traditional media narratives.

The launch garnered significant media attention, with coverage from various outlets praising Harper's commitment to redefining the media landscape. The tagline, "Where Every Voice Matters," resonated with audiences, setting the stage for the show's success.

Reception and Impact

Upon its premiere, *The Voice of Tomorrow* quickly gained traction, attracting a diverse audience eager for substantive content. The show featured a mix of investigative journalism, human interest stories, and expert analyses, all framed within the context of social justice and accountability.

The impact of the show was profound:

- **Audience Engagement:** Viewers reported feeling more informed and empowered to engage with societal issues. The show's interactive format encouraged active participation, with many taking to social media to discuss episodes and share their perspectives.

- **Raising Awareness:** Each episode tackled critical issues such as climate change, political corruption, and systemic inequality, prompting viewers to question the status quo and seek change in their communities.

- **Inspiring Change:** The show inspired grassroots movements, with many viewers mobilizing to advocate for policy changes and hold their leaders accountable. The ripple effect of Harper's work extended far beyond the screen, igniting a passion for activism among a new generation.

Conclusion

The launch of *The Voice of Tomorrow* was not merely the debut of a television program; it was the inception of a movement aimed at transforming the media landscape. Harper Sato's innovative approach and unwavering commitment to ethical journalism established new standards for the industry, proving that media could be a powerful tool for social change. As the show gained momentum, it became clear that Harper's vision was not just about reporting the news; it was about creating a platform for justice, equity, and the celebration of diverse voices.

In summary, the successful launch of *The Voice of Tomorrow* exemplified Harper's ability to navigate the complexities of the media industry while staying true to her core values. It set the stage for a new era in journalism, one where the voices of the marginalized were amplified, and the pursuit of truth was held in the highest regard.

Early Challenges and Triumphs

As Harper Sato embarked on her ambitious project, "The Voice of Tomorrow," she quickly encountered a myriad of challenges that tested her resolve and vision. The media landscape was fraught with obstacles, from financial constraints to the entrenched interests of established media conglomerates. This section delves into the early hurdles Harper faced and the triumphs that emerged from her tenacity and innovative spirit.

Financial Constraints

One of the most pressing issues Harper faced was securing funding for her revolutionary media initiative. Traditional media outlets often relied on advertising revenue, which posed a significant challenge for a new show aiming to prioritize ethical reporting over sensationalism. The initial funding came from a combination of small donations, crowdfunding campaigns, and grants from non-profit organizations dedicated to media reform. This funding strategy not only provided the necessary capital but also established a community of supporters who believed in Harper's vision.

$$\text{Funding} = \text{Crowdfunding} + \text{Grants} + \text{Small Donations} \qquad (4)$$

This equation illustrates the diversified funding model that became crucial for the survival of "The Voice of Tomorrow." By engaging with her audience and potential supporters, Harper was able to cultivate a sense of ownership among viewers, fostering a loyal community that would champion her cause.

Resistance from Established Media

Another significant challenge was the resistance from established media institutions. Harper's innovative approach threatened the status quo, leading to pushback from traditional media executives who viewed her as a disruptor. They employed various tactics to undermine her credibility, including smear campaigns and attempts to discredit her reporting.

For instance, during the launch phase of "The Voice of Tomorrow," Harper faced criticism for her focus on marginalized voices and underreported stories. Critics accused her of being too idealistic, arguing that her approach would not attract viewers in a ratings-driven industry. However, Harper remained undeterred, believing that authentic storytelling would resonate with audiences seeking deeper connections with the news.

Technological Challenges

In addition to financial and institutional barriers, Harper also grappled with technological challenges. The rapid evolution of media technology required her to adapt quickly to new platforms and formats. Initially, "The Voice of Tomorrow" struggled to establish a strong online presence, with technical glitches and platform integration issues hampering viewer engagement.

To address these challenges, Harper assembled a team of tech-savvy individuals who shared her vision. Together, they developed a robust digital strategy that leveraged social media platforms, podcasts, and live streaming to reach a broader audience. This innovative approach not only enhanced the show's visibility but also allowed for real-time interaction with viewers, creating a more dynamic and engaging experience.

Triumphs in Audience Engagement

Despite these early challenges, Harper celebrated several key triumphs that solidified the show's impact on media culture. One of the most significant accomplishments was the successful launch of a campaign called #VoicesUnheard, which aimed to amplify the stories of marginalized communities. This initiative not only garnered widespread attention but also fostered a sense of community among viewers who felt represented for the first time.

The campaign's success can be quantified through increased viewer engagement metrics, which demonstrated a growing audience eager for diverse narratives. For example, within the first six months of the show's launch, social media engagement increased by over 200%, and viewership ratings surpassed initial projections by 150%.

$$\text{Engagement Rate} = \frac{\text{Total Interactions}}{\text{Total Followers}} \times 100 \tag{5}$$

This equation highlights how effective engagement strategies can lead to a more connected audience, ultimately contributing to the show's growth and influence.

Building a Supportive Community

Harper's ability to cultivate a supportive community around "The Voice of Tomorrow" was instrumental in overcoming early challenges. By prioritizing transparency and open dialogue, she fostered trust with her audience, encouraging them to participate actively in discussions and share their own stories. This community-driven approach not only enriched the content of the show but also created a sense of belonging among viewers.

In conclusion, the early challenges faced by Harper Sato and her team were significant, yet they were met with resilience and innovation. Through strategic funding, technological adaptation, and a commitment to audience engagement, Harper transformed obstacles into opportunities. The triumphs of "The Voice of Tomorrow" set the stage for a new era in media, one that prioritized ethical reporting and the amplification of diverse voices, ultimately redefining the media landscape for generations to come.

Captivating Audiences Worldwide

In the rapidly evolving landscape of media, Harper Sato's show, *The Voice of Tomorrow*, emerged as a beacon of innovation and engagement, captivating audiences not only locally but also on a global scale. This phenomenon can be understood through various theoretical frameworks, including the Uses and Gratifications Theory, which posits that audiences actively seek out media that fulfills their needs for information, personal identity, integration, and social interaction [?].

Global Reach and Accessibility

From its inception, *The Voice of Tomorrow* was designed with accessibility in mind. Harper recognized that the traditional broadcasting model often excluded large segments of the population, particularly marginalized communities. By leveraging digital platforms, the show reached audiences in remote areas, where conventional media was either unavailable or biased. This approach aligns with the concept of *media democratization*, which advocates for equal access to information and diverse viewpoints [?].

The show's online streaming capabilities allowed it to transcend geographical boundaries. For instance, during its first season, viewership statistics indicated that over 50% of the audience was from outside the host country, with significant numbers tuning in from regions like Southeast Asia and Africa [?]. This not only broadened the audience base but also enriched the content with diverse perspectives, fostering a more inclusive dialogue.

Engaging Content and Storytelling Techniques

Harper's unique storytelling approach played a crucial role in captivating audiences. By employing narrative techniques that resonate emotionally, such as personal anecdotes and compelling visuals, the show effectively engaged viewers. Theories of narrative transportation suggest that when audiences become emotionally involved in a story, they are more likely to change their attitudes and beliefs [?].

For example, in one episode, Harper featured a segment on climate refugees, sharing the poignant story of a family displaced by rising sea levels. This personal narrative not only humanized the issue but also sparked discussions on climate justice across social media platforms, illustrating the power of storytelling in evoking empathy and mobilizing action.

Interactive Engagement and Community Building

Another significant aspect of *The Voice of Tomorrow* was its commitment to interactive engagement. Utilizing social media platforms, Harper encouraged viewers to participate in discussions, share their stories, and even propose topics for future episodes. This participatory model aligns with the concept of *media convergence*, where traditional media and new media intersect, allowing for greater audience interaction [?].

The show implemented live Q&A sessions, where viewers could ask Harper questions in real-time, fostering a sense of community and belonging. This interactive approach not only enhanced viewer loyalty but also created a feedback loop that informed future content, ensuring that the show remained relevant and responsive to audience needs.

Addressing Global Issues with Local Perspectives

Harper's ability to address global issues through local perspectives was another key factor in captivating audiences. By featuring grassroots activists and local leaders, the show highlighted the interconnectedness of global challenges such as climate change, political corruption, and social justice. This approach resonates with the *glocalization* theory, which emphasizes the importance of local context in global discourse [?].

For instance, an episode focused on plastic pollution featured local community leaders from coastal towns who were implementing innovative waste management solutions. By showcasing these local initiatives, Harper not only informed viewers about the global crisis but also inspired action at the community level, demonstrating that change is possible regardless of scale.

Measuring Impact and Audience Reception

To assess the impact of *The Voice of Tomorrow*, Harper's team employed various metrics, including viewer ratings, social media engagement, and audience surveys. The show's success was evident in its ratings, which consistently ranked among the top programs in its time slot, alongside positive audience feedback that highlighted the show's role in raising awareness and inspiring action.

The equation for measuring audience engagement can be represented as:

$$E = \frac{I + C + R}{T} \qquad (6)$$

Where:

- E = Engagement level
- I = Information retention
- C = Community interaction
- R = Response to calls to action
- T = Total viewership

In a survey conducted after the first season, 75% of respondents reported feeling more informed about critical issues, while 60% indicated that they had taken action based on the show's content, such as participating in local activism or engaging in discussions with peers [?].

Conclusion

In summary, Harper Sato's *The Voice of Tomorrow* captivated audiences worldwide through its innovative approach to media reform, engaging storytelling, and commitment to inclusivity. By harnessing the power of digital platforms, interactive engagement, and local perspectives, the show not only informed viewers but also inspired them to participate actively in the global discourse on pressing issues. Harper's vision for a better media landscape has undoubtedly left a lasting impact, paving the way for future innovators in the realm of journalism and activism.

Harper's Influence on Media Culture

Redefining Journalism Standards

In the era of rapid technological advancement and the proliferation of information, Harper Sato emerged as a pivotal figure in redefining journalism standards. The traditional paradigms of journalism, often characterized by objectivity, neutrality, and a rigid adherence to facts, were increasingly challenged by the complexities of modern media landscapes. Harper recognized that the evolution of journalism required a paradigm shift, one that embraced transparency, accountability, and inclusivity.

Theoretical Foundations

The foundation of Harper's approach can be traced back to several key theories in journalism ethics and media studies. One significant framework is the *Social Responsibility Theory*, which posits that media should serve the public good by providing accurate information, fostering public discourse, and being accountable to the communities they serve. This theory emphasizes the role of journalists not merely as reporters of facts but as active participants in shaping societal narratives.

Moreover, the *Critical Media Theory* highlights the importance of examining power dynamics within media institutions. It critiques the ways in which corporate interests can shape news coverage, often at the expense of marginalized voices. Harper's commitment to redefining journalism standards was deeply rooted in these theoretical frameworks, as she sought to challenge the status quo and promote a more equitable media landscape.

Identifying Problems in Traditional Journalism

The traditional journalism model faced numerous challenges that necessitated a redefinition of standards. Among these challenges were:

- **Misinformation and Disinformation:** The rise of social media and digital platforms has led to an unprecedented spread of misinformation. Journalists were often seen as mere conduits of information rather than as fact-checkers and truth-seekers. This resulted in a crisis of credibility, with audiences increasingly skeptical of news sources.

- **Lack of Diversity:** Mainstream media has historically underrepresented diverse voices, leading to a narrow portrayal of issues affecting various communities. This lack of representation perpetuated stereotypes and marginalized important narratives.

- **Corporate Influence:** The consolidation of media ownership has raised concerns about the influence of corporate interests on news coverage. Journalists faced pressures to prioritize sensationalism and profitability over responsible reporting.

- **Ethical Dilemmas:** Journalists often grappled with ethical dilemmas regarding privacy, sensationalism, and the balance between public interest and individual rights. The absence of clear ethical guidelines contributed to a culture of ambiguity in reporting practices.

Harper's Vision for Journalism

Harper's vision for redefining journalism standards was multifaceted, focusing on several key areas:

1. **Promoting Transparency:** Harper advocated for transparency in journalistic practices, encouraging news organizations to disclose their sources, funding, and decision-making processes. By fostering an environment of openness, she aimed to rebuild public trust in journalism.

2. **Prioritizing Ethical Reporting:** Harper emphasized the importance of ethical reporting, urging journalists to adhere to a strict code of conduct that prioritizes accuracy, fairness, and respect for individuals' rights. This included a commitment to fact-checking and rigorous editorial standards.

3. **Encouraging Diversity and Inclusion:** Recognizing the importance of diverse perspectives, Harper championed initiatives to increase representation within newsrooms. She believed that a diverse media landscape would lead to more comprehensive and accurate reporting.

4. **Engaging Audiences:** Harper promoted the idea of journalism as a dialogue rather than a monologue. She encouraged journalists to engage with their audiences, fostering a sense of community and collaboration in the pursuit of truth.

Examples of Redefined Standards in Practice

Harper's influence on journalism standards can be seen in several notable examples:

- **The Launch of "The Voice of Tomorrow":** Harper's groundbreaking show exemplified her vision for a new kind of journalism. By prioritizing investigative reporting, ethical storytelling, and the amplification of marginalized voices, the show set a new standard for media accountability.

- **Collaborations with Fact-Checking Organizations:** Harper partnered with independent fact-checking organizations to ensure the accuracy of information presented in her reporting. This collaboration not only enhanced the credibility of her work but also served as a model for other journalists.

- **Community Engagement Initiatives:** Under Harper's leadership, news organizations implemented community engagement initiatives that encouraged audience participation in the news-gathering process. This approach fostered a sense of ownership among viewers and contributed to more relevant and impactful reporting.

- **Diversity Training Programs:** Harper advocated for diversity training programs within newsrooms, emphasizing the need for journalists to understand the cultural contexts of the stories they cover. This initiative aimed to reduce bias and promote more nuanced reporting.

Conclusion

Harper Sato's efforts to redefine journalism standards represent a significant shift in the media landscape. By prioritizing transparency, ethical reporting, diversity, and audience engagement, she not only addressed the pressing challenges facing journalism but also laid the groundwork for a more responsible and inclusive media future. Her legacy serves as a reminder that journalism is not merely a profession but a vital public service that demands constant reflection, adaptation, and commitment to the truth.

Promoting Ethical Reporting

In an age where misinformation proliferates like weeds in a neglected garden, Harper Sato emerges as a beacon of ethical journalism. Promoting ethical reporting is not merely a noble aspiration; it is a critical necessity for the integrity of media and the health of democracy. Ethical reporting encompasses a framework of principles that guide journalists in their pursuit of truth, accuracy, and fairness, while also safeguarding the rights and dignity of individuals and communities.

Theoretical Foundations of Ethical Reporting

At the core of ethical reporting lies the concept of journalistic integrity, which can be understood through the lens of various ethical theories. One prominent theory is Kantian ethics, which emphasizes the importance of duty and adherence to universal moral principles. According to Kant, journalists have a duty to report the truth, as truth-telling is a categorical imperative that upholds the dignity of individuals and society as a whole.

Another relevant framework is utilitarianism, which posits that actions should be evaluated based on their consequences. In the context of journalism, this means that ethical reporting should aim to maximize societal well-being by providing accurate information that enables informed decision-making. By promoting ethical reporting, Harper advocates for a media landscape that prioritizes the public good over sensationalism or profit-driven motives.

Challenges to Ethical Reporting

Despite the clear theoretical foundations for ethical reporting, numerous challenges persist in the media landscape. One significant problem is the pressure to produce sensational content that captures audience attention, often at the expense of accuracy. This phenomenon is exacerbated by the rise of social media, where the speed of information dissemination can lead to the spread of false narratives before thorough fact-checking can occur.

Moreover, the concentration of media ownership poses a substantial threat to ethical reporting. When a handful of corporations control the majority of news outlets, there is a risk that editorial decisions will be influenced by commercial interests rather than journalistic integrity. This creates a conflict of interest that can undermine the credibility of news organizations and erode public trust.

Harper's Initiatives for Ethical Reporting

Recognizing these challenges, Harper Sato spearheads initiatives aimed at promoting ethical reporting within her organization, "The Voice of Tomorrow." One such initiative is the establishment of an internal ethics board, composed of experienced journalists and ethicists, tasked with reviewing content for adherence to ethical standards. This board serves as a safeguard against bias and misinformation, ensuring that all reporting meets rigorous ethical criteria.

Additionally, Harper emphasizes the importance of ongoing training and education for journalists. Workshops and seminars on ethical reporting practices are regularly conducted, covering topics such as fact-checking, source verification, and the ethical implications of reporting on sensitive issues. By fostering a culture of ethical awareness, Harper empowers her team to navigate the complexities of modern journalism with integrity.

Examples of Ethical Reporting in Action

To illustrate the impact of ethical reporting, consider the case of a high-profile political scandal involving allegations of corruption. In this scenario, many media outlets rushed to publish sensational headlines based on unverified information, leading to widespread public outrage and misinformation. However, Harper's team took a different approach. They conducted thorough investigations, verified sources, and sought multiple perspectives before publishing their report.

As a result, "The Voice of Tomorrow" produced a comprehensive and balanced article that not only presented the facts but also contextualized the implications of the scandal. This commitment to ethical reporting not only preserved the integrity of the journalism but also enhanced the public's trust in the media. The article became a reference point for other news outlets, demonstrating the power of ethical reporting to inform and educate the public.

The Importance of Accountability

Another critical aspect of promoting ethical reporting is accountability. Harper advocates for transparency in journalistic practices, encouraging journalists to disclose their sources and methodologies whenever possible. This transparency not only bolsters the credibility of the reporting but also allows the public to critically assess the information presented.

In instances where errors occur, Harper emphasizes the importance of issuing corrections promptly and transparently. This practice not only rectifies misinformation but also reinforces the media's commitment to ethical standards. By holding herself and her team accountable, Harper sets a precedent for responsible journalism that prioritizes truth and integrity.

Conclusion

Promoting ethical reporting is a cornerstone of Harper Sato's vision for a better media landscape. By grounding her initiatives in solid ethical theories, addressing the challenges of modern journalism, and fostering a culture of accountability, Harper paves the way for a new era of journalism that prioritizes truth, accuracy, and the public good. In doing so, she not only transforms her organization but also inspires a generation of journalists to embrace the principles of ethical reporting, ensuring that the voice of tomorrow remains a powerful force for positive change in society.

Challenging Misinformation

In an era where information is disseminated at an unprecedented speed, the challenge of misinformation has become a critical concern for media professionals and consumers alike. Harper Sato recognized early on that misinformation not only undermines public trust in media but also poses a significant threat to democratic processes and societal cohesion. This section explores the theoretical frameworks surrounding misinformation, the problems it presents, and the innovative strategies employed by Harper and her team to combat it.

Theoretical Frameworks

Misinformation can be understood through various theoretical lenses, including the **Information Disorder Model** proposed by Claire Wardle and Hossein Derakhshan. This model categorizes information into three types: misinformation (false information shared without harmful intent), disinformation (false information shared with the intent to deceive), and mal-information (true information shared to cause harm). Understanding these distinctions is essential for media reformers like Harper, as it informs the approaches they take in addressing each type.

Moreover, the **Social Media Ecosystem Theory** posits that social media platforms serve as both amplifiers and moderators of information. This dual role complicates the landscape of misinformation, as algorithms prioritize engagement over accuracy, often promoting sensational or misleading content. Harper's approach to challenging misinformation involved not only addressing the content itself but also scrutinizing the platforms that facilitate its spread.

Identifying the Problems

The proliferation of misinformation has led to several pressing problems:

1. **Erosion of Trust**: Public trust in media has significantly declined, with studies showing that a majority of Americans believe misinformation is a serious problem. According to a 2020 Pew Research Center survey, 59% of Americans say they often see conflicting reports about the same topic, leading to confusion and skepticism about credible news sources.

2. **Polarization**: Misinformation contributes to societal polarization, as individuals increasingly consume news that aligns with their pre-existing beliefs. This phenomenon is exacerbated by echo chambers and filter bubbles, where algorithms curate content that reinforces users' views, making it challenging for them to encounter diverse perspectives.

3. **Public Health Risks**: The COVID-19 pandemic highlighted the dangers of misinformation, particularly regarding health-related topics. False claims about the virus, vaccines, and treatments proliferated on social media, leading to public confusion and hesitancy, which had direct consequences on public health efforts.

Harper's Strategies

To combat misinformation effectively, Harper implemented a multi-faceted strategy that included the following components:

1. Promoting Media Literacy   One of Harper's key initiatives was the promotion of media literacy among the public. By educating audiences on how to critically evaluate sources, identify bias, and discern credible information from misinformation, Harper aimed to empower individuals to become informed consumers of media. Workshops, online courses, and interactive content were developed to engage diverse demographics, particularly younger audiences who are more susceptible to misinformation.

2. Fact-Checking Partnerships   Recognizing the importance of collaboration, Harper forged partnerships with established fact-checking organizations. By integrating fact-checking into her media platform, Harper ensured that claims made in news stories were subject to rigorous scrutiny. This not only enhanced the credibility of her outlet but also provided a model for other media organizations to follow. For instance, a collaborative project with FactCheck.org led to the development of a real-time fact-checking tool that provided context and verification for trending news stories.

3. Engaging with Technology Companies   Harper understood that addressing misinformation required engagement with technology companies that host and distribute content. She advocated for greater transparency in algorithms, emphasizing the need for platforms to prioritize accuracy over engagement. Her efforts included public campaigns and discussions with tech leaders, pushing for policies that would mitigate the spread of misinformation, such as labeling false information and promoting authoritative sources.

4. Amplifying Credible Voices   To counteract misinformation, Harper's platform made a concerted effort to amplify credible voices in journalism, academia, and public health. By featuring expert opinions and evidence-based reporting, her media outlet provided audiences with reliable information and context. This approach not only enriched the discourse but also served to diminish the influence of sensationalist narratives.

Case Studies and Examples

Several case studies illustrate the effectiveness of Harper's strategies in challenging misinformation:

- **The Vaccine Misinformation Campaign**: During the COVID-19 pandemic, Harper's team launched a comprehensive campaign to address vaccine misinformation. By partnering with health organizations and utilizing social media influencers, they disseminated accurate information about vaccine safety and efficacy. The campaign resulted in a measurable increase in vaccine uptake in targeted communities.

- **Political Misinformation During Elections**: In the lead-up to the elections, Harper's platform dedicated resources to fact-checking political advertisements and statements. By publicly debunking false claims and providing context, they played a crucial role in informing voters. A post-election analysis revealed that their efforts contributed to a more informed electorate, with a notable increase in public awareness about the importance of verifying political information.

Conclusion

Challenging misinformation is an ongoing battle that requires vigilance, innovation, and collaboration. Harper Sato's commitment to media reform and her proactive strategies have set a precedent for future media professionals. By promoting media literacy, forging partnerships, engaging with technology companies, and amplifying credible voices, Harper has not only addressed the immediate challenges of misinformation but has also laid the groundwork for a more informed and resilient society. As misinformation continues to evolve, so too must the strategies to combat it, ensuring that the public remains equipped to navigate the complex information landscape of the future.

Amplifying Marginalized Voices

In an era where media representation is often skewed towards dominant narratives, Harper Sato recognized the critical need to amplify marginalized voices. This endeavor not only aligns with her vision for a more equitable media landscape but also addresses the systemic inequalities that have long persisted in journalism. By prioritizing the stories and perspectives of underrepresented communities, Harper sought to reshape the media's role in society and promote social justice.

Theoretical Framework

The concept of amplifying marginalized voices can be understood through the lens of critical media theory, which posits that media institutions often reflect and reinforce societal power dynamics. According to Hall's (1980) encoding/decoding model, media messages are encoded with specific meanings by their producers and decoded by audiences in various ways. This process highlights the importance of representation, as marginalized groups frequently find their narratives misrepresented or ignored altogether.

Furthermore, the theory of intersectionality, introduced by Crenshaw (1989), emphasizes that individuals experience multiple, overlapping identities (such as race, gender, class, and sexuality) that shape their experiences and access to power. By amplifying marginalized voices, Harper aimed to create a more nuanced understanding of social issues that considers these intersecting identities.

Identifying Problems in Media Representation

The media landscape has historically marginalized voices based on race, gender, socioeconomic status, and other identity markers. Studies have shown that:

- **Underrepresentation in News Coverage:** Research indicates that people of color are often underrepresented in news stories, particularly in positions of authority or expertise (Dixon, 2008).

- **Stereotyping and Misrepresentation:** Marginalized groups are frequently depicted through stereotypes, which can perpetuate harmful narratives and reinforce societal biases (Entman, 1990).

- **Access to Media Platforms:** Many marginalized voices lack access to mainstream media platforms, limiting their ability to share their stories and perspectives (McChesney, 2000).

These issues contribute to a media environment that fails to reflect the diversity of society, leading to a skewed understanding of social realities.

Harper's Approach to Amplification

Harper's commitment to amplifying marginalized voices involved several strategic initiatives:

1. **Inclusive Storytelling:** Harper emphasized the importance of inclusive storytelling practices, ensuring that the narratives of marginalized communities were told by those who lived them. This approach not only fosters authenticity but also empowers individuals to reclaim their narratives.

2. **Collaborative Journalism:** By collaborating with grassroots organizations and community leaders, Harper facilitated partnerships that allowed for the co-production of media content. This method ensured that the voices of marginalized groups were not only included but were central to the storytelling process.

3. **Training and Mentorship:** Understanding the barriers to entry in the media industry, Harper established training programs aimed at aspiring journalists from marginalized backgrounds. These programs focused on skill development, mentorship, and providing access to resources, thereby cultivating a new generation of diverse media professionals.

4. **Utilizing Digital Platforms:** Harper leveraged digital media platforms to amplify marginalized voices, recognizing that social media can serve as a powerful tool for grassroots activism. By creating spaces where underrepresented individuals could share their stories, she democratized access to media production.

Case Studies and Impact

Several case studies illustrate the effectiveness of Harper's initiatives in amplifying marginalized voices:

- **The "Voices of the Unheard" Series:** This series featured personal stories from individuals in marginalized communities, addressing issues such as systemic racism, economic inequality, and gender discrimination. The series garnered significant attention and sparked national conversations about social justice.

- **Collaboration with Indigenous Activists:** Harper partnered with Indigenous activists to cover environmental issues affecting their lands. This collaboration not only highlighted the struggles faced by Indigenous communities but also brought attention to the intersection of environmental justice and Indigenous rights.

- **Youth-Led Climate Initiatives:** By amplifying the voices of young climate activists, Harper's media platform featured the perspectives of those most affected by climate change. This initiative not only empowered youth but also contributed to a broader movement for climate justice.

Challenges and Resistance

Despite her efforts, Harper faced significant challenges in amplifying marginalized voices:

- **Institutional Resistance:** Established media institutions often resisted changes to traditional storytelling practices, viewing Harper's initiatives as a threat to their authority and legitimacy.
- **Backlash from Powerful Interests:** Harper's commitment to amplifying marginalized voices frequently put her at odds with powerful interests that sought to maintain the status quo. This resistance manifested in attempts to discredit her work and silence her platform.
- **Sustainability of Initiatives:** Ensuring the sustainability of programs designed to amplify marginalized voices proved challenging, particularly in an industry driven by profit motives. Harper had to navigate funding constraints while maintaining the integrity of her mission.

Conclusion

Harper Sato's dedication to amplifying marginalized voices represents a transformative approach to media reform. By prioritizing inclusivity and collaboration, she not only challenged the dominant narratives within the media landscape but also fostered a more equitable representation of society. As the media continues to evolve, Harper's legacy serves as a reminder of the importance of amplifying diverse voices to create a more just and informed world.

Inspiring Future Journalists

Harper Sato's influence on the media landscape extends far beyond her own achievements; she has become a beacon of inspiration for aspiring journalists around the globe. Through her innovative approach to journalism and her unwavering commitment to ethical reporting, Harper has ignited a passion for truth-seeking in countless young minds. This section explores the ways in which

Harper has inspired future journalists, the challenges they face, and the theoretical frameworks that underpin their aspirations.

Theoretical Framework: The Role of Journalism in Democracy

At the heart of Harper's influence lies the fundamental theory that journalism serves as a cornerstone of democracy. According to the *Social Responsibility Theory*, the media has an obligation to act in the public interest, providing information that empowers citizens to make informed decisions. This theory posits that journalists are not merely reporters but custodians of democracy, tasked with holding power accountable and amplifying marginalized voices. Harper embodies this principle, demonstrating that journalism is not just a profession but a vital societal function.

Empowering Young Voices

One of the most significant ways Harper has inspired future journalists is by empowering young voices. She has actively engaged with students through workshops, mentorship programs, and public speaking events, encouraging them to explore their passion for storytelling. By sharing her own journey—filled with both triumphs and setbacks—Harper illustrates that the path to becoming a journalist is not linear but rather a mosaic of experiences.

For example, during a workshop at a local university, Harper shared her experience of investigating a high-profile corruption case. She emphasized the importance of perseverance, stating, "Every 'no' I encountered was just a stepping stone to the next 'yes.'" This candidness not only demystifies the challenges of journalism but also inspires students to embrace resilience as they pursue their careers.

Challenging Misinformation

In an era where misinformation runs rampant, Harper has made it her mission to challenge false narratives and promote media literacy among young journalists. She has initiated campaigns aimed at educating students about the importance of fact-checking and critical thinking. By collaborating with educational institutions, Harper has developed curricula that equip future journalists with the skills needed to navigate the complexities of modern media.

For instance, her partnership with the *Global Media Literacy Alliance* has resulted in the creation of a comprehensive online resource that provides students with tools to identify credible sources, discern bias, and understand the implications of misinformation. This initiative not only empowers young journalists but also fosters a more informed public, ultimately strengthening democracy.

Creating Inclusive Spaces

Harper's commitment to diversity in journalism has also inspired future journalists to advocate for inclusive media representation. Recognizing that diverse perspectives enrich storytelling, she has championed initiatives aimed at increasing the representation of underrepresented groups in the media.

Through her platform, Harper has highlighted the stories of marginalized communities, demonstrating the power of inclusive narratives. She often cites the work of journalists like *Ida B. Wells* and *George Seldes*, who paved the way for investigative journalism that addresses social injustices. By showcasing these historical figures, Harper instills a sense of responsibility in young journalists to continue this legacy of inclusivity and advocacy.

Real-World Examples of Inspired Action

The impact of Harper's mentorship is evident in the actions of her protégés. For instance, *Maya Chen*, a young journalist inspired by Harper's work, launched a grassroots campaign called *Voices Unheard*, aimed at amplifying the stories of immigrant communities facing discrimination. This initiative not only provides a platform for these voices but also encourages young journalists to engage in activism through their reporting.

Similarly, *Lucas Martinez*, a student journalist, credits Harper's teachings for his investigative piece on environmental injustices in his hometown. His work, which exposed the detrimental effects of industrial pollution on low-income neighborhoods, garnered national attention and sparked discussions about environmental equity. Lucas attributes his success to Harper's emphasis on ethical reporting and the importance of community engagement.

Conclusion: A Legacy of Inspiration

In conclusion, Harper Sato's legacy as an inspiring figure for future journalists is firmly rooted in her commitment to ethical journalism, empowerment, and inclusivity. By providing mentorship, challenging misinformation, and advocating for diverse representation, Harper has ignited a passion for truth-seeking in a new generation of journalists. As they navigate the complexities of the media landscape, these aspiring journalists carry forward Harper's vision of a more just and equitable society, ensuring that the voice of tomorrow continues to resonate with integrity and purpose.

In the words of Harper herself, "The future of journalism lies not in the stories we tell, but in the stories we choose to listen to." This ethos encapsulates the essence of her influence, inspiring young journalists to not only seek the truth but also to elevate the voices that have long been silenced.

Transforming the News Landscape

Shaking Up Established Media Institutions

The advent of Harper Sato's revolutionary media platform, "The Voice of Tomorrow," marked a significant turning point in the landscape of established media institutions. This section delves into the profound changes initiated by Harper, examining the theoretical underpinnings, the challenges faced, and the tangible examples that illustrate her impact on traditional media paradigms.

Theoretical Framework

To understand Harper's influence, we must first consider the theoretical frameworks that underpin media reform. Theories of media pluralism and democratic communication suggest that a diverse media landscape is essential for a healthy democracy. According to McQuail (2010), media pluralism ensures that multiple voices are represented, allowing for a more informed public. Harper's approach can be seen as a direct application of this theory, as she sought to dismantle monopolistic practices that stifled diversity in media representation.

Moreover, the concept of media hegemony, as articulated by Gramsci (1971), posits that dominant media narratives often reflect the interests of the powerful. Harper's mission was to challenge this hegemony by amplifying marginalized voices and promoting alternative narratives. In doing so, she aimed to create a more equitable media landscape that reflected the complexities of contemporary society.

Challenges to Established Norms

Despite her ambitious vision, Harper faced numerous challenges in shaking up established media institutions. One of the primary obstacles was the entrenched power of traditional media conglomerates, which often wield significant influence over public discourse. These institutions were resistant to change, viewing Harper's efforts as a threat to their longstanding practices.

Additionally, Harper encountered skepticism from within the industry. Many established journalists and media executives questioned her unconventional methods, perceiving them as disruptive rather than innovative. This resistance highlighted a broader tension between traditional journalistic standards and the evolving demands of a rapidly changing media landscape.

Examples of Disruption

Harper's impact on established media institutions can be illustrated through several key initiatives that exemplified her commitment to reform.

1. **The Rise of Independent Media** One of Harper's most significant achievements was the promotion of independent media outlets. By providing a platform for grassroots journalists and citizen reporters, she challenged the dominance of corporate media. For instance, the launch of the "Voices Unheard" segment on "The Voice of Tomorrow" showcased stories from underrepresented communities, highlighting issues often ignored by mainstream outlets. This initiative not only diversified the media landscape but also empowered individuals to share their narratives, fostering a sense of agency among marginalized groups.

2. **Ethical Journalism Standards** Harper's emphasis on ethical journalism practices further disrupted established norms. In response to the rampant spread of misinformation, she championed a rigorous fact-checking protocol that became a hallmark of her platform. This approach was not merely a reaction to the crisis of credibility in journalism; it was a proactive measure to restore public trust. By prioritizing transparency and accountability, Harper set a new standard for journalistic integrity that challenged the lax practices of many traditional media institutions.

3. **Audience Engagement and Interactivity** Another innovative aspect of Harper's approach was her focus on audience engagement. Recognizing the shift towards digital media consumption, she implemented interactive features that allowed viewers to participate in the news-making process. For example, the "Your Voice, Your News" initiative encouraged audiences to submit story ideas and questions, fostering a collaborative relationship between journalists and the public. This model not only democratized the news but also provided a counter-narrative to the passive consumption of information often perpetuated by established media.

Measuring Impact

To quantify the impact of Harper's reforms, we can employ the following equation, which assesses the relationship between media diversity (D), public trust (T), and audience engagement (E):

$$I = f(D, T, E)$$

Where: - I represents the overall impact of media reform, - D is the level of media diversity, - T is the degree of public trust in media, - E is the extent of audience engagement.

As Harper's initiatives led to increased media diversity through the rise of independent outlets, improvements in public trust due to ethical journalism practices, and heightened audience engagement via interactive platforms, we can observe a positive correlation in the impact of her reforms on the media landscape.

Conclusion

In conclusion, Harper Sato's efforts to shake up established media institutions were marked by a commitment to diversity, ethical standards, and audience engagement. By challenging the status quo and promoting a more inclusive media landscape, she not only transformed the way news was produced and consumed but also inspired a new generation of journalists to prioritize integrity and accountability. The legacy of her work continues to resonate, as the media landscape evolves in response to the demands of a more informed and engaged public.

The Fight for Advertising Transparency

In the rapidly evolving landscape of media, advertising transparency has emerged as a critical issue, particularly in light of the pervasive influence that corporate interests exert on news content. Harper Sato recognized early on that the lack of transparency in advertising practices not only undermined the integrity of journalism but also eroded public trust in media institutions. This section explores the theoretical foundations, the problems associated with opaque advertising practices, and the innovative strategies employed by Harper and her team to advocate for transparency in advertising.

Theoretical Foundations of Advertising Transparency

Advertising transparency can be understood through the lens of media ethics and accountability. Theories such as *stakeholder theory* suggest that media organizations have a responsibility to all stakeholders, including the audience, advertisers, and society at large. According to *stakeholder theory*, the interests of all parties must be considered, fostering an environment where ethical practices can flourish. This theory posits that transparency in advertising not only benefits consumers but also enhances the credibility of the media outlet itself.

Moreover, the *social contract theory* posits that media organizations operate under an implicit agreement with society, which includes the expectation of honesty and integrity in their operations. When media outlets fail to disclose their advertising relationships, they violate this social contract, leading to a breakdown in trust and credibility.

Problems Associated with Opaque Advertising Practices

The lack of transparency in advertising can lead to several significant problems:

- **Misinformation and Deceptive Practices:** Many media outlets engage in practices that obscure the distinction between editorial content and advertising. This can lead to audiences being misled about the nature of the information they are consuming. For example, sponsored content may be presented as news, causing viewers to accept biased information as factual reporting.

- **Conflict of Interest:** When media organizations rely heavily on advertising revenue from specific corporations, they may face conflicts of interest that compromise their journalistic integrity. This dependence can lead to self-censorship or the omission of critical coverage that could jeopardize lucrative advertising contracts.

- **Erosion of Public Trust:** As audiences become increasingly aware of the blurring lines between advertising and editorial content, trust in media organizations diminishes. A survey conducted by the *Pew Research Center* in 2021 revealed that 70% of respondents believed that news organizations were influenced by advertisers, highlighting the urgent need for reform.

Harper's Advocacy for Advertising Transparency

Recognizing these challenges, Harper Sato launched a multi-faceted campaign to promote advertising transparency. Her approach included:

- **Establishing Clear Guidelines:** Harper and her team developed a set of guidelines for ethical advertising practices that emphasized the importance of clear labeling of sponsored content. These guidelines were disseminated widely within the media industry, encouraging other organizations to adopt similar standards.

- **Public Awareness Campaigns:** To educate the public about the importance of advertising transparency, Harper initiated campaigns that highlighted the dangers of deceptive advertising practices. These campaigns utilized social media, public service announcements, and community engagement to reach a broad audience.

- **Collaborating with Regulatory Bodies:** Harper actively collaborated with regulatory bodies to advocate for stronger regulations on advertising practices. She lobbied for policies that would require media outlets to disclose their advertising relationships and provide clear distinctions between news and sponsored content.

- **Leveraging Technology:** Harper's team harnessed technology to create tools that would allow consumers to easily identify sponsored content. By developing browser extensions and mobile applications that flagged advertising, they empowered audiences to make informed choices about the information they consumed.

Case Studies and Examples

The impact of Harper's fight for advertising transparency can be illustrated through several key case studies:

- **The "AdWatch" Initiative:** One of Harper's most successful projects was the launch of the *AdWatch* initiative, which aimed to track and analyze the advertising practices of major media organizations. This initiative provided a platform for consumers to report instances of misleading advertising, fostering accountability among media outlets.

- **Partnership with Independent Media:** Harper partnered with independent media outlets to create a coalition focused on promoting advertising transparency. This coalition shared best practices and resources, helping smaller organizations implement ethical advertising standards despite limited resources.

- **Legislative Changes:** Harper's advocacy efforts contributed to significant legislative changes that mandated greater transparency in advertising practices. In 2023, a landmark bill was passed requiring all media organizations to disclose their advertising relationships prominently, a testament to the effectiveness of her campaign.

Conclusion

Harper Sato's unwavering commitment to advertising transparency has transformed the media landscape. By addressing the theoretical underpinnings of transparency, exposing the problems associated with opaque practices, and implementing innovative solutions, Harper has set a new standard for ethical advertising in journalism. Her legacy serves as a reminder that transparency is not just a regulatory requirement but a fundamental principle that upholds the integrity of the media and fosters trust within society.

Through her efforts, Harper has not only reshaped the dialogue around advertising practices but has also inspired a new generation of journalists and media professionals to prioritize transparency and accountability in their work. As we move forward, it is imperative that the fight for advertising transparency continues, ensuring that the media serves as a reliable source of information in an increasingly complex world.

Combatting Corporate Control of News

In an age where information is a commodity, the control of news by corporate interests poses a significant threat to the integrity of journalism and the democratic process. The phenomenon of corporate control over news media has been widely analyzed through various theoretical frameworks, including media concentration theory, propaganda model, and critical media studies. These frameworks highlight the systemic issues arising from the intertwining of media ownership and corporate interests, which ultimately undermines the public's right to unbiased information.

Theoretical Frameworks

One of the foundational theories in understanding corporate control of news is the **Propaganda Model** proposed by Edward Herman and Noam Chomsky in their seminal work, *Manufacturing Consent*. This model posits that mass media serves as a propaganda system that primarily serves the interests of elite groups, particularly large corporations and government entities. The model identifies five filters through which news passes, including the size and ownership of media companies, advertising as the primary revenue source, reliance on information from government and corporate sources, and the anti-communism and fear ideologies that shape public discourse.

Mathematically, this can be represented as:

$$N = f(O, A, I, F, C)$$

where N is the news output, O represents ownership structure, A is the influence of advertising, I signifies information sources, F denotes ideological filters, and C encapsulates the cultural context. The function f describes how these elements interact to shape the news narrative.

Problems Arising from Corporate Control

The problems stemming from corporate control of news are manifold. Firstly, there is a significant **concentration of media ownership**, where a handful of corporations dominate the news landscape. For instance, in the United States, companies like Comcast, Disney, and AT&T control vast segments of the media, limiting the diversity of viewpoints presented to the public. This concentration leads to a homogenization of content, where dissenting voices and alternative perspectives are marginalized.

Secondly, the reliance on **advertising revenue** leads to a conflict of interest. Media outlets often prioritize content that attracts advertisers over content that serves the public interest. This results in a sensationalized news cycle, where clickbait headlines and entertainment news overshadow critical reporting on issues like climate change, social justice, and political corruption.

Moreover, the reliance on **corporate-sponsored information** can create a cycle of misinformation. Journalists often depend on press releases and information provided by corporations, which may be biased or incomplete. For example, during the COVID-19 pandemic, many news outlets relied heavily on information from pharmaceutical companies, which raised concerns about transparency and the potential for conflicts of interest.

Examples of Corporate Control in Action

One notable example of corporate control influencing news coverage is the case of the 2010 Deepwater Horizon oil spill. Major media outlets, which had financial ties to the oil industry, were criticized for downplaying the environmental impact of the disaster. Investigative reports revealed that some news organizations received advertising revenue from BP, leading to questions about their objectivity in reporting on the spill.

Another example is the coverage of climate change. Research has shown that news organizations with corporate ties to fossil fuel companies often present climate change as a debatable issue, despite the overwhelming scientific consensus. This has contributed to public confusion and a lack of urgency in addressing the climate crisis.

Harper Sato's Response

Harper Sato recognized the dangers posed by corporate control of news and took a proactive stance against it. Through her platform, "The Voice of Tomorrow," she advocated for **independent journalism** and the establishment of media outlets free from corporate influence. She emphasized the importance of transparency in media ownership and called for policies that promote media diversity.

Sato also championed the idea of **public funding for journalism**, arguing that a well-informed public is essential for a functioning democracy. By supporting independent journalism through public grants, she aimed to reduce reliance on advertising revenue and corporate sponsorships, thereby allowing journalists to focus on investigative reporting without fear of reprisal from corporate interests.

In her efforts, Sato highlighted the role of **community-supported media** as a viable alternative to corporate-controlled news. By encouraging local communities to invest in and support their own media outlets, she aimed to foster a more diverse and representative media landscape.

Conclusion

Combatting corporate control of news is a critical issue that requires a multifaceted approach. By understanding the theoretical underpinnings of media concentration, recognizing the problems associated with corporate influence, and implementing innovative solutions such as public funding and community-supported media, advocates like Harper Sato are working to reclaim the integrity of journalism. As the media landscape continues to evolve, the fight for independent and ethical reporting remains more important than ever.

The Power of Independent Media

Independent media plays a crucial role in shaping public discourse, providing a platform for diverse voices, and promoting accountability in both journalism and governance. As traditional media outlets increasingly fall under the influence of corporate interests, independent media emerges as a bastion of truth, integrity, and social justice. This section delves into the theoretical underpinnings of independent media, the challenges it faces, and the transformative examples that highlight its power.

Theoretical Framework

The significance of independent media can be understood through various theoretical lenses. One of the foundational theories is the **Public Sphere Theory**, proposed by Jürgen Habermas, which posits that a vibrant public sphere is essential for democracy. Habermas argues that independent media serves as a platform for rational-critical debate, allowing citizens to engage with issues that affect their lives. This engagement is vital for informed citizenship and the functioning of a healthy democracy.

Another relevant theory is the **Media Dependency Theory**, which suggests that the more a person depends on media for information, the more influence that media has on their beliefs and behaviors. In contexts where mainstream media is biased or controlled, independent media becomes indispensable, as it provides alternative narratives and fosters critical thinking among audiences.

Challenges Facing Independent Media

Despite its importance, independent media faces numerous challenges that threaten its viability and effectiveness.

- **Funding and Sustainability:** Many independent media outlets struggle with financial instability due to a lack of funding sources. Unlike mainstream media, which often relies on advertising revenue, independent outlets frequently depend on donations, grants, or crowdfunding. This precarious financial situation can compromise their independence and editorial integrity.

- **Censorship and Repression:** Independent journalists often face threats from both governmental and non-governmental entities. Censorship, harassment, and even violence are common tactics used to silence dissenting voices. For instance, the case of *Maria Ressa*, co-founder of the independent news site Rappler in the Philippines, illustrates the dangers faced by independent journalists. Ressa has been subjected to multiple legal challenges and threats for her reporting on the Duterte administration's controversial policies.

- **Digital Disruption:** The rise of social media and digital platforms has transformed the media landscape, creating both opportunities and challenges for independent media. While these platforms can amplify independent voices, they can also lead to misinformation, echo chambers, and algorithmic biases that undermine the credibility of independent journalism.

Examples of Impact

Independent media has demonstrated its power through various impactful initiatives and movements.

- **The #MeToo Movement:** Independent media outlets played a crucial role in amplifying the voices of survivors of sexual harassment and assault, leading to a global reckoning with issues of gender-based violence. Investigative reporting by independent journalists uncovered systemic abuses in various industries, challenging powerful figures and institutions.

- **The Arab Spring:** Independent media, particularly through social media platforms, was instrumental in mobilizing protests and disseminating information during the Arab Spring. Activists used independent news outlets and social media to bypass state-controlled media, sharing real-time updates and organizing demonstrations against oppressive regimes.

- **Environmental Journalism:** Independent media has been at the forefront of environmental reporting, exposing corporate malfeasance and advocating for climate justice. Outlets like *Grist* and *Inside Climate News* have provided in-depth coverage of environmental issues, influencing public opinion and policy decisions.

Conclusion

The power of independent media lies in its ability to challenge the status quo, promote transparency, and foster civic engagement. As Harper Sato exemplifies, independent media can redefine journalism standards and hold power accountable. In an era where misinformation and corporate control threaten the integrity of news, supporting independent media is essential for the preservation of democracy and social justice.

The resilience of independent media in the face of adversity reaffirms its critical role in society. As we continue to navigate complex global challenges, the voices of independent journalists will be paramount in shaping a more informed and equitable world.

$$\text{Impact of Independent Media} \propto \frac{\text{Diversity of Voices}}{\text{Corporate Influence}} \quad (7)$$

This equation illustrates that the impact of independent media increases as the diversity of voices rises while corporate influence decreases, highlighting the need for a robust independent media landscape.

Harper's Legacy in Media Reform

Harper Sato's impact on media reform is a multifaceted legacy that transcends her immediate contributions to journalism. Her work has not only reshaped the landscape of media but has also laid the groundwork for future generations to engage critically with information. This section explores the key elements of Harper's legacy, focusing on her influence on journalistic standards, the promotion of ethical reporting, and the empowerment of marginalized voices.

Redefining Journalistic Standards

One of Harper's most significant contributions to media reform was her commitment to redefining journalistic standards. In an era where sensationalism often overshadowed factual reporting, Harper championed the principles of accuracy, fairness, and accountability. She argued that the core of journalism should be rooted in the pursuit of truth, a notion that resonates with the foundational theories of journalism ethics, such as those proposed by the Society of Professional Journalists (SPJ).

$$\text{Truth} + \text{Transparency} = \text{Trust} \quad (8)$$

In this equation, Harper emphasized that trust in media is built through a steadfast commitment to truth and transparency. Her initiatives included the establishment of rigorous editorial guidelines that mandated fact-checking and source verification, leading to a marked decline in the publication of misleading information.

Promoting Ethical Reporting

Harper's advocacy for ethical reporting was further exemplified through her campaigns against misinformation and disinformation. In a time when "fake news" became a pervasive term, she launched the "Verify First" initiative, which encouraged journalists to prioritize verification before dissemination. This initiative not only educated reporters but also engaged the public in understanding the importance of scrutinizing information sources.

For instance, during the 2024 election cycle, Harper's team uncovered a series of misleading advertisements funded by shadowy organizations. By employing investigative techniques rooted in ethical journalism, they exposed the truth behind these ads, which led to significant public outcry and a call for regulatory reforms in political advertising. This case exemplifies how Harper's ethical framework led to tangible changes in media practices.

Amplifying Marginalized Voices

Another cornerstone of Harper's legacy is her dedication to amplifying marginalized voices within the media landscape. Recognizing the historical underrepresentation of certain demographics, Harper implemented programs that provided platforms for diverse voices. This initiative was grounded in the theory of media pluralism, which posits that a diverse media landscape is essential for a healthy democracy.

Harper's commitment to diversity was operationalized through the creation of the "Voices of the Unheard" segment on her show, which featured stories from individuals in marginalized communities. This segment not only highlighted social injustices but also fostered a sense of community and solidarity among viewers. As a result, many grassroots organizations reported increased visibility and support, illustrating the profound impact of inclusive media representation.

Institutional Changes and Independent Media

In addition to her direct influence on journalistic practices, Harper's legacy also includes significant institutional changes within media organizations. She advocated for the establishment of independent media outlets that prioritize public interest over corporate profit. This movement aligns with the concept of media independence, which is crucial for fostering a democratic society.

Harper's efforts led to the creation of several independent news platforms that emerged in the wake of her reforms. These platforms not only adhered to her ethical guidelines but also actively engaged in investigative journalism that challenged corporate narratives. For example, the independent outlet "Truth Unfiltered," launched in 2025, became known for its in-depth investigative pieces that scrutinized corporate malfeasance, a direct result of Harper's influence.

A Lasting Influence on Future Generations

Harper's legacy is not merely confined to her achievements; it extends into the future through the inspiration she provided to aspiring journalists and media reformers. By establishing mentorship programs and workshops, she cultivated a new generation of media professionals who are equipped with the tools to challenge the status quo.

The impact of Harper's work is evident in the increasing number of journalism students who prioritize ethical reporting and social justice in their careers. Many of these students cite Harper as a pivotal figure in their decision to pursue journalism, demonstrating the enduring nature of her influence.

$$\text{Inspiration} \rightarrow \text{Action} \rightarrow \text{Change} \tag{9}$$

This equation encapsulates the essence of Harper's legacy—her ability to inspire action that leads to meaningful change in media practices and societal norms.

In conclusion, Harper Sato's legacy in media reform is characterized by her unwavering commitment to truth, ethical reporting, and the amplification of marginalized voices. Through her efforts, she not only transformed the media landscape but also inspired future generations to continue the fight for a more just and equitable society. The principles she championed remain relevant today, serving as a guiding light for those who seek to uphold the integrity of journalism in an increasingly complex world.

Overcoming Adversity

Facing Backlash from Powerful Interests

The ascent of Harper Sato as a transformative figure in media reform did not come without its share of challenges. As she began to challenge the status quo, she inevitably faced significant backlash from powerful interests entrenched in the traditional media landscape. This backlash was multifaceted, involving corporate entities, political figures, and even segments of the public who were resistant to change.

The Nature of the Backlash

The backlash against Harper can be understood through several theoretical frameworks, including the *Theory of Structural Power* and the *Public Choice Theory*. Structural power, as discussed by scholars such as Susan Strange, posits that certain actors in society have the ability to shape the rules of the game to their advantage, often at the expense of others. In Harper's case, established media conglomerates wielded their structural power to undermine her initiatives, fearing that her reforms would disrupt their monopolistic control over information dissemination.

Public Choice Theory, articulated by economists like James Buchanan and Gordon Tullock, provides another lens through which to view the backlash. This theory suggests that individuals in positions of power act primarily out of self-interest. Political figures aligned with corporate interests viewed Harper's advocacy for transparency and ethical reporting as a direct threat to their political capital and financial backing. As a result, they mobilized resources to counter her influence.

Examples of Backlash

One of the most notable instances of backlash occurred when Harper's investigative team exposed a major corporation's involvement in a scandal involving environmental violations. The corporation, fearing reputational damage and financial repercussions, launched a smear campaign against Harper. This included targeted advertisements that misrepresented her motives and questioned her credibility. The campaign was not just a public relations effort; it was a calculated move to intimidate her and deter others from pursuing similar investigations.

In another instance, Harper faced legal challenges from a powerful political figure who was implicated in corruption. This figure attempted to silence her through a series of lawsuits aimed at discrediting her work and hindering her ability to report on the issue. The legal strategy was based on the premise that prolonged litigation would drain her resources and divert her focus from her investigative work. This tactic is a common method employed by those in power to suppress dissent and maintain the status quo.

Theoretical Implications

The backlash Harper faced illustrates the dynamics of power and resistance in a democratic society. According to the *Social Movement Theory*, successful social movements often encounter opposition from established interests. This opposition can manifest in various forms, including legal challenges, media smear campaigns, and even threats of violence. The resilience of a movement, therefore, is often contingent upon its ability to navigate and counteract this backlash.

Moreover, Harper's experience aligns with the *Resource Mobilization Theory*, which emphasizes the importance of resources—both material and social—in sustaining movements against powerful adversaries. Harper's ability to garner support from grassroots organizations and the global community was crucial in countering the backlash. By mobilizing resources, she was able to amplify her voice and maintain momentum in her reform efforts.

Conclusion

Facing backlash from powerful interests was an inevitable part of Harper Sato's journey as a media reformer. The interplay of structural power and self-interest created a challenging environment for her initiatives. However, through strategic mobilization of resources and community support, Harper not only weathered the storm but also emerged as a resilient leader in the fight for media reform. This chapter of her biography serves as a testament to the complexities of advocating for change in a landscape often dominated by entrenched interests, and highlights the importance of solidarity and resilience in the face of adversity.

Threats and Attacks on Harper's Life

As Harper Sato's influence in the media landscape grew, so too did the threats against her life. The intersection of journalism and activism often places individuals in peril, particularly when they challenge powerful interests. This section explores the various forms of threats and attacks that Harper faced, illustrating the precarious balance between the pursuit of truth and personal safety in an increasingly polarized society.

The Nature of Threats

The threats against Harper were multifaceted, ranging from online harassment to physical intimidation. As she began to expose political corruption and corporate malfeasance, she became a target for those whose interests were threatened. The use of social media as a tool for both connection and conflict became evident as Harper received numerous threats via platforms such as Twitter and Facebook.

$$\text{Threat Level} = f(\text{Public Exposure}, \text{Political Climate}, \text{Corporate Interests}) \quad (10)$$

Where: - Public Exposure refers to the visibility of Harper's work. - Political Climate indicates the degree of political polarization. - Corporate Interests represents the extent to which corporate entities feel threatened by her revelations.

In Harper's case, as her public exposure increased, so did the threat level, resulting in a dangerous environment where her safety was compromised.

Physical Attacks

The most alarming threats materialized as physical attacks. On several occasions, Harper faced direct confrontations that escalated to violence. For instance, during a public speaking event aimed at discussing media ethics, she was confronted by a group of individuals associated with a corporation she had previously criticized. Eyewitnesses reported that the confrontation quickly turned aggressive, requiring security intervention to ensure her safety.

In one notable incident, as she left a press conference, an assailant attempted to physically intimidate her, shouting threats and attempting to block her exit. Fortunately, due to prior warnings and security arrangements, Harper was escorted to safety. This incident illustrated the tangible risks faced by journalists who dare to challenge the status quo.

Psychological Warfare

Beyond physical confrontations, Harper also endured psychological warfare. The constant barrage of online threats created a climate of fear and anxiety. The psychological impact of such harassment is profound, often leading to stress-related health issues, as outlined by the following model:

$$\text{Psychological Impact} = \alpha \cdot \text{Frequency of Threats} + \beta \cdot \text{Severity of Threats} \quad (11)$$

Where: - α and β are constants that represent the sensitivity of the individual to threats.

For Harper, the psychological toll was exacerbated by the isolation that often accompanies high-profile activism. The fear of potential attacks not only affected her mental health but also her ability to engage fully in her work, creating a paradox where the very act of speaking out could lead to silence.

Institutional Responses

In response to the threats against her, Harper sought to implement institutional measures to enhance her security. This included working with law enforcement and private security firms to develop a comprehensive safety plan. Additionally, she advocated for policies that protect journalists from harassment and violence, emphasizing the need for a supportive environment in which the press can operate without fear.

The lack of adequate protections for journalists is a systemic issue that has been highlighted by various organizations. According to the Committee to Protect Journalists (CPJ), the increasing number of attacks on journalists worldwide reflects a broader trend of impunity for those who threaten press freedom. Harper's case became emblematic of this crisis, drawing attention to the urgent need for reform.

Solidarity and Support

Despite the threats, Harper found solace in the solidarity of her peers and the global community. Organizations dedicated to press freedom rallied around her, providing support and resources. This collective action underscored the importance of community in the face of adversity.

For instance, after a particularly severe threat was made against her, a coalition of journalists and activists organized a public demonstration to show their support. The event not only raised awareness about the threats faced by journalists but also served as a powerful reminder that the fight for media reform is a shared struggle.

In conclusion, the threats and attacks on Harper Sato's life illustrate the dangerous landscape that journalists must navigate in the pursuit of truth. While her work has inspired countless others, it has also placed her in the crosshairs of those resistant to change. The resilience she demonstrated in the face of such adversity serves as both a cautionary tale and a beacon of hope for future innovators in the field of media and activism.

The Importance of Freedom of the Press

The concept of freedom of the press is a cornerstone of democratic societies and plays a pivotal role in ensuring accountability, transparency, and the dissemination of information. It allows journalists to investigate and report on matters of public interest without undue interference from government or corporate entities. This subsection delves into the theoretical frameworks surrounding press freedom, the challenges faced by journalists, and the real-world implications of a free press, particularly in the context of Harper Sato's media reforms.

Theoretical Frameworks

Freedom of the press is often grounded in several key theories of democracy and communication. One prominent theory is the **Marketplace of Ideas**, proposed by

John Stuart Mill. Mill argued that in a free society, all ideas should be allowed to compete in the public sphere, and through this competition, the best ideas will prevail. This concept underscores the importance of a diverse media landscape that enables various viewpoints to be heard.

Another relevant theory is the **Social Responsibility Theory**, which posits that the press has an obligation to serve the public good by providing accurate information, fostering public debate, and acting as a watchdog over government and powerful interests. This theory emphasizes that while the press should be free from censorship, it also carries a responsibility to ensure that its reporting is ethical and serves the interests of society as a whole.

Challenges to Press Freedom

Despite its importance, freedom of the press faces numerous challenges globally. These challenges can be categorized into several areas:

- **Government Censorship:** In many countries, government entities impose restrictions on what can be reported, often justifying such measures in the name of national security or public order. For instance, in authoritarian regimes, journalists may face imprisonment or violence for exposing government corruption or human rights abuses.

- **Corporate Influence:** Media consolidation has led to a few corporations controlling a significant portion of news outlets. This concentration can result in biased reporting, as corporate interests may prioritize profit over journalistic integrity. The case of Sinclair Broadcast Group, which has been criticized for promoting a conservative agenda across its local news stations, exemplifies this concern.

- **Threats and Violence Against Journalists:** Journalists often face physical threats, harassment, and even murder for their work. According to the Committee to Protect Journalists (CPJ), over 1,000 journalists were killed between 1992 and 2021, highlighting the dangerous environment in which many reporters operate.

Real-World Implications

The implications of a free press are profound. A robust press serves as a check on power, ensuring that government officials and corporate leaders are held accountable for their actions. For example, investigative journalism has played a crucial role in exposing corruption, as seen in the Watergate scandal, which ultimately led to the resignation of President Richard Nixon.

Moreover, a free press fosters informed citizenry, which is essential for the functioning of a democracy. The ability of citizens to access diverse and accurate information enables them to make informed decisions at the ballot box. In contrast, when press freedom is curtailed, misinformation can proliferate, leading to public distrust in institutions and a disinformed electorate.

Harper Sato's Advocacy for Press Freedom

Harper Sato's media reforms highlight the critical importance of press freedom in contemporary society. By advocating for ethical journalism, transparency, and the amplification of marginalized voices, Harper has positioned herself as a champion of press freedom. Her efforts to combat misinformation and challenge corporate control of news media resonate with the foundational principles of a democratic society.

Furthermore, Harper's work serves as a reminder that the fight for press freedom is ongoing. Her resilience in the face of threats and backlash underscores the necessity of protecting journalists and ensuring that they can operate without fear. As Harper navigates the challenges posed by powerful interests, her story exemplifies the courage and determination required to uphold the vital tenets of a free press.

Conclusion

In conclusion, the importance of freedom of the press cannot be overstated. It is essential for democracy, accountability, and social justice. The theoretical frameworks surrounding press freedom, coupled with the challenges faced by journalists, illustrate the complexities of maintaining an independent media landscape. Harper Sato's advocacy for press freedom embodies the ongoing struggle for a media environment that prioritizes truth, transparency, and the public interest. As future innovators and leaders arise, the lessons learned from Harper's journey will serve as a guiding light for those committed to upholding the principles of a free and responsible press.

Support and Solidarity from the Global Community

In an era where media figures often face intense scrutiny and backlash, Harper Sato's journey was notably bolstered by an outpouring of support from the global community. This solidarity not only served as a shield against the adversities she faced but also illustrated the interconnectedness of media reform and global activism.

The Power of Collective Action

The phenomenon of collective action is a key theoretical framework that helps explain the support Harper received. According to Mancur Olson's *The Logic of Collective Action*, individuals are more likely to contribute to a cause when they perceive a common interest and a potential for meaningful impact. Harper's commitment to media reform resonated with individuals and organizations worldwide who recognized the need for transparency, ethical reporting, and the amplification of marginalized voices.

$$C = \frac{n}{1 + \frac{b}{r}} \tag{12}$$

Where C is the level of collective action, n is the number of individuals involved, b is the perceived benefit of the collective action, and r is the perceived cost. In Harper's case, as the number of supporters grew (n), the perceived benefit (b) of her reforms increased, encouraging even more individuals to join the movement.

Global Movements and Networks

The rise of social media platforms has significantly altered the landscape of activism, allowing movements to transcend geographical boundaries. Harper's message was amplified through various global networks, including organizations like *Reporters Without Borders* and the *International Federation of Journalists*, which rallied behind her cause. These organizations not only provided moral support but also mobilized resources, organized campaigns, and facilitated dialogues on media freedom.

For instance, during a pivotal moment when Harper faced threats from powerful interests, a social media campaign titled *#StandWithHarper* gained traction, garnering thousands of tweets and posts from supporters around the world. This campaign not only raised awareness of her plight but also pressured political leaders to take a stand for press freedom.

Solidarity in Action: International Responses

The global community's solidarity manifested in various forms, from public statements by international leaders to grassroots movements advocating for media reform. For example, the European Parliament passed a resolution condemning the attacks on journalists, specifically citing Harper's case as emblematic of the broader issue of press freedom under threat.

$$R = P \cdot E \qquad (13)$$

Where R represents the resolution passed, P is the pressure from the public, and E is the engagement of external entities. The resolution served as a powerful reminder that the fight for media reform is a shared responsibility that transcends national borders.

Building a Culture of Support

Harper's experience highlights the importance of building a culture of support for journalists and activists. This culture is characterized by a shared understanding of the role of media in democracy and the necessity of protecting those who dare to challenge the status quo. Educational initiatives, workshops, and seminars organized by global organizations have played a crucial role in fostering this culture, encouraging individuals to advocate for media freedom in their own communities.

One notable example is the *Global Media Freedom Conference*, which brought together journalists, policymakers, and activists to discuss strategies for protecting media freedom. Harper was invited as a keynote speaker, where she shared her experiences and inspired attendees to take action. The conference not only provided a platform for dialogue but also resulted in actionable commitments from participating nations to uphold press freedom.

Conclusion: A Testament to Global Solidarity

The support and solidarity Harper Sato received from the global community underscore the notion that media reform is not an isolated endeavor but a collective struggle that requires the involvement of diverse stakeholders. As Harper continued to face adversity, the unwavering backing from individuals and organizations worldwide fortified her resolve and amplified her message.

In conclusion, the global community's solidarity with Harper serves as a powerful reminder of the potential for collective action to effect change. It illustrates that when individuals unite for a common cause, they can challenge entrenched systems and advocate for a future where media serves as a pillar of democracy rather than a tool of oppression. Harper's legacy, therefore, is not just her own but a testament to the enduring power of global solidarity in the fight for media reform.

Harper's Courage and Resilience

Harper Sato's journey through the tumultuous landscape of media reform and political advocacy is a testament to her extraordinary courage and resilience. In an era marked by rampant misinformation, corporate influence, and political corruption, Harper emerged as a beacon of hope, embodying the spirit of a new generation of activists who refuse to be silenced. Her story is not just one of triumph over adversity; it is a profound exploration of the human capacity for resilience in the face of overwhelming odds.

The Definition of Courage and Resilience

Courage can be defined as the ability to confront fear, pain, or adversity, while resilience refers to the capacity to recover quickly from difficulties. Together, these traits create a powerful combination that enables individuals to navigate the challenges of life. In Harper's case, her courage was evident in her willingness to challenge the status quo, while her resilience shone through in her ability to withstand the backlash from powerful interests.

Facing Backlash from Powerful Interests

As Harper began to gain traction with her media reforms and investigations into political corruption, she quickly became a target for those whose interests were threatened by her work. Powerful corporations and political figures launched a coordinated campaign to discredit her, employing tactics ranging from smear campaigns to legal threats. Harper's ability to confront these challenges head-on is a testament to her courage.

For instance, when a major corporation attempted to silence her by threatening legal action over a report she published exposing unethical practices, Harper did not back down. Instead, she rallied her team and the public to support her cause, turning the threat into an opportunity to highlight the importance of journalistic integrity. This incident exemplifies the psychological theory of resilience, which posits that individuals who view challenges as opportunities for growth are better equipped to overcome adversity.

Threats and Attacks on Harper's Life

The stakes escalated when Harper's investigations began to unveil deep-seated corruption within the government. As she delved deeper into the nexus between political power and corporate greed, the threats against her became increasingly severe. Reports of harassment, intimidation, and even physical threats against her life emerged, painting a chilling picture of the risks faced by those who dare to challenge the powerful.

In one particularly harrowing incident, Harper received a direct threat from an anonymous source warning her to cease her investigations or face dire consequences. Rather than succumbing to fear, Harper used this experience to galvanize her supporters and raise awareness about the dangers faced by journalists and activists. This act of defiance not only reinforced her courage but also highlighted the broader issue of press freedom, drawing international attention to her cause.

The Importance of Freedom of the Press

Harper's experiences underscore the vital role of a free press in a democratic society. The threats she faced serve as a stark reminder of the lengths to which those in power will go to maintain their control. Her resilience in the face of such adversity became a rallying cry for advocates of press freedom worldwide. According to the *Committee to Protect Journalists*, over 250 journalists were imprisoned globally in 2020 alone, demonstrating the precarious position of media professionals who dare to speak truth to power.

Harper's advocacy for freedom of the press was not merely a personal endeavor; it became a movement. She worked tirelessly to create alliances with other journalists, media organizations, and civil society groups to promote the importance of press freedom as a cornerstone of democracy. Her efforts culminated in the establishment of the "Harper Sato Foundation for Press Freedom," which supports journalists facing persecution and advocates for policy changes that protect media professionals.

Support and Solidarity from the Global Community

In response to the threats against her, Harper received an outpouring of support from both local and international communities. Activists, journalists, and ordinary citizens rallied around her, organizing protests and campaigns to raise awareness about the dangers of censorship and the importance of a free press. This solidarity not only bolstered Harper's resolve but also highlighted the collective power of individuals united by a common cause.

One notable example of this global solidarity was the "Stand with Harper" campaign, which saw thousands of people take to the streets in major cities around the world. The movement emphasized the importance of standing up for truth and justice, showcasing the interconnectedness of struggles faced by journalists globally. This phenomenon aligns with the theory of social identity, which posits that individuals derive a sense of self from their group memberships. Harper's ability to unite diverse groups under a shared vision exemplifies the power of collective action in the face of oppression.

Harper's Courage and Resilience in Action

Ultimately, Harper's courage and resilience are not just traits; they are the driving forces behind her impactful work. Her ability to confront powerful interests, endure threats, and galvanize global support has made her a symbol of hope for many. She has shown that resilience is not merely about enduring hardships but also about transforming challenges into opportunities for growth and change.

In conclusion, Harper Sato's journey illustrates the profound impact of courage and resilience in the pursuit of justice. Her story serves as an inspiration for future generations of activists, reminding us that even in the face of adversity, one person's commitment to truth and integrity can ignite a movement that transcends borders and empowers others to stand up for what is right. As we reflect on Harper's legacy, we are reminded that courage and resilience are not just personal attributes; they are essential qualities for anyone seeking to effect change in the world.

Harper Takes on Political Corruption

Unveiling the Truth

Investigating Political Links to Big Corporations

The intertwining of political entities and corporate interests has long been a contentious issue in democratic societies. As Harper Sato embarked on her journey to expose these connections, she faced a complex landscape filled with challenges and ethical dilemmas. This section delves into the methodologies employed by Harper and her team to investigate political links to big corporations, the theoretical frameworks that underpin these investigations, the problems encountered, and notable examples that illustrate the pervasive nature of corporate influence in politics.

Theoretical Frameworks

To understand the implications of corporate influence on politics, it is essential to consider several theoretical frameworks. One of the most prominent theories is the **Iron Triangle Theory**, which posits that a stable relationship exists between bureaucratic agencies, congressional committees, and interest groups, particularly corporations. This triangle creates a closed system where mutual interests are served, often at the expense of public welfare.

Interest Groups $\rightarrow$ Bureaucratic Agencies $\rightarrow$ Congressional Committees   (14)

Another relevant framework is the **Political Economy of Media**, which examines how media institutions are influenced by corporate funding and advertising. This theory highlights the role of media in shaping public perception and political discourse, often leading to a biased representation of issues that favor corporate interests.

Methodologies Employed by Harper

Harper Sato utilized a multi-faceted approach to investigate the links between political figures and large corporations. Her methods included:

- **Data Analysis:** Harper's team collected and analyzed vast amounts of data, including campaign finance records, lobbying disclosures, and corporate tax filings. By employing data mining techniques, they identified patterns of financial contributions that correlated with legislative outcomes.

- **Investigative Journalism:** Utilizing traditional investigative journalism techniques, Harper and her team conducted interviews with whistleblowers, former politicians, and corporate insiders. These narratives provided crucial insights into the clandestine interactions between corporations and government officials.

- **Public Records Requests:** Harper's team made extensive use of Freedom of Information Act (FOIA) requests to obtain documents related to government contracts, communications between politicians and corporate lobbyists, and any undisclosed meetings that could indicate collusion.

- **Collaboration with NGOs:** Partnering with non-governmental organizations focused on transparency and accountability, Harper's investigations were bolstered by the expertise and resources of these groups, which often had access to proprietary databases and legal expertise.

Challenges and Problems Encountered

Investigating political links to big corporations is fraught with challenges. Harper faced numerous obstacles, including:

- **Access to Information:** Many corporations employ legal tactics to shield their dealings from public scrutiny, including non-disclosure agreements and lobbying to weaken transparency laws. This made it difficult for Harper to obtain critical information.

- **Political Retaliation:** As Harper began to uncover significant links between politicians and corporations, she faced threats and intimidation from both corporate entities and political allies of those implicated. This highlighted the risks associated with investigative journalism in the current political climate.

- **Public Skepticism:** Despite the evidence gathered, Harper encountered public skepticism regarding the credibility of her findings. Misinformation campaigns orchestrated by powerful interests aimed to discredit her work and undermine public trust in her investigations.

Notable Examples

Several high-profile cases exemplify the type of political-corporate links that Harper sought to expose:

- **The Case of the Pharmaceutical Industry:** Harper investigated the pharmaceutical industry's lobbying efforts to influence healthcare legislation. Her team uncovered evidence of substantial campaign contributions made to key legislators who subsequently voted in favor of legislation that benefited the industry, including measures that limited drug price negotiations.

$$\text{Legislation} \propto \text{Campaign Contributions} \qquad (15)$$

- **Environmental Regulations and Fossil Fuels:** Another investigation revealed how fossil fuel companies funded political campaigns to secure favorable regulatory environments. Harper's findings illustrated a direct correlation between campaign donations and the weakening of environmental protections.

$$\text{Environmental Protections} \downarrow \text{ as Campaign Donations} \uparrow \qquad (16)$$

- **Tech Giants and Privacy Legislation:** Harper's team also focused on the influence of major tech companies on privacy legislation. By tracing the flow of money from these corporations to lawmakers, they exposed how corporate interests often dictated the terms of privacy protections, leading to legislation that favored corporate data collection practices over individual rights.

Conclusion

The investigation of political links to big corporations is not merely an academic exercise; it is a crucial endeavor that holds the potential to reshape public policy and restore trust in democratic institutions. Harper Sato's relentless pursuit of truth in the face of adversity exemplifies the role of investigative journalism in promoting transparency and accountability. By employing rigorous methodologies and confronting formidable challenges, Harper's work illuminates the intricate web of influence that shapes our political landscape and underscores the necessity for ongoing vigilance in the defense of democratic principles.

Exposing Government Cover-ups

The act of exposing government cover-ups is a critical aspect of investigative journalism, particularly in the context of political corruption. Harper Sato, through her relentless pursuit of truth, became a beacon of hope for those disillusioned by the opacity of governmental operations. This subsection delves into the theories, problems, and notable examples surrounding the exposure of government cover-ups, illustrating the profound impact of Harper's work on public consciousness and political accountability.

Theoretical Framework

The foundation of exposing government cover-ups lies in the principles of transparency and accountability, which are essential for a functioning democracy. Theories of democratic governance emphasize the role of an informed citizenry in holding power to account. According to [?], a democracy thrives when citizens have access to information that enables them to make informed decisions. This aligns with the concept of the *public sphere*, as articulated by [?], where open discourse is necessary for the health of democratic processes.

In this context, investigative journalism serves as a watchdog, tasked with uncovering hidden truths that powerful entities may wish to conceal. The *fourth estate* theory posits that the press acts as a check on government power, ensuring that citizens are informed about potential abuses. This theoretical framework underscores the significance of Harper's investigations into government cover-ups, as they not only reveal misconduct but also empower the public to demand accountability.

Challenges in Exposing Cover-ups

Despite the noble intentions behind investigative journalism, exposing government cover-ups presents numerous challenges:

- **Access to Information:** One of the primary obstacles is the lack of access to public records. Government entities often employ tactics to withhold information, citing national security or privacy concerns. The Freedom of Information Act (FOIA) is a tool that journalists like Harper utilize, yet it is frequently met with bureaucratic delays and redactions.

- **Threats to Journalists:** Investigative journalists often face intimidation and threats from powerful interests seeking to silence dissent. Harper's own experiences with threats highlight the personal risks involved in exposing government malfeasance.

- **Public Apathy:** In an era of information overload, the public may become desensitized to political scandals, leading to apathy towards government accountability. Harper's challenge was not only to uncover the truth but also to engage the public in meaningful discourse about these issues.

Notable Examples of Government Cover-ups

Several high-profile cases illustrate the importance of exposing government cover-ups and the impact of Harper's work:

- **Watergate Scandal:** One of the most notorious government cover-ups in U.S. history, the Watergate scandal involved a break-in at the Democratic National Committee headquarters and subsequent attempts by the Nixon administration to cover it up. Investigative journalists Bob Woodward and Carl Bernstein played a pivotal role in uncovering the truth, leading to President Nixon's resignation. This case exemplifies the power of journalism in holding government officials accountable and restoring public trust.

- **The Pentagon Papers:** In 1971, Daniel Ellsberg leaked classified documents detailing the U.S. government's misleading portrayal of the Vietnam War. The subsequent publication of the Pentagon Papers by The New York Times revealed the extent of government deception, igniting public outrage and skepticism towards official narratives. Harper often cited this case as a source of inspiration, emphasizing the necessity of transparency in governance.

- **Flint Water Crisis:** In Flint, Michigan, government officials attempted to cover up the contamination of the city's water supply, which resulted in a public health crisis. Investigative journalism played a crucial role in bringing the issue to light, ultimately leading to legal actions against those responsible. Harper's reporting on similar environmental injustices underscored the interconnectedness of governmental accountability and public health.

Impact of Harper's Investigations

Harper's commitment to exposing government cover-ups resonated with audiences, fostering a culture of accountability and transparency. Her investigations not only revealed systemic corruption but also empowered citizens to demand change. The following impacts can be observed:

- **Increased Public Awareness:** Harper's work raised awareness about government cover-ups, prompting public discourse on the importance of transparency. Her ability to present complex issues in an accessible manner allowed citizens to engage with critical topics.

- **Policy Changes:** The fallout from Harper's investigations led to calls for legislative reforms aimed at enhancing government transparency. Initiatives such as the strengthening of FOIA provisions and the establishment of independent oversight bodies emerged as a direct response to her findings.

- **A New Generation of Journalists:** Harper's influence inspired a new wave of journalists dedicated to investigative reporting. Her mentorship and advocacy for ethical journalism practices fostered a generation committed to uncovering the truth, ensuring that the fight for accountability continues.

Conclusion

Exposing government cover-ups is an essential function of journalism that upholds the principles of democracy. Harper Sato's fearless investigations not only illuminated the dark corners of political corruption but also empowered citizens to demand accountability from their leaders. As the landscape of media continues to evolve, the need for transparency remains paramount, and Harper's legacy serves as a guiding light for future innovators in the field of journalism.

Uncovering Bribery and Kickback Schemes

In the intricate web of political maneuvering, bribery and kickback schemes often lurk in the shadows, undermining the integrity of democratic institutions. Harper Sato, with her unwavering commitment to uncovering the truth, embarked on a relentless investigation into these clandestine practices that have plagued governance at various levels.

Theoretical Framework

Bribery can be defined as the act of offering something of value, typically money, to influence the actions of an official in a position of authority. Kickback schemes, on the other hand, involve the return of a portion of the money received in a transaction as a reward for facilitating that transaction. Both practices violate ethical standards and legal statutes, often leading to a cycle of corruption that erodes public trust.

The principal-agent theory elucidates the dynamics at play in bribery and kickback schemes. In this context, the "principal" is the public or the electorate, while the "agent" is the elected official or bureaucrat. The misalignment of incentives can lead to situations where agents prioritize personal gain over the public good, resulting in corrupt practices.

Identifying the Problem

The prevalence of bribery and kickback schemes poses significant challenges to governance. These schemes not only distort policy outcomes but also perpetuate inequality, as those with financial resources can exert disproportionate influence over decision-making processes. For instance, in the construction industry, it is not uncommon for contractors to offer kickbacks to government officials in exchange for lucrative contracts. This practice not only inflates project costs but also compromises the quality of public infrastructure.

Case Studies

One notable example of such corruption was the investigation into the city of Springfield's public works department, where officials were found to be accepting kickbacks from contractors. Harper uncovered documents that illustrated a pattern of inflated bids, with the excess funds being funneled back to the officials involved. This scandal not only resulted in the indictment of several city officials but also sparked public outrage, leading to calls for comprehensive reforms in procurement processes.

Another significant case involved a large healthcare conglomerate accused of bribing state legislators to pass favorable legislation. Harper's investigative team obtained emails revealing a coordinated effort to influence policy through financial incentives. The fallout from this revelation led to a statewide investigation and the eventual passage of stricter laws governing lobbying and campaign financing.

Methodologies for Uncovering Corruption

To effectively expose bribery and kickback schemes, Harper employed a multifaceted approach:

- **Data Analysis:** By analyzing public records, campaign finance reports, and contract awards, Harper's team identified anomalies that suggested corrupt practices. Statistical methods, such as regression analysis, were utilized to detect patterns indicative of bribery.

- **Whistleblower Testimonies:** Harper established a secure channel for whistleblowers to report corruption without fear of retaliation. Many insiders provided crucial information that corroborated the evidence gathered through data analysis.

- **Collaboration with Law Enforcement:** Partnering with investigative agencies allowed Harper to leverage additional resources and expertise. This collaboration was instrumental in conducting raids and gathering physical evidence.

The Impact of Investigations

The impact of uncovering bribery and kickback schemes extends beyond individual cases. Harper's investigations catalyzed a broader movement advocating for transparency and accountability in government. The exposure of corruption not only led to criminal charges against wrongdoers but also prompted legislative reforms aimed at curbing the influence of money in politics.

For instance, following the Springfield scandal, new regulations were enacted requiring greater transparency in public contracts and stricter penalties for officials found guilty of accepting bribes. These reforms aimed to restore public trust and ensure that government officials are held accountable for their actions.

Conclusion

Harper Sato's dedication to uncovering bribery and kickback schemes exemplifies the crucial role of investigative journalism in upholding democratic values. By exposing corruption, she not only brought accountability to those in power but also inspired a generation of activists and journalists to continue the fight for transparency and integrity in governance. The battle against bribery and kickbacks remains ongoing, but with advocates like Harper leading the charge, there is hope for a more equitable and just political landscape.

$$\text{Corruption Index} = \frac{\text{Total Instances of Corruption}}{\text{Total Government Transactions}} \times 100 \qquad (17)$$

Tirelessly Pursuing the Facts

In the realm of investigative journalism, the pursuit of truth is not merely a profession; it is a relentless quest that requires tenacity, courage, and an unwavering commitment to the facts. Harper Sato epitomizes this ethos, embodying the idea that factual integrity is the bedrock of a functioning democracy. This section delves into her methodical approach to uncovering truths, the theoretical frameworks underpinning her work, the challenges faced in the process, and real-world examples that illustrate her impact.

Theoretical Frameworks of Investigative Journalism

At the heart of Harper's pursuit of facts lies a theoretical foundation rooted in several key principles:

- **The Public Interest:** Investigative journalism serves the public interest by exposing corruption, injustice, and abuse of power. According to the *Societal Responsibility Theory*, media must act as a watchdog, ensuring that those in power are held accountable.

- **Transparency and Accountability:** The *Accountability Journalism* model emphasizes the necessity of transparency in governance. By pursuing facts, journalists like Harper ensure that the public is informed about the workings of their government, fostering a culture of accountability.

- **Critical Thinking and Skepticism:** The *Critical Theory* of media encourages journalists to question dominant narratives and challenge the status quo. Harper's investigative approach is characterized by a healthy skepticism towards official narratives, prompting her to seek out multiple sources and perspectives.

Challenges in Pursuing the Facts

Despite her commitment to uncovering the truth, Harper faced numerous challenges that threatened her investigative efforts:

- **Access to Information:** One of the primary obstacles in investigative journalism is the lack of access to critical information. Government agencies often employ bureaucratic barriers to limit transparency. Harper navigated these hurdles by utilizing the Freedom of Information Act (FOIA), enabling her to obtain documents that would otherwise remain hidden.

- **Intimidation and Threats:** Investigative journalists frequently encounter intimidation from powerful entities whose interests are threatened by exposure. Harper was no exception; she faced harassment and threats aimed at silencing her voice. However, her steadfast commitment to the truth only strengthened her resolve.

- **Misinformation and Disinformation:** In the digital age, the spread of misinformation poses a significant challenge to factual reporting. Harper employed rigorous fact-checking methodologies and collaborated with fact-checking organizations to combat the spread of false narratives, ensuring that her reporting was grounded in verifiable evidence.

Real-World Examples of Harper's Investigative Work

Harper's tireless pursuit of the facts is exemplified in several high-profile investigations that not only uncovered corruption but also sparked public discourse and reform:

- **The Corporate Influence Scandal:** In a groundbreaking investigation, Harper exposed the intricate web of corporate influence over local government decisions. Through meticulous research and interviews, she uncovered a series of clandestine meetings between corporate lobbyists and elected officials, revealing a pattern of bribery and unethical behavior. Her findings led to widespread public outrage and prompted legislative reforms aimed at increasing transparency in lobbying practices.

- **The Environmental Cover-Up:** Harper's investigation into a major environmental disaster showcased her relentless pursuit of the truth. By analyzing public records and conducting interviews with whistleblowers, she uncovered evidence that a corporation had knowingly concealed information about hazardous waste disposal. Her reporting not only held the corporation accountable but also galvanized community action, leading to stricter environmental regulations.

- **Voter Suppression Tactics:** In another notable investigation, Harper focused on voter suppression tactics employed in several states. Through data analysis and interviews with affected voters, she documented instances of disenfranchisement and intimidation at polling places. Her findings were pivotal in raising awareness about the issue, leading to advocacy for voting rights protections and reforms.

Conclusion

Harper Sato's tireless pursuit of the facts exemplifies the critical role of investigative journalism in a democratic society. Her commitment to uncovering the truth, despite the challenges she faced, serves as an inspiration for aspiring journalists and advocates for transparency. By adhering to the principles of public interest, accountability, and critical inquiry, Harper not only reshaped the media landscape but also empowered citizens to demand accountability from their leaders. As she continues her work, her legacy will undoubtedly inspire future generations to uphold the values of truth and integrity in journalism.

Gaining Public Trust and Support

In an era marked by skepticism towards media and political institutions, Harper Sato's journey towards gaining public trust and support stands as a testament to the power of integrity, transparency, and community engagement. This subsection delves into the strategies and challenges Harper faced in building a solid foundation of trust with the public, which was crucial for her success in exposing political corruption and advocating for climate justice.

The Importance of Trust in Media

Trust is a fundamental component of effective journalism and public discourse. According to the *Trust in Media* report by the Reuters Institute for the Study of Journalism, public trust in news media has been declining globally, with only 38%

of respondents expressing confidence in the media's ability to report news accurately. This decline creates a challenging landscape for journalists like Harper, who seek to inform and engage the public on critical issues.

To counteract this trend, Harper employed several key strategies:

- **Transparency:** Harper made it a priority to be open about her methods and sources. By providing clear explanations of her investigative processes, she fostered an environment of trust where the public felt informed rather than manipulated.

- **Engagement:** Understanding the importance of community, Harper actively engaged with her audience through social media platforms, town hall meetings, and public forums. This two-way communication allowed her to address concerns directly and demonstrate her commitment to the public's interests.

- **Credibility:** Harper consistently adhered to high journalistic standards, including fact-checking and ethical reporting. By prioritizing accuracy over sensationalism, she established herself as a credible voice in a crowded media landscape.

Building a Community of Support

Harper recognized that gaining public trust required more than just individual efforts; it necessitated building a community of support. This was particularly evident during her investigations into political corruption, where she faced significant backlash from powerful interests.

Mobilizing Grassroots Support One of the most effective ways Harper garnered public trust was by mobilizing grassroots support. She organized community events, workshops, and forums to educate citizens about the issues at stake and the importance of transparency in government. By empowering individuals to become advocates for change, she cultivated a sense of ownership and responsibility among her supporters.

For instance, during her investigation into a local government cover-up involving environmental regulations, Harper partnered with local environmental groups to raise awareness about the issue. This collaboration not only amplified her reach but also demonstrated her commitment to the community's well-being.

Utilizing Social Media In the digital age, social media emerged as a powerful tool for Harper to connect with the public. By leveraging platforms such as Twitter, Instagram, and Facebook, she shared updates on her investigations, engaged in discussions, and responded to public inquiries. This accessibility helped demystify the journalistic process and fostered a sense of trust among her followers.

Overcoming Challenges to Trust

Despite her efforts, Harper faced significant challenges in gaining public trust. Misinformation and disinformation campaigns, often fueled by political adversaries, sought to undermine her credibility. In response, Harper adopted a proactive approach to counteract these narratives:

- **Fact-Checking Initiatives:** Harper established a dedicated team to fact-check claims made about her work, providing the public with clear, evidence-based rebuttals to false narratives.

- **Collaborative Journalism:** By partnering with other reputable media outlets and organizations, Harper expanded her reach and reinforced her credibility. Collaborative efforts not only diversified perspectives but also created a network of support against misinformation.

The Role of Ethical Reporting

Ethical reporting played a crucial role in Harper's ability to gain public trust. By adhering to principles of fairness, accuracy, and impartiality, she demonstrated her commitment to serving the public interest rather than catering to sensationalist tendencies.

As noted by the *Society of Professional Journalists Code of Ethics*, journalists are tasked with seeking truth and reporting it, minimizing harm, and acting independently. Harper's adherence to these principles became a cornerstone of her identity as a journalist and a leader in media reform.

Examples of Success

Harper's efforts to gain public trust culminated in several notable successes:

- **Public Support for Investigative Reporting:** Following her exposé on political corruption, public opinion polls indicated a significant increase in trust towards her reporting. A survey conducted by a local university found that 72% of respondents expressed confidence in Harper's ability to report accurately on political issues.

- **Community Engagement Initiatives:** The community events Harper organized not only increased awareness about critical issues but also fostered a sense of solidarity among attendees. Many participants reported feeling more empowered to engage in civic activities and advocate for change.

Conclusion

In conclusion, Harper Sato's journey to gain public trust and support serves as a powerful example of the importance of integrity, transparency, and community engagement in journalism. By prioritizing ethical reporting, mobilizing grassroots support, and effectively utilizing social media, Harper successfully navigated the challenges of a skeptical public. Her legacy underscores the vital role that trust plays in fostering a healthy democracy and empowering citizens to advocate for accountability and change.

The Fallout from Harper's Investigations

Political Backlash and Retaliation

In the wake of Harper Sato's groundbreaking investigations into political corruption, the backlash from those in power was both swift and severe. This section examines the multifaceted nature of the political retaliation that Harper faced, highlighting the mechanisms of power, the consequences of her revelations, and the broader implications for democratic governance.

The Nature of Political Backlash

Political backlash can be defined as the adverse reactions from political entities and their supporters in response to actions or disclosures that threaten their interests. In Harper's case, her investigative journalism exposed significant ties between government officials and corporate entities, leading to a series of retaliatory measures aimed at discrediting her and undermining her work.

The backlash manifested in various forms, including:

- **Public Discrediting:** Political opponents and allies of the implicated officials launched smear campaigns against Harper, questioning her credibility and motives. This included the dissemination of false narratives that painted her as a partisan activist rather than an impartial journalist.

- **Legal Threats:** In an attempt to silence her, powerful political figures initiated legal actions against Harper and her media outlet. These lawsuits often hinged on defamation claims, asserting that her reporting was misleading or factually incorrect. The legal costs and the threat of punitive damages served to intimidate her and her team.

- **Institutional Retaliation:** Harper faced pushback from established media institutions that were hesitant to support her due to fear of losing access to political sources or advertising revenue. Some media outlets chose to distance themselves from her investigations, reflecting a broader trend of self-censorship within the industry.

Theoretical Framework

The backlash against Harper can be analyzed through the lens of *power dynamics* in political communication. According to *Foucault's theory of power*, power is not merely held but is exercised through a network of relationships and discourses. In this context, Harper's revelations disrupted the established power relations, prompting those in authority to mobilize their resources to reassert control.

Furthermore, the *spiral of silence theory* posits that individuals are less likely to express their opinions if they believe they are in the minority. The backlash against Harper created a chilling effect, discouraging other journalists from pursuing similar investigative paths for fear of facing similar retaliation.

Case Studies and Examples

Several high-profile cases illustrate the nature of political backlash against journalists who challenge the status quo:

1. **The Case of Maria Ressa:** The Philippine journalist and CEO of Rappler, Maria Ressa, faced multiple legal challenges and threats of imprisonment after her outlet reported on government corruption and the Duterte administration's war on drugs. Ressa's experience parallels Harper's in that both faced a coordinated effort to undermine their credibility while navigating a hostile political landscape.

2. **The Assassination of Daphne Caruana Galizia:** The Maltese journalist was killed in a car bomb attack after exposing corruption at the highest levels of

government. Her murder highlighted the extreme lengths to which those in power may go to silence dissenting voices, underscoring the risks faced by journalists like Harper.

Consequences of Retaliation

The political backlash against Harper had several significant consequences:

- **Increased Vigilance Among Journalists:** The retaliation served as a wake-up call for many journalists, prompting a reevaluation of safety protocols and the need for solidarity within the media community. Journalists began to form networks of support, sharing resources and strategies to combat intimidation.

- **Public Awareness and Advocacy:** Harper's struggle against political retaliation resonated with the public, leading to increased advocacy for press freedom and the protection of journalists. Grassroots movements emerged, demanding accountability from political leaders and support for investigative journalism.

- **Legislative Changes:** In response to the outcry over retaliatory actions against journalists, some governments proposed new legislation aimed at protecting press freedoms. However, these measures often faced significant opposition from political factions resistant to transparency.

Conclusion

The political backlash and retaliation faced by Harper Sato exemplify the challenges that journalists encounter when exposing corruption and advocating for accountability. As she navigated this treacherous landscape, her resilience not only highlighted the importance of a free press but also galvanized public support for media reform. The implications of her experiences extend beyond her individual story, serving as a critical reminder of the ongoing struggle for journalistic integrity in the face of political power.

$$\text{Political Backlash} = f(\text{Power Dynamics, Public Perception, Media Influence}) \tag{18}$$

This equation encapsulates the complex interplay of factors that contribute to the backlash against journalists like Harper, underscoring the necessity of vigilance and advocacy in preserving the freedoms that underpin democratic society.

Attempts to Silence Harper

The journey of Harper Sato, a relentless journalist and media reform advocate, was not without peril. As she began to expose the intricate web of political corruption and corporate influence, it became increasingly clear that powerful interests would stop at nothing to silence her voice. This section delves into the various attempts made by these entities to undermine Harper's work, employing tactics ranging from intimidation to legal threats, all aimed at quashing her influence and stifling the truth.

The Nature of Threats

In the realm of investigative journalism, the line between uncovering the truth and facing retaliation is often perilously thin. The threats against Harper were not merely abstract notions; they were concrete and multifaceted. These threats can be categorized into three primary forms: **physical intimidation**, **legal harassment**, and **media smear campaigns**.

Physical Intimidation

One of the most alarming tactics employed by those seeking to silence Harper was physical intimidation. After a particularly revealing exposé regarding a local politician's ties to a major corporation, Harper began receiving anonymous threats. These threats escalated from ominous phone calls to more direct confrontations, such as being followed home from work. In one incident, Harper's car was vandalized, a clear message intended to instill fear and compel her to reconsider her journalistic pursuits.

The psychological impact of such intimidation cannot be overstated. According to the *Journal of Media Ethics*, journalists facing threats often experience heightened anxiety and stress, which can impair their ability to report effectively [?]. Harper, however, chose to confront these threats with resilience. She understood that giving in would not only endanger her career but also compromise the integrity of the information she sought to bring to light.

Legal Harassment

In addition to physical threats, Harper faced a barrage of legal harassment. Powerful individuals and corporations often wield legal action as a weapon against journalists, hoping to drain their resources and deter them from pursuing their investigations. In Harper's case, she was served with multiple lawsuits alleging defamation and invasion of privacy, all of which were transparently aimed at silencing her voice.

The legal landscape can be a daunting battleground for journalists, as the costs associated with defending against such lawsuits can be crippling. In a study conducted by the *Committee to Protect Journalists*, it was found that nearly 70% of journalists who face legal challenges report a significant impact on their reporting due to the stress and financial burden of litigation [?]. Harper, however, sought pro bono legal assistance and utilized her platform to raise awareness about the chilling effects of such tactics on press freedom.

Media Smear Campaigns

Simultaneously, Harper was subjected to media smear campaigns designed to undermine her credibility. As she garnered more attention for her investigations, detractors began to circulate false narratives about her character and motivations. Misinformation spread like wildfire across social media platforms, with opponents portraying her as a biased and unreliable source, intent on pursuing a personal agenda rather than the truth.

The impact of these smear campaigns can be profound. According to a report by the *Pew Research Center*, 54% of Americans have encountered misinformation about a public figure, which can significantly influence public perception and trust [?]. Harper's response was strategic; she leveraged her media platform to directly address these falsehoods, providing evidence and context to counter the narratives being spun against her.

The Role of Support Networks

Despite the relentless attempts to silence her, Harper found strength in her support networks. Fellow journalists, advocacy groups, and civil society organizations rallied around her, providing both moral and practical support. This solidarity was crucial in helping her withstand the pressures of intimidation and harassment.

For instance, organizations like *Reporters Without Borders* and the *Committee to Protect Journalists* not only condemned the attacks against her but also helped amplify her voice, ensuring that her story remained in the public eye. This collective action underscored the importance of community in the fight for press freedom.

Conclusion

In conclusion, the attempts to silence Harper Sato serve as a stark reminder of the challenges faced by journalists in the pursuit of truth. Through physical intimidation, legal harassment, and media smear campaigns, powerful interests sought to undermine her credibility and stifle her voice. However, Harper's resilience, coupled with the support of her peers and the public, enabled her to continue her work, ultimately highlighting the vital role of investigative journalism in a democratic society. As she often stated, "The truth is not just a story; it is a lifeline for those who have none."

Harper's Resilience in the Face of Adversity

In the tumultuous landscape of modern journalism, where the truth is often obscured by layers of political maneuvering and corporate interests, Harper Sato emerged as a beacon of resilience. Her journey through adversity is not merely a narrative of personal strength but a profound commentary on the systemic challenges faced by journalists today. This section delves into the trials Harper encountered and the strategies she employed to navigate these turbulent waters, ultimately highlighting her unwavering commitment to truth and transparency.

The Nature of Adversity in Journalism

The contemporary media landscape is fraught with challenges that threaten the integrity of journalism. Adversity manifests in various forms, from direct threats to personal safety to the insidious pressure of corporate sponsorship influencing editorial independence. Harper's experiences epitomize these struggles. For instance, upon exposing a major political scandal involving a prominent corporation, she faced not only public backlash but also targeted harassment from those seeking to silence her voice.

Psychological Resilience: A Theoretical Framework

Psychological resilience, defined as the ability to adapt well in the face of adversity, trauma, tragedy, threats, or significant sources of stress, is crucial for journalists operating in high-stakes environments. According to the American Psychological Association, resilience encompasses behaviors, thoughts, and actions that can be learned and developed in anyone. Harper's resilience can be understood through various psychological theories, including:

- **Cognitive Behavioral Theory (CBT):** This theory posits that our thoughts influence our feelings and behaviors. Harper utilized CBT principles to reframe negative experiences, focusing on her mission rather than the obstacles.

- **Resilience Theory:** This theory emphasizes the importance of social support systems. Harper cultivated a network of allies in journalism, advocacy, and academia, providing her with emotional and professional backing during challenging times.

- **Post-Traumatic Growth Theory:** This concept suggests that individuals can experience positive growth following adversity. Harper's experiences not only strengthened her resolve but also deepened her understanding of the societal impact of her work.

Harper's Strategies for Resilience

Harper's resilience was not a passive trait; it was actively cultivated through various strategies:

1. **Building a Support Network:** Harper recognized the importance of surrounding herself with like-minded individuals. She formed alliances with fellow journalists, activists, and legal experts who provided emotional support and strategic advice. This network proved invaluable when she faced threats, as they rallied to defend her and amplify her voice.

2. **Maintaining a Focus on the Mission:** Harper consistently reminded herself of her purpose: to uncover the truth and promote accountability. This focus helped her navigate periods of intense pressure and doubt. By keeping her goals in sight, she was able to endure the backlash and continue her investigations.

3. **Engaging in Self-Care Practices:** Understanding the toll that her work took on her mental health, Harper incorporated self-care practices into her routine. This included mindfulness meditation, physical exercise, and seeking professional counseling when necessary. These practices equipped her to manage stress and maintain her emotional well-being.

4. **Leveraging Public Support:** Harper adeptly used social media to connect with her audience, turning her adversities into opportunities for engagement. By sharing her experiences and the challenges she faced, she garnered public sympathy and support, which not only bolstered her resolve but also increased pressure on her adversaries.

5. **Continuous Learning and Adaptation:** Harper viewed challenges as opportunities for growth. She actively sought feedback on her work and

adapted her strategies based on the evolving media landscape. This flexibility allowed her to stay relevant and effective in her advocacy.

Case Studies of Resilience in Action

Several key incidents illustrate Harper's resilience:

Case Study 1: The Corporate Backlash After releasing a documentary exposing corrupt ties between local politicians and a multinational corporation, Harper faced a coordinated smear campaign. Rather than retreating, she organized a public forum to discuss the implications of corporate influence in politics. This event not only showcased her courage but also galvanized community support, leading to increased viewership and engagement with her content.

Case Study 2: Personal Threats Following a series of threatening messages, Harper was advised to reduce her public presence. Instead, she chose to increase transparency by sharing her experiences with her audience. This act of vulnerability not only humanized her but also inspired her followers to rally behind her cause, further solidifying her position as a leader in the fight for media integrity.

The Broader Implications of Harper's Resilience

Harper's resilience extends beyond her individual experiences; it serves as a powerful example for journalists and activists worldwide. Her story underscores the importance of fostering resilience within the media community. As the threats to journalistic integrity continue to evolve, the cultivation of resilience will be crucial in ensuring that the truth prevails.

In conclusion, Harper Sato's journey through adversity is emblematic of the challenges faced by modern journalists. Her resilience, built through strategic support networks, a clear focus on her mission, and adaptive learning, not only enabled her to overcome personal and professional challenges but also inspired a generation of activists and journalists. As we reflect on her contributions, it becomes clear that resilience is not merely a personal trait but a collective necessity in the pursuit of truth and justice in an increasingly complex world.

The Impact of Harper's Revelations on the Political Landscape

Harper Sato's groundbreaking investigations into political corruption served as a catalyst for profound changes within the political landscape. Her revelations not only exposed the intertwining of government and corporate interests but also ignited a public discourse surrounding accountability, transparency, and the ethical responsibilities of public officials. This section explores the multifaceted impact of Harper's work on the political arena, examining both the immediate consequences of her findings and the long-term shifts in public perception and policy.

The Shift in Public Perception

Prior to Harper's revelations, a significant portion of the public harbored skepticism towards politicians, viewing them through a lens of cynicism. However, the detailed exposés she published transformed this skepticism into a more active demand for accountability. As her investigations revealed the depths of corruption, public trust in government institutions began to wane, leading to a surge in civic engagement.

For instance, the case of the *Corporate Influence Scandal*, which Harper uncovered, illustrated the extent to which lobbyists had infiltrated legislative processes. The scandal involved a series of undisclosed payments to politicians in exchange for favorable legislation. Following Harper's reports, public outcry led to protests demanding reforms in campaign financing, demonstrating a direct correlation between her work and increased political activism.

Legislative Reforms and New Policies

Harper's investigations prompted lawmakers to reevaluate existing policies regarding campaign finance and lobbying. In the wake of her findings, several states introduced legislation aimed at increasing transparency in political donations. For example, the *Transparency in Political Funding Act* mandated that all political donations over a certain threshold be publicly disclosed, a move that aligned with Harper's advocacy for greater governmental transparency.

The impact of Harper's revelations extended beyond state legislation; it influenced national discourse as well. The federal government initiated a review of lobbying regulations, leading to the introduction of stricter rules governing the interactions between lawmakers and lobbyists. This shift reflected a growing acknowledgment of the need to safeguard democratic processes from undue corporate influence.

Grassroots Movements and Activism

The revelations also catalyzed the formation of grassroots movements aimed at combating political corruption. Organizations such as *Citizens for Ethical Governance* emerged in response to Harper's findings, mobilizing citizens to advocate for systemic reforms. These movements utilized social media platforms to amplify their message, creating a digital space for dialogue and activism.

One notable campaign, #EndCorruptionNow, gained traction as citizens shared personal stories of how political corruption affected their communities. This campaign not only highlighted the real-world implications of Harper's investigations but also fostered a sense of collective responsibility among individuals who felt empowered to demand change.

The Role of Media in Shaping Political Discourse

Harper's work underscored the critical role of media in shaping political discourse. By providing a platform for investigative journalism, she demonstrated how media could serve as a watchdog, holding power accountable. The subsequent rise of independent media outlets, inspired by Harper's model, further diversified the landscape of political reporting.

The impact of this shift was evident in the way political stories were covered. Journalists began to adopt a more critical approach, prioritizing investigative reporting over sensationalism. This change not only enhanced the quality of political coverage but also encouraged a more informed electorate.

Long-term Implications for Political Culture

The long-term implications of Harper's revelations on political culture are profound. By challenging the status quo and exposing the vulnerabilities within political systems, she laid the groundwork for a more engaged and informed citizenry. The demand for accountability and transparency has become a cornerstone of contemporary political discourse, influencing the expectations that citizens hold for their elected officials.

Moreover, Harper's legacy continues to inspire future generations of journalists and activists. Her work serves as a reminder of the power of investigative journalism in fostering democratic ideals and promoting social justice. As new challenges arise in the political landscape, the principles championed by Harper remain relevant, guiding the ongoing struggle for integrity in governance.

In conclusion, Harper Sato's revelations had a transformative impact on the political landscape, reshaping public perception, prompting legislative reforms, and inspiring grassroots activism. Her legacy endures as a testament to the power of truth-telling in the pursuit of a more just and accountable political system.

A Call for Accountability and Change

In the wake of Harper Sato's groundbreaking investigations into political corruption, a clarion call for accountability and change resonated across the nation. This call was not merely a response to the scandals unearthed by Harper; it represented a broader demand for a systemic overhaul of the political landscape, urging citizens and institutions alike to recognize their roles in fostering a more transparent and equitable society.

Theoretical Framework for Accountability

At the heart of Harper's advocacy lies the theoretical framework of *social accountability*, which posits that citizens have the right and responsibility to hold their governments accountable for their actions. This framework draws upon theories of participatory democracy, which emphasize the importance of active citizen engagement in governance. According to [1], social accountability mechanisms enable citizens to monitor public officials and demand responsiveness, thereby enhancing the legitimacy of democratic institutions.

Problems of Accountability in Politics

Despite the theoretical underpinnings of accountability, the reality is often starkly different. Political corruption, characterized by bribery, nepotism, and the manipulation of public resources for private gain, undermines trust in governmental institutions. The findings of Harper's investigations revealed a disturbing trend: the intertwining of political power and corporate interests, leading to a culture of impunity where public officials felt emboldened to act without fear of repercussions.

One striking example of this phenomenon is the case of the *Bribery Scandal of 2025*, where multiple high-ranking officials were implicated in accepting kickbacks from major corporations in exchange for favorable legislation. This scandal not only eroded public trust but also highlighted the urgent need for mechanisms to ensure accountability.

A Framework for Change

In response to these challenges, Harper championed a multi-faceted approach to reform that included:

- **Strengthening Whistleblower Protections:** Ensuring that individuals who expose corruption are safeguarded from retaliation is crucial for fostering an environment where accountability can flourish. Harper advocated for comprehensive legislation that would protect whistleblowers in both the public and private sectors.

- **Implementing Transparency Measures:** Harper called for the adoption of robust transparency measures, such as mandatory disclosure of campaign financing and lobbying activities. These measures would enable citizens to track the flow of money in politics, making it more difficult for corrupt practices to go unnoticed.

- **Encouraging Civic Engagement:** A vibrant democracy requires active participation from its citizens. Harper emphasized the importance of civic education initiatives aimed at informing citizens about their rights and responsibilities, thereby empowering them to demand accountability from their leaders.

- **Establishing Independent Oversight Bodies:** The creation of independent commissions tasked with investigating allegations of corruption would serve as a critical check on political power. These bodies would operate free from political influence, ensuring impartiality and integrity in their investigations.

Case Studies of Successful Accountability Initiatives

Harper's call for accountability found resonance in various grassroots movements and initiatives across the globe. For instance, the *Citizens Against Corruption* movement in Brazil successfully mobilized citizens to demand greater transparency in government spending, resulting in significant reforms in public procurement processes. Similarly, in South Korea, the *Candlelight Revolution* led to the impeachment of a corrupt president, showcasing the power of collective action in holding leaders accountable.

Conclusion: A Collective Responsibility

Ultimately, the call for accountability and change is not solely the responsibility of journalists like Harper; it requires a collective effort from all sectors of society. Citizens, civil society organizations, and political leaders must work in tandem to dismantle the structures that perpetuate corruption. As Harper eloquently stated, "Accountability is not a privilege; it is a fundamental right of every citizen." The path to a more transparent and just political landscape is fraught with challenges, but with unwavering commitment and collective action, it is a journey that can be undertaken.

Bibliography

[1] Fung, A. (2006). *Varieties of Participation in Complex Governance*. Public Administration Review, 66(s1), 66-75.

Harper's Advocacy for Government Transparency

Pushing for Open Records and Freedom of Information

In the realm of journalism and media reform, the push for open records and freedom of information (FOI) stands as a cornerstone of transparency and accountability in government. Harper Sato recognized that without access to information, democracy is merely a facade, akin to a stage play where the audience is left in the dark about the script. The importance of FOI is underscored by the principle that citizens have the right to know how their government operates, what decisions are being made, and how public funds are being utilized.

Theoretical Framework

The theoretical underpinning of FOI is rooted in the concept of *democratic accountability*. According to the *Social Contract Theory*, citizens consent to be governed in exchange for transparency and accountability in governance. This social contract necessitates that public officials operate under scrutiny, and the public must have the means to access information that affects their lives.

The *Public's Right to Know* is enshrined in various legal frameworks globally, with the United States' Freedom of Information Act (FOIA) of 1966 serving as a seminal example. FOIA mandates that federal agencies disclose records requested by the public, unless the information falls under specific exemptions. This act has been pivotal in uncovering government malfeasance and fostering an informed citizenry.

Challenges to Open Records

Despite the theoretical and legal foundations supporting FOI, Harper faced numerous challenges in her advocacy for open records. One significant problem is the *culture of secrecy* that pervades many government institutions. Bureaucratic resistance often manifests in the form of delayed responses, excessive redactions, and outright denials of requests for information. For instance, a 2019 report by the National Security Archive revealed that nearly 75% of FOIA requests to the Department of Defense were either denied or not fully answered, highlighting the systemic barriers that obstruct transparency.

Moreover, the advent of digital technology has introduced complications regarding information accessibility. While digital records have the potential to streamline access, they also create opportunities for *data manipulation* and *surveillance*. Governments may leverage technology to obscure information rather than enhance transparency. For example, the use of encryption and secure servers can prevent public access to critical data, raising ethical concerns about the balance between national security and public accountability.

Case Studies and Examples

Harper's commitment to pushing for open records was exemplified in her investigation into the funding of political campaigns. By utilizing FOI requests, she uncovered a web of financial contributions from corporate entities to politicians, revealing the extent of corporate influence in governance. One notable case involved a major energy company that had funneled millions into a political action committee (PAC) that supported candidates opposing climate legislation. This revelation not only informed the public but also galvanized grassroots movements advocating for campaign finance reform.

Another significant example was Harper's collaboration with whistleblowers who provided crucial information about government contracts awarded without competitive bidding. This investigation led to a series of articles that detailed the misuse of public funds and prompted congressional hearings on procurement practices. The ensuing public outcry resulted in legislative changes aimed at increasing transparency in government contracting.

The Role of Technology in FOI Advocacy

In the digital age, technology plays a dual role in the pursuit of open records. On one hand, it enhances the ability of journalists and citizens to file FOI requests and access information. Online platforms and tools like *FOIAonline* and *MuckRock* have simplified the process, allowing users to track requests and responses in real time.

On the other hand, technology can also be weaponized against transparency. The proliferation of *fake news* and misinformation campaigns can obscure the truth, making it increasingly difficult for the public to discern credible sources of information. Harper understood that combating misinformation was integral to her FOI advocacy. She utilized her platform to educate the public about the importance of verifying sources and understanding the implications of FOI laws.

Conclusion

Harper Sato's relentless push for open records and freedom of information not only transformed the landscape of journalism but also empowered citizens to demand accountability from their government. By challenging the culture of secrecy and advocating for transparency, she laid the groundwork for a more informed and engaged populace. The legacy of her efforts continues to inspire a new generation of journalists and activists committed to the principles of open government, ensuring that the public's right to know remains a fundamental tenet of democracy.

$$\text{Transparency} \propto \frac{\text{Accountability}}{\text{Public Engagement}} \tag{19}$$

This equation illustrates the direct relationship between transparency and accountability, moderated by the level of public engagement. As public engagement increases, the demand for accountability grows, thereby enhancing transparency in government operations.

Collaborating with Whistleblowers

The role of whistleblowers in the pursuit of transparency and accountability cannot be overstated. They serve as critical informants who expose unethical practices, corruption, and malpractice within organizations, often at great personal risk. In this section, we explore how Harper Sato strategically collaborated with whistleblowers to unveil political corruption and corporate malfeasance, thereby reinforcing her commitment to government transparency and ethical journalism.

The Importance of Whistleblowers

Whistleblowers are individuals who report misconduct within their organization, which can include illegal activities, violations of regulations, or threats to public safety. Their actions are often motivated by a moral obligation to expose wrongdoing, even when it puts their careers and personal safety in jeopardy. According to the *Whistleblower Protection Act* of 1989 in the United States, whistleblowers are protected from retaliation, which encourages individuals to come forward with information that can lead to significant reforms.

Theoretical Framework

The collaboration between journalists and whistleblowers can be understood through the lens of *social responsibility theory*. This theory posits that the media has an obligation to act in the public interest, which includes exposing corruption and holding power accountable. When journalists like Harper Sato work alongside whistleblowers, they fulfill this responsibility by ensuring that critical information reaches the public domain.

$$P = \frac{C}{R} \qquad (20)$$

Where:

- P = Public interest
- C = Credibility of the information provided by whistleblowers
- R = Risks taken by whistleblowers in exposing wrongdoing

This equation illustrates that as the credibility of the whistleblower's information increases, so does the public interest in the issue, despite the risks involved.

Challenges Faced by Whistleblowers

Despite the protections in place, whistleblowers often face significant challenges, including:

- **Retaliation:** Many whistleblowers encounter hostile work environments, demotions, or even termination after coming forward.
- **Legal Battles:** Whistleblowers may find themselves embroiled in lengthy legal disputes as they fight for their rights and protections.
- **Public Scrutiny:** The act of whistleblowing can lead to public vilification, where the whistleblower is portrayed as a traitor rather than a hero.

Harper Sato recognized these challenges and worked to provide a safe platform for whistleblowers to share their stories without fear of retribution.

Case Studies of Collaboration

One notable instance of Harper's collaboration with a whistleblower involved the exposure of a government contract awarded to a major corporation under suspicious circumstances. The whistleblower, a former employee of the corporation, approached Harper with documents that revealed a series of unethical practices, including bribery and falsified reports.

- **Document Verification:** Harper's team conducted thorough investigations to verify the authenticity of the documents provided by the whistleblower. This included cross-referencing information with public records and interviewing other sources.

- **Building Trust:** Harper established a rapport with the whistleblower, ensuring them that their identity would be protected. This trust was crucial in obtaining additional evidence and testimonies.

- **Public Disclosure:** After gathering sufficient evidence, Harper aired a segment on "The Voice of Tomorrow," detailing the findings and the whistleblower's account. This segment not only informed the public but also prompted governmental investigations into the matter.

The outcome was a significant political fallout, leading to the resignation of several high-ranking officials and a renewed focus on ethical governance.

The Broader Impact of Collaboration

Harper's collaboration with whistleblowers extended beyond individual cases; it sparked a movement that encouraged more individuals to come forward. The visibility of these collaborations in her media reforms helped to normalize whistleblowing as a courageous act of civic responsibility rather than a betrayal.

$$I = E \cdot C \tag{21}$$

Where:

- I = Impact of whistleblower collaboration
- E = Exposure provided by media
- C = Credibility of the whistleblower

This equation suggests that the impact of whistleblower collaboration is maximized when credible information is effectively exposed through media channels.

Conclusion

Harper Sato's commitment to collaborating with whistleblowers exemplifies the vital role that journalists play in fostering transparency and accountability in government and corporate practices. By providing a platform for whistleblowers, Harper not only amplified their voices but also reinforced the importance of ethical journalism in a democratic society. Her efforts have encouraged a culture where whistleblowing is recognized as an essential mechanism for promoting justice and integrity, paving the way for future innovations in media reform and political accountability.

The Fight Against Secretive Political Dealings

In an age where information is power, the fight against secretive political dealings has become a crucial battleground for advocates of transparency and accountability. Harper Sato emerged as a formidable force in this struggle, championing the cause of open governance and shining a spotlight on the murky waters of political transactions that often escape public scrutiny.

The Nature of Secretive Dealings

Secretive political dealings typically encompass a range of covert activities, including backroom negotiations, undisclosed lobbying efforts, and undisclosed financial contributions to political campaigns. These dealings are often facilitated by a lack of transparency in government processes, allowing powerful interests to manipulate political outcomes without public knowledge. The consequences of such secrecy can be dire, leading to policies that favor the few over the many, eroding public trust in institutions, and ultimately undermining democracy itself.

Theoretical Framework

The theoretical underpinning of Harper's fight against secretive political dealings can be found in the principles of *public choice theory*. This theory posits that politicians, like all individuals, are motivated by self-interest, often leading to a misalignment between their actions and the public's interest. The theory suggests that when political transactions are shrouded in secrecy, the potential for corruption increases, as the accountability mechanisms that would normally check such behavior are weakened.

Mathematically, we can represent the relationship between transparency and corruption as follows:

$$C = f(T, I) \tag{22}$$

where C represents the level of corruption, T represents the degree of transparency, and I represents the level of institutional integrity. As T increases, C is expected to decrease, assuming I remains constant. This relationship illustrates that greater transparency can lead to reduced corruption, supporting Harper's advocacy for open governance.

Problems Associated with Secretive Dealings

The problems associated with secretive political dealings are manifold:

1. **Erosion of Public Trust**: When citizens perceive that decisions are made behind closed doors, trust in political institutions diminishes. This erosion of trust can lead to increased cynicism and disengagement from the political process.

2. **Policy Distortion**: Secretive dealings often result in policies that favor special interests rather than the public good. For instance, the influence of lobbying groups can lead to legislation that benefits a small segment of the population while neglecting broader societal needs.

3. **Inequality**: The lack of transparency can exacerbate social inequalities, as those with financial resources can exert undue influence on political outcomes. This creates a feedback loop where the interests of the wealthy are prioritized over those of marginalized communities.

4. **Impunity**: When political dealings are hidden from view, it becomes easier for corrupt practices to flourish without consequence. This impunity can perpetuate a cycle of corruption that is difficult to break.

Examples of Secretive Dealings

Harper's investigative efforts uncovered numerous instances of secretive political dealings. One notable example involved a major corporation's undisclosed financial contributions to a political campaign. Through meticulous research and collaboration with whistleblowers, Harper revealed that these contributions were aimed at securing favorable legislation that would benefit the corporation at the expense of public health and safety.

Another example was Harper's exposure of a covert lobbying effort aimed at influencing environmental regulations. By obtaining documents through freedom of information requests, she was able to demonstrate how corporate interests had secretly shaped policy decisions, undermining efforts to combat climate change.

Strategies for Combatting Secretive Dealings

Harper's approach to combatting secretive political dealings involved several key strategies:

1. **Advocacy for Transparency Legislation**: Harper lobbied for laws that would require greater transparency in political financing, including the disclosure of campaign contributions and lobbying activities. This push for transparency was grounded in the belief that informed citizens are better equipped to hold their representatives accountable.

2. **Public Awareness Campaigns**: Recognizing the power of public opinion, Harper launched campaigns to educate citizens about the dangers of secretive dealings. By using social media and traditional media platforms, she aimed to mobilize public support for transparency initiatives.

3. **Collaboration with Whistleblowers**: Harper actively sought out whistleblowers willing to expose corrupt practices. By providing a safe space for these individuals to share their stories, she was able to gather critical information that would otherwise remain hidden.

4. **Engagement with Grassroots Movements**: Harper understood that change often begins at the grassroots level. She collaborated with community organizations to empower citizens to demand transparency from their elected officials, fostering a culture of accountability.

Conclusion

The fight against secretive political dealings is a vital component of Harper Sato's broader mission for government transparency and accountability. By exposing the hidden machinations of power, advocating for legislative reforms, and mobilizing public support, Harper has not only challenged the status quo but has also inspired a new generation of activists to continue the struggle for a more open and equitable political landscape. As we reflect on her contributions, it is clear that the battle for transparency is far from over; it is an ongoing fight that requires vigilance, courage, and unwavering commitment to the principles of democracy.

Engaging the Public in Government Oversight

Engaging the public in government oversight is a cornerstone of a healthy democracy and a critical component of Harper Sato's advocacy for transparency. This engagement not only empowers citizens but also holds government officials accountable for their actions. In this section, we will explore the theoretical underpinnings, the challenges faced, and the successful strategies implemented to facilitate public participation in government oversight.

Theoretical Framework

The concept of public engagement in governance is grounded in several key theories:

- **Participatory Democracy:** This theory posits that democracy is most effective when citizens actively participate in decision-making processes. Participatory democracy encourages transparency and accountability, fostering a political environment where public input is valued.

- **Deliberative Democracy:** This theory emphasizes the importance of discussion and deliberation among citizens and policymakers. Deliberative democracy advocates for informed public debate as a means of enhancing civic engagement and ensuring that diverse perspectives are considered in governance.

- **Social Capital Theory:** This theory highlights the value of social networks and relationships in facilitating collective action. High levels of social capital can lead to greater community engagement and trust in government institutions, thereby enhancing oversight efforts.

Challenges to Public Engagement

Despite the theoretical support for public engagement, several challenges hinder effective participation in government oversight:

- **Information Asymmetry:** Often, the public lacks access to critical information regarding government actions, decisions, and processes. This lack of transparency creates a barrier to informed participation.

- **Political Apathy:** Many citizens may feel disillusioned or apathetic towards the political process, believing that their voices do not matter. This disengagement can result in low participation rates in oversight initiatives.

- **Complexity of Government Processes:** The intricate nature of government operations can be daunting for the average citizen. Without adequate education and resources, individuals may struggle to understand how to engage meaningfully in oversight activities.

- **Institutional Resistance:** Government institutions may resist public engagement efforts, viewing them as threats to established power dynamics. This resistance can manifest in bureaucratic hurdles that limit public participation.

Strategies for Engaging the Public

To overcome these challenges, several strategies have been successfully implemented to engage the public in government oversight:

- **Open Data Initiatives:** Governments can promote transparency by making data publicly accessible. By providing open datasets, citizens can analyze government activities, track spending, and identify irregularities. For example, the U.S. government's Data.gov platform allows users to access a wealth of information related to federal spending, public services, and more.

- **Public Forums and Town Halls:** Hosting public forums and town hall meetings allows citizens to voice their concerns and ask questions directly to government officials. These events can foster dialogue and build trust between the public and policymakers. Harper's initiatives often included such forums, encouraging community members to engage with their representatives.

- **Citizen Advisory Boards:** Establishing citizen advisory boards can provide a structured way for the public to contribute to government decision-making. These boards can offer insights and recommendations on various issues, ensuring that diverse perspectives are considered.

- **Digital Engagement Platforms:** Utilizing technology to create online platforms for public engagement can enhance participation. Websites and applications that allow citizens to report issues, provide feedback, and engage in discussions can significantly increase oversight efforts. For instance, platforms like SeeClickFix enable citizens to report local issues directly to their municipalities.

- **Educational Campaigns:** Raising awareness about government processes and the importance of civic engagement is crucial. Educational campaigns can empower citizens with the knowledge they need to participate effectively in oversight initiatives. Harper's organization frequently collaborated with local schools and community organizations to provide workshops and resources on government transparency.

Case Studies and Examples

Several notable examples illustrate the success of public engagement in government oversight:

- **The City of Boston's Open Data Initiative:** Boston has implemented an open data platform that allows residents to access information on city services, budgets, and performance metrics. This initiative has fostered greater transparency and enabled citizens to hold the city accountable for its actions.

- **The Participatory Budgeting Movement:** Cities like New York and Paris have adopted participatory budgeting processes, allowing citizens to directly decide how to allocate a portion of the municipal budget. This approach not only increases public engagement but also enhances accountability, as residents can see the direct impact of their decisions.

- **The Role of Nonprofits:** Organizations like the Sunlight Foundation work to promote transparency in government by advocating for open data policies and providing tools for public engagement. Their efforts have led to increased awareness of government activities and greater citizen involvement in oversight.

- **Social Media Campaigns:** Harper's organization effectively utilized social media platforms to engage the public in discussions about government transparency. By creating hashtags and online campaigns, they mobilized citizens to demand accountability and participate in oversight efforts.

- **Whistleblower Protections:** Strengthening protections for whistleblowers encourages individuals to report misconduct without fear of retaliation. Harper advocated for legislation that safeguards whistleblowers, thereby enhancing public oversight of government actions.

Conclusion

Engaging the public in government oversight is essential for fostering transparency, accountability, and trust in democratic institutions. By implementing effective strategies and overcoming challenges, advocates like Harper Sato have demonstrated that citizen participation can significantly enhance government oversight efforts. As we move forward, it is vital to continue exploring innovative ways to engage the public and ensure that their voices are heard in the democratic process.

Harper's Impact on Government Accountability

Harper Sato's relentless pursuit of transparency and accountability within government institutions has profoundly reshaped the political landscape. By employing investigative journalism as a tool for social change, she has not only exposed corruption but has also fostered a culture of accountability that resonates through various levels of government. This section explores the theoretical frameworks underpinning Harper's impact, the systemic problems she aimed to address, and the tangible outcomes of her advocacy.

Theoretical Frameworks

Harper's approach to government accountability can be examined through the lens of several theoretical frameworks, including the *Social Contract Theory* and *Accountability Theory*.

- **Social Contract Theory:** This theory posits that individuals consent, either explicitly or implicitly, to surrender some freedoms in exchange for the protection of their remaining rights. Harper emphasized that government officials are accountable to the public, reinforcing the idea that transparency is essential for the legitimacy of governmental authority.

- **Accountability Theory:** This framework suggests that accountability involves holding individuals or institutions responsible for their actions. Harper's investigations into political corruption illustrated how a lack of accountability can lead to abuses of power, thereby necessitating mechanisms that ensure government officials are answerable to the citizenry.

Systemic Problems Addressed

Harper's work highlighted several systemic problems that undermined government accountability:

- **Corruption and Misuse of Power:** Harper's investigations revealed widespread corruption, including bribery and kickbacks, which eroded public trust. For example, her exposé on a major political figure's illicit ties to corporate donors shed light on how financial incentives can distort public policy.

- **Lack of Transparency:** Many governmental processes were shrouded in secrecy, leading to a culture of mistrust. Harper advocated for the implementation of open records and freedom of information laws, arguing that transparency is foundational to a functioning democracy.

- **Public Apathy and Disengagement:** Harper recognized that public disengagement was partly due to a lack of accessible information regarding government actions. By making complex political issues understandable, she aimed to re-engage citizens in the democratic process.

Tangible Outcomes of Harper's Advocacy

The impact of Harper's work on government accountability can be categorized into several key outcomes:

- **Legislative Changes:** Harper's advocacy contributed to the passage of several key pieces of legislation aimed at increasing government transparency. For instance, her campaign for the *Government Accountability Act* led to stricter regulations on lobbying and campaign financing, ensuring that citizens have greater insight into the relationships between politicians and special interest groups.

- **Strengthened Whistleblower Protections:** By collaborating with whistleblowers, Harper helped to establish stronger legal protections for individuals who expose wrongdoing within government. This has encouraged more individuals to come forward with information about corruption, thereby enhancing accountability.

- **Increased Civic Engagement:** Harper's work inspired a wave of grassroots activism focused on government accountability. Organizations dedicated to civic education and engagement have proliferated, fostering a more informed electorate that actively participates in the democratic process.

- **Media as a Watchdog:** Harper's success in investigative journalism has reinforced the role of the media as a watchdog in democracy. Her work has inspired a new generation of journalists to pursue stories that hold power accountable, thereby contributing to a culture of scrutiny that deters corruption.

Conclusion

In conclusion, Harper Sato's impact on government accountability is both profound and multifaceted. Through her commitment to transparency, she has challenged entrenched systems of corruption and fostered a culture of accountability that empowers citizens. By utilizing theoretical frameworks that emphasize the importance of social contracts and accountability, she has addressed systemic problems that hinder democratic governance. The tangible outcomes of her advocacy, from legislative changes to increased civic engagement, underscore the critical role of investigative journalism in shaping a more transparent and accountable government. As Harper continues to influence the political landscape, her legacy serves as a reminder of the power of informed citizens and the media in holding governments accountable for their actions.

The Grassroots Movement Inspired by Harper

Activists Mobilize for Political Reform

In the wake of Harper Sato's groundbreaking media reforms, a new wave of political activism emerged, catalyzing a grassroots movement that sought to challenge entrenched political structures and advocate for meaningful reform. This mobilization was characterized by a collective recognition of the urgent need for transparency, accountability, and ethical governance in the face of rampant political corruption and corporate influence.

Theoretical Framework

The mobilization of activists for political reform can be understood through the lens of social movement theory, which posits that collective action arises in response to perceived injustices and the desire for social change. According to Tilly and Tarrow (2015), social movements are characterized by their organization, sustained interaction, and shared purpose, often fueled by a shared grievance. In this context, activists rallied around the common goal of dismantling the systemic barriers that perpetuated corruption and hindered democratic processes.

Identifying Core Problems

The activists identified several core problems that necessitated reform:

1. **Corporate Influence in Politics**: The overwhelming power of corporate interests in shaping policy decisions often sidelined the needs and voices of ordinary citizens. This phenomenon, termed *corporate capture*, manifested in lobbying efforts that prioritized profit over public welfare.

2. **Voter Suppression**: Systematic efforts to disenfranchise marginalized communities, including restrictive voter ID laws and gerrymandering, undermined the democratic process and perpetuated inequality.

3. **Lack of Transparency**: The opacity of government operations, particularly regarding campaign financing and decision-making processes, eroded public trust and accountability.

4. **Inequitable Representation**: The political landscape often failed to reflect the diversity of the populace, leading to policies that did not address the needs of all constituents, particularly those from underrepresented communities.

Mobilization Strategies

Activists employed a variety of strategies to mobilize for political reform:

1. **Grassroots Campaigning**: Local organizations and community leaders played a pivotal role in mobilizing citizens at the grassroots level. Through town hall meetings, workshops, and community forums, activists educated the public about the importance of political engagement and the need for reform.

2. **Digital Organizing**: The rise of social media platforms provided activists with powerful tools for mobilization. Campaigns such as #OurDemocracy and #VoteForChange gained traction online, allowing activists to reach a broader audience and galvanize support for reform initiatives.

3. **Coalition Building**: Recognizing the interconnectedness of various issues, activists formed coalitions across different movements—environmentalists, civil rights advocates, and labor unions—creating a unified front for political reform. This intersectional approach highlighted the importance of solidarity in addressing systemic injustices.

4. **Direct Action**: Activists organized protests, sit-ins, and demonstrations to draw attention to the urgent need for reform. These actions not only raised awareness but also applied pressure on lawmakers to prioritize reform efforts.

Case Studies and Examples

Several notable examples illustrate the effectiveness of activist mobilization for political reform:

- **The Fight for Campaign Finance Reform**: In the wake of the Supreme Court's decision in *Citizens United v. FEC* (2010), which allowed for unlimited corporate spending in elections, activists launched campaigns advocating for constitutional amendments to overturn this ruling. Organizations such as *Common Cause* and *Move to Amend* mobilized citizens nationwide, leading to increased public discourse on the influence of money in politics.

- **Youth-Led Movements**: Inspired by Harper's commitment to social justice, young activists organized movements such as *March for Our Lives* and *Fridays for Future*, demanding accountability from political leaders on issues ranging from gun control to climate action. These movements harnessed the power of youth voices, emphasizing the importance of civic engagement in shaping the future.

- **Local Initiatives**: In cities across the nation, activists successfully campaigned for measures such as ranked-choice voting and independent redistricting commissions, which aimed to enhance democratic participation and reduce the influence of partisan politics.

Conclusion

The mobilization of activists for political reform represents a critical response to the challenges posed by corruption and corporate influence in governance. Through grassroots organizing, digital strategies, coalition building, and direct action, activists have demonstrated their ability to effect change and inspire a new generation of civic engagement. The legacy of Harper Sato's media reforms served as a catalyst for this movement, illustrating the profound impact that informed and passionate individuals can have in shaping the political landscape for the better. As activists continue to push for reform, their efforts remind us of the enduring importance of accountability, transparency, and equitable representation in a functioning democracy.

Grassroots Campaigns for Campaign Finance Reform

The issue of campaign finance reform has been a contentious topic in American politics, often drawing attention to the influence of money on electoral processes and the potential for corruption. Grassroots campaigns have emerged as vital vehicles for advocating change, driven by a collective desire to restore democratic integrity and ensure that political representation reflects the will of the people rather than the financial interests of a few.

Theoretical Background

Campaign finance refers to the funds raised to promote candidates, political parties, or policies in elections. Theories surrounding campaign finance reform often hinge on the principles of democratic equality and political accountability. According to *Theories of Justice* by John Rawls, a fair political system must ensure that all individuals have an equal opportunity to influence political outcomes, which is severely undermined when wealth translates into political power.

The **Citizens United v. FEC** (2010) Supreme Court ruling marked a significant turning point in campaign finance, allowing corporations and unions to spend unlimited funds on political advocacy. This decision, rooted in the First Amendment's protection of free speech, has led to the rise of Super PACs, which can raise and spend unlimited amounts of money, often obscuring the sources of their funding. The ruling has intensified calls for reform, as critics argue that it undermines the democratic process by enabling wealthy individuals and entities to drown out the voices of ordinary citizens.

Problems with Current Campaign Finance Systems

The current landscape of campaign finance presents several critical problems:

1. **Inequality in Political Influence**: Wealthy donors can exert disproportionate influence over candidates and elected officials, leading to policies that favor corporate interests over public welfare. 2. **Lack of Transparency**: Many campaign finance mechanisms lack adequate disclosure requirements, allowing donors to remain anonymous and hindering public accountability. 3. **Corruption Risks**: The intersection of money and politics creates opportunities for quid pro quo arrangements, where financial contributions are exchanged for political favors, eroding public trust in government.

These issues have galvanized grassroots movements across the nation, as citizens increasingly recognize the need for systemic change.

Examples of Grassroots Campaigns

Several grassroots campaigns have emerged to address the flaws in the campaign finance system, mobilizing citizens to advocate for reform:

1. **Move to Amend**: This campaign seeks to amend the U.S. Constitution to clarify that corporations do not possess the same rights as individuals and to establish that money is not equivalent to speech. Through local resolutions and national advocacy, Move to Amend aims to dismantle the legal framework that allows for unlimited corporate spending in elections.

2. **Public Campaign**: Founded in 2002, Public Campaign advocates for public financing of elections, arguing that it would level the playing field for candidates from diverse backgrounds. Their model promotes a system where candidates can receive public funds if they demonstrate grassroots support, thereby reducing reliance on large donations.

3. **Wolf-PAC**: This organization focuses on the goal of a constitutional amendment to overturn Citizens United. Wolf-PAC mobilizes volunteers to lobby state legislatures to pass resolutions calling for an amendment, emphasizing the need for a united front against corporate influence in politics.

4. **The RepresentUs Movement**: RepresentUs combines a variety of grassroots efforts to combat political corruption through comprehensive reforms, including campaign finance reform. Their strategy involves engaging citizens in local campaigns, passing anti-corruption laws, and promoting ballot initiatives aimed at reducing the influence of money in politics.

Impact of Grassroots Campaigns

Grassroots campaigns have demonstrated significant potential to influence public discourse and policy regarding campaign finance reform. By mobilizing citizens, these movements have achieved notable successes:

- **Increased Awareness**: Grassroots efforts have raised awareness about the detrimental effects of money in politics, prompting public discussions and debates on the issue. - **Legislative Changes**: Some states have enacted reforms, such as public financing of campaigns and stricter disclosure requirements for campaign contributions, as a direct result of grassroots advocacy. - **Engagement of Young Activists**: Grassroots movements have inspired a new generation of activists who are passionate about political reform, utilizing social media and digital platforms to organize and spread their message.

Conclusion

Grassroots campaigns for campaign finance reform represent a vital force in the ongoing struggle for political equality and accountability. By challenging the status quo and advocating for systemic change, these movements embody the spirit of democratic participation. As Harper Sato's influence grows, her commitment to amplifying these grassroots voices will be crucial in shaping a future where political power is not dictated by wealth but by the collective will of the people.

Through the lens of grassroots activism, the fight for campaign finance reform is not merely a political issue; it is a fundamental battle for the soul of democracy itself. As citizens continue to mobilize and demand change, the hope for a more equitable political landscape remains alive and vibrant.

Increasing Civic Engagement and Voter Education

In the contemporary political landscape, civic engagement and voter education stand as pivotal elements in fostering a robust democracy. As Harper Sato championed media reforms and transparency, she also recognized the critical need for an informed electorate capable of actively participating in the democratic process. This section delves into the theories underpinning civic engagement, the prevalent challenges in voter education, and real-world examples that illustrate Harper's profound impact on these areas.

Theoretical Frameworks

Civic engagement is often grounded in several theoretical frameworks, including the **Social Capital Theory**, which posits that social networks have value. According to Robert Putnam, social capital facilitates coordination and cooperation for mutual benefit, thereby enhancing community engagement and political participation. Putnam's seminal work, *Bowling Alone*, highlights the decline of social capital in the United States, correlating it with decreased civic participation and voter turnout.

Furthermore, the **Civic Voluntarism Model** developed by Verba, Schlozman, and Brady emphasizes three key factors influencing civic engagement: resources (time, money, and civic skills), psychological engagement (interest in politics), and recruitment networks (influence of social networks). This model illustrates how disparities in these factors can lead to unequal levels of civic engagement across different demographics.

Challenges to Civic Engagement and Voter Education

Despite the theoretical frameworks supporting civic engagement, several challenges persist:

- **Misinformation:** In the digital age, misinformation spreads rapidly, undermining informed decision-making. A study by the Pew Research Center found that 64% of Americans believe that made-up news has caused confusion about basic facts of current events. This phenomenon has a direct impact on voter education, as individuals may base their decisions on false information.

- **Voter Apathy:** A significant portion of the electorate feels disillusioned with the political process. According to the U.S. Census Bureau, only 66.8% of eligible voters participated in the 2020 presidential election, indicating a persistent trend of voter apathy. Factors contributing to this apathy include a lack of trust in government institutions and a belief that individual votes do not matter.

- **Barriers to Access:** Structural barriers such as voter ID laws, limited access to polling places, and complicated registration processes disproportionately affect marginalized communities. The Brennan Center for Justice reports that states with strict voter ID laws experienced a 2-3% decrease in turnout among minority voters.

Harper's Initiatives for Civic Engagement and Voter Education

Recognizing these challenges, Harper Sato implemented several initiatives aimed at increasing civic engagement and voter education:

- **Community Workshops:** Harper launched a series of workshops designed to educate citizens on the voting process, including registration, understanding ballot measures, and the importance of local elections. These workshops emphasized the role of civic engagement in shaping community outcomes and encouraged participants to take an active role in local governance.

- **Digital Literacy Campaigns:** In response to the rampant spread of misinformation, Harper's team developed digital literacy campaigns aimed at teaching citizens how to critically evaluate news sources and discern factual information from falsehoods. These campaigns utilized social media platforms to reach a broader audience, particularly younger voters who are increasingly consuming news online.

- **Partnerships with Local Organizations:** Harper fostered partnerships with grassroots organizations focused on voter registration and education. By collaborating with established community groups, Harper's initiatives were able to leverage existing networks and resources, amplifying their reach and impact. For instance, a partnership with the League of Women Voters resulted in the successful registration of over 50,000 new voters in a single election cycle.

Case Studies and Impact

The effectiveness of Harper's initiatives can be illustrated through various case studies:

- **The Youth Voter Engagement Initiative:** In 2022, Harper's campaign targeted college campuses to boost youth voter turnout. By organizing events that combined entertainment with educational components, such as live music and guest speakers, the initiative saw a 30% increase in voter registration among college students compared to the previous election cycle.

- **The Misinformation Response Team:** In 2023, Harper established a rapid response team to counteract misinformation during election seasons. This team utilized social media to debunk false claims and provided accurate information about the voting process. As a result, surveys indicated a 40% increase in respondents' confidence in their understanding of the electoral process.

Conclusion

Increasing civic engagement and voter education are essential for a healthy democracy. Harper Sato's multifaceted approach to these issues not only addressed the immediate challenges posed by misinformation and voter apathy but also laid the groundwork for a more informed and active electorate. By fostering community involvement and enhancing voter education, Harper has inspired a generation to reclaim their agency in the political process, ensuring that the voice of tomorrow is indeed heard today. As we reflect on her contributions, it becomes clear that the legacy of civic engagement is not merely about participation but about empowering individuals to shape the future of their communities and society at large.

A New Era of Grassroots Activism

In the wake of Harper Sato's impactful journalism and advocacy, a new era of grassroots activism emerged, characterized by heightened public engagement, innovative strategies, and a collective push for systemic change. This section explores the theoretical foundations, challenges, and real-world examples that define this transformative movement.

Theoretical Foundations of Grassroots Activism

Grassroots activism is rooted in the theory of participatory democracy, which emphasizes the importance of citizen involvement in political processes. According to [?], participatory democracy not only empowers individuals but also enhances the legitimacy of democratic institutions. The rise of digital technology has further fueled this movement, enabling activists to organize, mobilize, and disseminate information rapidly.

The **Networked Public Sphere** theory posits that the internet has created a space where diverse voices can converge, allowing for the amplification of grassroots movements. [?] argues that this shift has democratized information dissemination, making it possible for grassroots organizations to challenge established narratives and mobilize support for their causes.

Challenges Faced by Grassroots Movements

Despite the promising landscape for grassroots activism, numerous challenges persist. One significant issue is the **digital divide**, which refers to the gap between those who have access to digital technology and those who do not. As [?] highlights, this divide can limit the effectiveness of grassroots efforts, particularly in marginalized communities.

Additionally, grassroots movements often face **institutional resistance** from established political and corporate entities. These institutions may employ tactics such as disinformation campaigns, legal challenges, and even intimidation to undermine grassroots efforts. For instance, the backlash against the Black Lives Matter movement illustrates how entrenched systems can mobilize against grassroots activism to maintain the status quo.

Innovative Strategies in Grassroots Activism

In response to these challenges, grassroots activists have employed innovative strategies to enhance their effectiveness. One notable approach is the use of **social** media platforms for organizing and mobilization. Activists have harnessed platforms like Twitter, Instagram, and TikTok to raise awareness, share information, and build community. The viral nature of social media campaigns, such as the #MeToo movement, demonstrates the potential for grassroots activism to reach a global audience and effect change.

Another strategy involves **coalition-building** among diverse groups. By forming alliances with other organizations, grassroots movements can pool resources, share knowledge, and amplify their voices. The collaboration between environmental justice groups and indigenous activists during the Standing Rock protests exemplifies the power of coalition-building in confronting powerful interests.

Real-World Examples of Grassroots Activism

The resurgence of grassroots activism is evident in several contemporary movements. The **Fridays for Future** movement, initiated by climate activist Greta Thunberg, mobilized millions of young people worldwide to demand urgent action on climate change. This movement exemplifies how grassroots activism can leverage social media to mobilize a global audience and influence political discourse.

Similarly, the **Women's March** following the 2016 U.S. presidential election showcased the power of grassroots organization. Millions of participants united to advocate for women's rights and social justice, demonstrating that grassroots movements can effectively galvanize public support and influence policy discussions.

Conclusion

The emergence of a new era of grassroots activism, fueled by innovative strategies and the theoretical foundations of participatory democracy, has reshaped the landscape of social and political engagement. While challenges remain, the resilience and creativity of grassroots movements continue to inspire individuals to take action and advocate for change. As Harper Sato's legacy illustrates, the power of collective action is a driving force for accountability, transparency, and justice in society.

The Rise of a Socially Conscious Generation

In the wake of Harper Sato's groundbreaking work in media reform and political activism, a new generation has emerged, characterized by a heightened social consciousness and a commitment to effecting change. This evolution is not merely a cultural shift; it is a response to the pressing challenges of our time, including climate change, political corruption, and social inequality. The rise of this socially conscious generation can be understood through various theoretical frameworks, including social identity theory, the theory of planned behavior, and the concept of collective efficacy.

Social Identity Theory

Social identity theory posits that individuals derive a sense of self from their group memberships, which significantly influences their attitudes and behaviors. As young people increasingly identify with social movements—such as climate activism, racial justice, and gender equality—they develop a strong sense of belonging and purpose. This identification fosters collective action, as seen in the global climate strikes initiated by youth activists like Greta Thunberg. The slogan "We are the last generation that can save the planet" encapsulates the urgency felt by this generation, galvanizing them into action.

The Theory of Planned Behavior

The theory of planned behavior suggests that an individual's intention to engage in a behavior is influenced by their attitudes, subjective norms, and perceived behavioral control. As media narratives shift to emphasize the importance of social responsibility, young people are more likely to adopt pro-social behaviors. For instance, the widespread adoption of sustainable practices—such as reducing plastic use, supporting local businesses, and advocating for renewable energy—reflects a positive attitude towards environmental stewardship. The rise of social media platforms has amplified these norms, allowing young activists to share their values and mobilize peers, thereby increasing collective engagement in social causes.

Collective Efficacy

Collective efficacy refers to a group's shared belief in its ability to achieve goals. This concept is particularly relevant in the context of grassroots movements. The mobilization of young people around issues like climate justice and political transparency demonstrates a growing belief that their actions can lead to tangible change. For example, the success of the Sunrise Movement in the United States, which advocates for a Green New Deal, showcases how collective action among young activists can influence policy discussions at the highest levels of government.

Challenges Faced by the Socially Conscious Generation

While this generation is marked by its activism and awareness, it also faces significant challenges. One major issue is the overwhelming nature of the problems they seek to address. The scale of climate change, systemic racism, and economic inequality can lead to feelings of helplessness and burnout. Research indicates that eco-anxiety—a chronic fear of environmental doom—affects many young people, potentially hindering their ability to engage in activism effectively. Furthermore, the digital landscape, while a powerful tool for mobilization, can also perpetuate misinformation and create echo chambers that stifle diverse perspectives.

Examples of Activism and Engagement

The rise of a socially conscious generation is illustrated through various movements and initiatives. The March for Our Lives campaign, initiated by survivors of the Parkland school shooting, exemplifies youth-led activism aimed at addressing gun violence in America. Similarly, the Black Lives Matter movement has galvanized young people around issues of racial justice and police reform, showcasing their commitment to challenging systemic injustices. These movements not only reflect the values of a socially conscious generation but also highlight their ability to influence public discourse and policy.

Educational Initiatives and Social Responsibility

Educational institutions play a crucial role in fostering social consciousness among young people. Programs that emphasize critical thinking, civic engagement, and social responsibility encourage students to become active participants in their communities. Initiatives like service-learning, which combines community service with academic study, empower students to apply their knowledge to real-world challenges. By cultivating a sense of agency and responsibility, educational systems can help sustain the momentum of this socially conscious generation.

Conclusion

The rise of a socially conscious generation, inspired by the efforts of innovators like Harper Sato, represents a profound shift in societal values. As young people increasingly engage with pressing social and environmental issues, they demonstrate a commitment to creating a more equitable and sustainable future. While challenges remain, the theoretical frameworks of social identity, planned behavior, and collective efficacy provide valuable insights into the motivations driving this generation. As they continue to mobilize and advocate for change, the potential for transformative impact grows, signaling a hopeful trajectory for future generations.

Harper's Enduring Influence on Politics

Policies and Legislation Influenced by Harper's Efforts

Harper Sato's work has significantly influenced a range of policies and legislation aimed at enhancing transparency, accountability, and ethical standards within both media and political spheres. This subsection explores the specific policies that emerged as a direct result of her advocacy, the theoretical frameworks that underpin these changes, and the real-world implications of her efforts.

Theoretical Frameworks

Harper's initiatives can be examined through several theoretical lenses, including *public choice theory* and *social contract theory*. Public choice theory posits that political actors are primarily motivated by self-interest, leading to inefficiencies and corruption in governance. By advocating for transparency and accountability, Harper sought to counteract these tendencies, aiming to realign the incentives of public officials with the public good.

Social contract theory, on the other hand, emphasizes the agreement between the governed and the governing. Harper's calls for greater government transparency and accountability resonate with the principles of social contract theory, as she argued that citizens have the right to demand honesty and integrity from their leaders. This theoretical underpinning provided a moral foundation for her advocacy, emphasizing that a government's legitimacy is derived from its adherence to the principles of transparency and accountability.

Key Policies and Legislation

1. **The Transparency in Government Act:** One of the landmark pieces of legislation influenced by Harper's work is the Transparency in Government Act. This act mandates that all government agencies must publish their spending, contracts, and decision-making processes online, allowing citizens to easily access this information. The act was designed to combat the culture of secrecy that often surrounds government operations and to empower citizens to hold their leaders accountable.

$$\text{Transparency Score} = \frac{\text{Public Accessed Documents}}{\text{Total Documents}} \times 100 \qquad (23)$$

This equation represents the transparency score, which can be used to assess the effectiveness of the act in increasing public access to government documents.

2. **The Whistleblower Protection Act:** In response to Harper's investigations into political corruption, the Whistleblower Protection Act was enacted to safeguard individuals who expose wrongdoing within government agencies. This legislation not only provides legal protections to whistleblowers but also encourages a culture of accountability by ensuring that those who come forward with information about corruption are not subject to retaliation.

3. **Campaign Finance Reform Legislation:** Influenced by Harper's exposé of the corrupting influence of money in politics, various campaign finance reform measures were introduced. These measures include stricter limits on campaign contributions, increased transparency requirements for political donations, and the establishment of public financing options for candidates who agree to adhere to spending limits.

$$\text{Contribution Limit} = \text{Base Limit} \times (1 + \text{Inflation Rate})^n \qquad (24)$$

Here, the contribution limit is adjusted annually based on inflation, ensuring that the limits remain relevant and effective over time.

4. **The Media Accountability Act:** Harper's influence also extended to media reform with the introduction of the Media Accountability Act, which aims to enhance journalistic standards and practices. This act includes provisions for mandatory training in ethical journalism, requirements for fact-checking, and the establishment of independent review boards to assess media bias and accuracy.

Real-World Implications

The policies influenced by Harper's efforts have led to a measurable increase in public trust in government institutions. According to a recent survey, public confidence in government transparency rose by 30% following the implementation of the Transparency in Government Act. Furthermore, the Whistleblower Protection Act has resulted in a 40% increase in reported cases of corruption, demonstrating that individuals feel safer coming forward with information.

Moreover, the Campaign Finance Reform Legislation has led to a notable decrease in the influence of corporate money in politics, with independent candidates reporting a 50% increase in campaign contributions from small donors.

This shift has enabled a more diverse range of voices to enter the political arena, fostering a healthier democratic process.

Conclusion

In summary, Harper Sato's advocacy has catalyzed significant legislative changes that have reshaped the landscape of both media and politics. By grounding her efforts in robust theoretical frameworks and addressing the pressing issues of transparency and accountability, Harper has not only influenced specific policies but has also inspired a broader movement towards reform. The enduring impact of her work continues to resonate, highlighting the importance of vigilance and activism in the pursuit of a just and equitable society.

The Long-Term Impact on Political Corruption

The long-term impact of Harper Sato's investigative journalism on political corruption can be understood through several frameworks, including the theory of accountability, the role of media as a watchdog, and the evolving relationship between citizens and their governments. Harper's relentless pursuit of the truth not only exposed systemic corruption but also instigated a cultural shift in how political accountability is perceived and enacted.

Theoretical Framework of Accountability

The concept of accountability in governance is rooted in the idea that public officials must answer to the public for their actions. As noted by Bovens et al. (2008), accountability can be defined as the obligation of power holders to explain and justify their decisions and actions to their constituents. Harper's work exemplified this principle, as she illuminated the mechanisms of corruption that often operate in the shadows of political power.

$$\text{Accountability} = \frac{\text{Transparency} + \text{Responsiveness}}{\text{Corruption}} \qquad (25)$$

In this equation, the numerator represents the essential components that foster accountability, while the denominator indicates the hindrance posed by corruption. Harper's investigations significantly increased transparency in political processes, making it more difficult for corrupt practices to thrive without scrutiny.

Media as a Watchdog

Harper's influence on the media landscape reinforced the role of journalism as a watchdog. The watchdog theory of the press posits that the media serves as a guardian against abuses of power by holding public officials accountable. This theory is supported by empirical evidence demonstrating that investigative journalism can lead to significant policy changes and reforms (Bennett et al., 2012).

For instance, following Harper's exposé on political links to corporate bribery, several high-profile politicians were forced to resign, and new legislation was enacted to enhance transparency in campaign financing. The long-term effect of these changes has been a gradual decline in overtly corrupt practices, as politicians recognize that their actions will be scrutinized by a vigilant press and an informed public.

Changing Public Perception

Harper's advocacy for accountability has also contributed to a shift in public perception regarding political corruption. According to a study by the Pew Research Center (2019), citizens are increasingly aware of the implications of corruption and demand greater transparency from their leaders. This heightened awareness has led to a more engaged electorate, willing to challenge corrupt practices and hold officials accountable.

For example, grassroots movements inspired by Harper's work have emerged across various regions, advocating for campaign finance reform and demanding stricter regulations on lobbying activities. These movements have not only increased public participation in the political process but have also pressured lawmakers to enact reforms aimed at reducing corruption.

Institutional Reforms and Policy Changes

The long-term impact of Harper's investigations is also evident in the institutional reforms that have been implemented in the wake of her revelations. Following her exposé of government cover-ups and bribery schemes, several states enacted measures to strengthen their ethics commissions and improve the enforcement of anti-corruption laws.

One notable example is the introduction of the *Corruption Prevention Act* in 2022, which established stricter penalties for corrupt practices and mandated greater transparency in public procurement processes. This legislation has led to a measurable decrease in corrupt activities, as evidenced by a report from

Transparency International (2023), which indicated a 15% reduction in corruption cases in the first year following the act's passage.

The Role of Technology in Combating Corruption

In addition to traditional media, technological advancements have played a crucial role in combating political corruption. Harper's emphasis on digital transparency and the use of social media platforms has empowered citizens to expose corrupt practices more readily. The proliferation of smartphones and online platforms has made it easier for individuals to document and report instances of corruption, thereby increasing the pressure on public officials to act with integrity.

For instance, the rise of whistleblower platforms, such as *Whistleblower Hub*, has provided a secure space for individuals to report corruption anonymously, further enhancing the accountability framework established by Harper's work. This technological shift has made it increasingly difficult for corrupt practices to go unnoticed, as citizens now have the tools to hold their leaders accountable in real-time.

Conclusion

In conclusion, the long-term impact of Harper Sato's investigations on political corruption is profound and multifaceted. By promoting accountability, reinforcing the role of media as a watchdog, changing public perceptions, and instigating institutional reforms, Harper has significantly altered the landscape of political corruption. Her legacy continues to inspire a new generation of activists and journalists committed to fighting for transparency and justice in governance. As society moves forward, the principles championed by Harper will remain vital in the ongoing struggle against corruption, ensuring that power remains accountable to the people it serves.

Bibliography

[1] Bovens, M., Curtin, D., & Groenleer, M. (2008). *Accountability in the Contemporary World*. In The Oxford Handbook of Public Accountability.

[2] Bennett, W. L., Lawrence, R. G., & Livingston, S. (2012). *When the Press Fails: Political Power and the News Media from Iraq to Katrina*. University of Chicago Press.

[3] Pew Research Center. (2019). *Public Attitudes Toward Political Corruption*. Retrieved from https://www.pewresearch.org.

[4] Transparency International. (2023). *Global Corruption Report: Trends and Developments*. Retrieved from https://www.transparency.org.

Continuing to Hold Power Accountable

In the wake of Harper Sato's groundbreaking investigations and relentless pursuit of truth, the concept of accountability in power dynamics has taken on new dimensions. This section explores the mechanisms through which power can be held accountable, the theoretical frameworks that underpin these practices, and the real-world implications of Harper's legacy.

Theoretical Frameworks of Accountability

Accountability is a multifaceted concept rooted in various theoretical frameworks, including political theory, ethics, and sociology. At its core, accountability refers to the obligation of individuals, organizations, and institutions to explain their actions and decisions to stakeholders. The following theories provide a foundation for understanding accountability in the context of media and politics:

- **Social Contract Theory:** This theory posits that individuals consent, either explicitly or implicitly, to surrender some freedoms in exchange for protection of their remaining rights. In the context of media, this implies that journalists have a duty to the public to hold power accountable, ensuring that the social contract is honored.

- **Public Interest Theory:** This framework asserts that the primary role of media is to serve the public interest. Journalists, therefore, have an ethical responsibility to investigate and report on issues that affect society, including governmental and corporate malfeasance.

- **Stakeholder Theory:** This theory emphasizes the importance of considering all stakeholders in decision-making processes. It encourages media professionals to recognize the impact of their reporting on various groups, advocating for transparency and accountability.

Mechanisms for Holding Power Accountable

Harper's work has illuminated several mechanisms through which power can be held accountable. These mechanisms are crucial for ensuring that those in positions of authority are answerable to the public. Key mechanisms include:

- **Investigative Journalism:** As demonstrated by Harper, investigative journalism serves as a watchdog, uncovering abuses of power and corruption. The rigorous methods employed by investigative journalists—such as deep research, interviews, and data analysis—are essential for exposing wrongdoing.

- **Public Advocacy and Activism:** Grassroots movements inspired by Harper's findings have mobilized citizens to demand accountability from their leaders. These movements often utilize social media platforms to amplify their voices and organize protests, creating pressure on political entities to respond to public grievances.

- **Legal Frameworks:** Laws and regulations such as the Freedom of Information Act (FOIA) empower citizens and journalists to access government records, fostering transparency. Legal challenges against governmental overreach have also become a tool for accountability, as seen in several landmark cases that have set precedents for public access to information.

Challenges to Accountability

Despite the mechanisms in place, several challenges persist in the pursuit of accountability:

- **Misinformation and Disinformation:** The proliferation of misinformation complicates the landscape of accountability. As Harper emphasized, the challenge of combating false narratives requires a concerted effort from media professionals to uphold journalistic integrity and fact-checking.

- **Political Resistance:** Those in power often resist accountability measures, employing tactics such as intimidation, legal threats, and smear campaigns against journalists and activists. Harper faced significant backlash from powerful interests, illustrating the risks involved in holding the powerful accountable.

- **Public Apathy:** A disengaged public can undermine accountability efforts. Harper's advocacy for civic engagement highlights the importance of educating citizens about their rights and responsibilities in a democratic society. Only through active participation can the public hold power to account.

Examples of Continuing Accountability

Harper's influence has inspired numerous initiatives and movements aimed at holding power accountable. Notable examples include:

- **The #MeToo Movement:** This grassroots movement has empowered individuals to speak out against sexual harassment and assault, holding powerful figures accountable in various industries. The movement exemplifies the power of collective action in challenging systemic abuses.

- **Whistleblower Protections:** Legislative efforts to protect whistleblowers have gained traction, allowing individuals to report misconduct without fear of retaliation. Harper's collaboration with whistleblowers has underscored the importance of safeguarding those who expose wrongdoing.

- **Citizen Journalism:** The rise of citizen journalism has democratized information dissemination, allowing ordinary individuals to report on local issues and hold authorities accountable. This trend has been particularly impactful in regions with limited press freedom, where traditional media may be constrained.

Conclusion

Harper Sato's legacy is not merely one of individual achievement but rather a catalyst for a broader movement towards accountability in media and politics. Through her unwavering commitment to truth, she has inspired a generation of journalists and activists to continue the fight against corruption and injustice. As society grapples with the complexities of power dynamics, the principles of accountability remain more critical than ever. The ongoing efforts to hold power accountable will determine the health of democratic institutions and the integrity of the media landscape, ensuring that the voice of the people is heard loud and clear.

$$\text{Accountability} = \text{Transparency} + \text{Responsibility} + \text{Engagement} \qquad (26)$$

Harper's Role as a Mentor and Catalyst for Change

Harper Sato's influence extends far beyond her groundbreaking media reforms and political activism; she has emerged as a pivotal mentor and catalyst for change in the lives of countless individuals and communities. Her journey illustrates the profound impact that one determined individual can have on the trajectory of future leaders, activists, and innovators. This section explores the various dimensions of Harper's mentorship, her strategic approach to fostering change, and the tangible outcomes of her efforts.

The Philosophy of Mentorship

At the core of Harper's mentorship philosophy is the belief that empowerment is a collective endeavor. Drawing from the theoretical framework of *transformational leadership*, Harper embodies the qualities of a leader who inspires and motivates others to exceed their own expectations. According to Burns (1978), transformational leaders create significant change by fostering an environment where followers can develop their own leadership potential. Harper's approach aligns with this theory, as she prioritizes collaboration, inclusivity, and the cultivation of critical thinking skills among her mentees.

Mentorship Programs and Initiatives

To institutionalize her commitment to mentorship, Harper established several programs aimed at nurturing the next generation of innovators and activists. One notable initiative is the *Media for Change Fellowship*, which provides aspiring journalists and media professionals with hands-on experience in ethical reporting and investigative journalism. The fellowship emphasizes the importance of accountability and transparency in media, mirroring Harper's own principles.

The program's structure includes:

- **Workshops:** Participants engage in workshops focused on ethical journalism, media literacy, and the role of independent media in society.

- **Mentorship Pairing:** Each fellow is paired with a seasoned journalist or activist who provides guidance, feedback, and support throughout the fellowship.

- **Community Projects:** Fellows undertake community-based projects that address local issues, reinforcing the connection between media and social change.

The success of the Media for Change Fellowship is evidenced by the achievements of its alumni, many of whom have gone on to become influential voices in the media landscape, advocating for social justice and integrity in reporting.

Harper as a Catalyst for Change

Harper's role as a catalyst for change is not limited to her direct mentorship. She has also fostered a culture of activism through her public speaking engagements, workshops, and collaborations with grassroots organizations. By sharing her experiences and insights, she encourages others to challenge the status quo and pursue their passions fearlessly.

One example of Harper's catalytic influence is her collaboration with the *Youth for Climate Justice* movement. By providing a platform for young activists to share their stories and strategies, Harper amplifies their voices and empowers them to lead the charge for climate action. This initiative exemplifies the concept of *social capital*, as it builds networks of support and collaboration among diverse stakeholders.

Challenges and Resilience

While Harper's mentorship efforts have yielded significant positive outcomes, they have not been without challenges. The backlash from powerful interests threatened to undermine her initiatives, leading to attempts to discredit her work and silence her voice. However, Harper's resilience is a testament to her commitment to fostering change. She has navigated these challenges by:

- **Building Alliances:** Harper actively collaborates with other mentors, organizations, and community leaders to create a united front against adversity.

- **Encouraging Open Dialogue:** She promotes an environment where mentees can voice their concerns and experiences, fostering a sense of solidarity and shared purpose.

- **Leveraging Technology:** Harper utilizes social media and digital platforms to reach a wider audience, ensuring that her message of empowerment and resilience resonates globally.

Impact on Future Generations

The long-term impact of Harper's mentorship is evident in the growing movement of socially conscious leaders and activists inspired by her work. Many of her mentees have taken on prominent roles in various sectors, including journalism, environmental advocacy, and political reform. Their successes serve as a powerful reminder of the ripple effect that mentorship can create.

For instance, one of her former fellows, Maya Chen, has become a leading voice in the fight against climate change, successfully lobbying for legislation that promotes renewable energy initiatives in her community. Maya attributes her confidence and strategic thinking to the guidance she received from Harper, demonstrating how mentorship can shape the trajectory of individuals and movements alike.

Conclusion

In conclusion, Harper Sato's role as a mentor and catalyst for change underscores the importance of nurturing future leaders who are equipped to tackle the pressing challenges of our time. By fostering a culture of empowerment, collaboration, and resilience, Harper not only transforms individual lives but also contributes to the broader movement for social justice and accountability. Her legacy as a mentor will continue to inspire generations to come, reinforcing the idea that change is possible when individuals are empowered to take action.

Harper's Legacy in Political Reform

Harper Sato's journey through the tumultuous landscape of political reform has left an indelible mark on the fabric of democratic governance. Her legacy is characterized by a relentless pursuit of transparency, accountability, and civic engagement, reshaping how citizens interact with their governments and how those governments respond to their constituents.

Theoretical Framework

At the core of Harper's approach to political reform lies the theory of **deliberative democracy**, which emphasizes the importance of informed and thoughtful discussion among citizens as a means to achieve consensus and foster genuine political engagement. According to [?], deliberative democracy posits that "legitimacy arises from the participation of citizens in the public sphere." Harper's initiatives exemplified this theory by promoting platforms for dialogue and debate, ensuring that the voices of marginalized communities were included in the political discourse.

Identifying Problems

Harper's reform efforts were catalyzed by the recognition of several systemic problems within the political landscape:

- **Corruption and Lack of Accountability:** The pervasive influence of special interests and corporate lobbying had eroded public trust in government institutions. Harper's investigations into political corruption revealed the extent of bribery and kickback schemes, as exemplified by her exposé on the *Corruption in Politics Act*, which highlighted the collusion between politicians and corporate giants.

- **Voter Disenfranchisement:** Harper identified that many citizens, particularly from marginalized backgrounds, faced barriers to voting. Her advocacy for campaign finance reform aimed to dismantle the financial barriers that often disenfranchised voters, a problem underscored by [?], which found that low-income individuals were significantly less likely to vote.

- **Information Asymmetry:** The information gap between the political elite and the general populace resulted in a lack of informed citizenry. Harper's commitment to transparency sought to bridge this gap, ensuring that citizens had access to essential information regarding governmental operations and decision-making processes.

Examples of Reform

Harper's legacy is evident in several key reforms that emerged from her advocacy:

- **The Transparency in Government Act:** This landmark legislation mandated open records for governmental proceedings, empowering citizens to access information that was previously hidden. The act has been credited with increasing public engagement and trust in government, as citizens became more informed about policy decisions.

- **Grassroots Mobilization Initiatives:** Harper inspired a new generation of activists to advocate for political reform through grassroots movements. The *Citizens for Accountability* campaign mobilized thousands across the nation, resulting in significant changes in local and national governance structures. The campaign's success was illustrated by the election of several reform-minded candidates who prioritized transparency and accountability.

- **Educational Programs on Civic Engagement:** Harper established programs aimed at educating citizens about their rights and the importance of civic participation. Workshops and seminars, particularly in underserved communities, have led to increased voter turnout and engagement, as evidenced by a 25% increase in voter registration among participants in these programs, according to the [?].

Impact on Political Culture

Harper's influence on political culture is profound, fostering a climate where accountability is expected and transparency is demanded. Her efforts have contributed to the emergence of a **new political ethos** that prioritizes citizen engagement and ethical governance. The public's growing skepticism towards traditional political structures has led to a demand for reform, a shift that Harper has both anticipated and nurtured.

Conclusion

In conclusion, Harper Sato's legacy in political reform is characterized by her unwavering commitment to transparency, accountability, and civic engagement. Her efforts have not only reshaped the political landscape but have also inspired a generation of activists and citizens to demand better governance. As we reflect on her contributions, it becomes clear that Harper's vision for a more equitable and just political system will continue to resonate in the ongoing struggle for democratic renewal.

Harper's Quest for Climate Justice

Awakening to the Climate Crisis

Harper Discovers the Devastating Reality of Climate Change

Harper Sato's awakening to the reality of climate change was not merely an intellectual exercise; it was a visceral experience that reshaped her worldview and ignited her passion for environmental justice. Growing up in a rapidly urbanizing world, she was initially oblivious to the environmental degradation occurring around her. However, a pivotal moment during her college years catalyzed her understanding of the climate crisis.

The Initial Encounter

In her sophomore year, Harper participated in a field trip to a local coastal community that had been severely impacted by rising sea levels. The once-thriving village, known for its vibrant fishing industry, was now a shadow of its former self, with homes abandoned and livelihoods destroyed. Witnessing the despair etched on the faces of the residents, Harper felt a profound sense of urgency. This experience was not just an isolated incident; it was emblematic of a global crisis affecting millions.

Scientific Understanding

To comprehend the gravity of what she had witnessed, Harper delved into the scientific literature on climate change. She encountered the work of climate scientists who warned of the catastrophic consequences of inaction. According to the Intergovernmental Panel on Climate Change (IPCC), global temperatures are projected to rise by 1.5°C above pre-industrial levels by as early as 2030 if current trends continue. This seemingly modest increase could lead to:

$$\Delta T = T_f - T_i \tag{27}$$

where ΔT is the change in temperature, T_f is the future temperature, and T_i is the initial temperature. The implications of this change are staggering: increased frequency of extreme weather events, loss of biodiversity, and dire consequences for food security.

The Human Element

As Harper dug deeper, she discovered the human element behind the statistics. She learned about the concept of climate refugees—individuals forced to leave their homes due to climate-related events. The United Nations estimates that by 2050, there could be as many as 200 million climate migrants. This statistic struck Harper profoundly, as she realized that climate change is not just an environmental issue; it is a humanitarian crisis.

The Role of Media

With her newfound understanding, Harper recognized the critical role of media in shaping public perception of climate change. She began to scrutinize how mainstream media outlets reported on environmental issues, often relegating them to the back pages or framing them as distant threats. This misrepresentation, she believed, contributed to a lack of urgency among the public and policymakers alike.

A Call to Action

Determined to make a difference, Harper decided to leverage her skills in media to raise awareness about climate change. She envisioned a platform that would not only inform the public but also inspire action. Her mission was clear: to bridge the gap between scientific understanding and public engagement.

Conclusion

Harper's discovery of the devastating reality of climate change was a turning point that set her on a path towards activism and reform. It was a journey marked by a profound understanding of the interconnectedness of human and environmental health. This realization became the foundation of her later efforts, as she sought to amplify the voices of those most affected by climate change and advocate for sustainable solutions. As she often stated in her speeches, "Climate change is not a distant threat; it is a present reality that demands our immediate attention and action."

Through her work, Harper aimed to transform the narrative surrounding climate change, emphasizing that it is not just an environmental issue but a matter of social justice, equity, and survival for future generations.

The Urgency of Addressing the Global Crisis

The climate crisis is not merely a distant threat; it is a present reality that demands immediate action. The urgency of addressing this global crisis can be understood through a multifaceted lens encompassing scientific evidence, socioeconomic impacts, and ethical imperatives. In this section, we will explore the critical nature of the climate crisis, the consequences of inaction, and the theoretical frameworks that guide our understanding of this pressing issue.

Scientific Evidence of Climate Change

The scientific consensus on climate change is overwhelming. According to the Intergovernmental Panel on Climate Change (IPCC), global temperatures have risen approximately 1.1°C since the late 19th century, primarily due to human activities such as fossil fuel combustion, deforestation, and industrial processes [1]. This increase in temperature is linked to a range of catastrophic phenomena, including:

- **Extreme Weather Events:** The frequency and intensity of hurricanes, floods, and wildfires have surged. For example, Hurricane Harvey in 2017 caused unprecedented flooding in Houston, Texas, displacing thousands and resulting in billions of dollars in damages [2].

- **Melting Ice Caps and Rising Sea Levels:** The Arctic and Antarctic regions are experiencing rapid ice melt, contributing to rising sea levels. Projections indicate that global sea levels could rise by up to 1 meter by 2100, threatening coastal communities worldwide [3].

- **Biodiversity Loss:** Climate change is a leading factor in the extinction of species, with estimates suggesting that up to 1 million species are at risk of extinction due to changing habitats and environmental conditions [4].

Mathematically, the relationship between carbon dioxide levels and global temperatures can be modeled using the climate sensitivity equation:

$$\Delta T = \lambda \cdot \Delta F \qquad (28)$$

where ΔT is the change in global temperature, λ is the climate sensitivity parameter, and ΔF is the radiative forcing due to greenhouse gas emissions. This equation underscores the critical need to reduce emissions to mitigate temperature increases.

Socioeconomic Impacts

The socioeconomic ramifications of climate change are profound and far-reaching. Vulnerable populations, particularly in developing countries, are disproportionately affected. The World Bank estimates that climate change could push over 100 million people into extreme poverty by 2030 [5]. Key socioeconomic impacts include:

- **Food Security:** Climate change affects agricultural productivity, leading to food shortages and increased prices. For instance, droughts in sub-Saharan Africa have resulted in crop failures, exacerbating hunger and malnutrition [6].

- **Health Risks:** Rising temperatures contribute to the spread of infectious diseases, heat-related illnesses, and respiratory issues due to poor air quality. The World Health Organization (WHO) estimates that climate change will cause an additional 250,000 deaths per year between 2030 and 2050 [7].

- **Economic Instability:** The financial costs of climate change are staggering, with the potential to disrupt economies globally. The National Oceanic and Atmospheric Administration (NOAA) reported that the United States alone faced over $1 billion in damages from weather-related disasters in 2020 [8].

Ethical Imperatives

Addressing the climate crisis is not just a matter of practicality; it is an ethical obligation. The principle of intergenerational justice posits that current generations have a duty to protect the environment for future generations. This ethical framework emphasizes the need for sustainable practices that ensure the planet remains habitable.

Furthermore, the concept of environmental justice highlights the disproportionate impact of climate change on marginalized communities. These communities often lack the resources to adapt to climate impacts, making it imperative that climate action is inclusive and equitable. As articulated by the

United Nations Framework Convention on Climate Change (UNFCCC), "climate change is a common concern of humankind" [9], necessitating a collective response that prioritizes the needs of the most vulnerable.

Conclusion

The urgency of addressing the climate crisis cannot be overstated. Scientific evidence illustrates the dire consequences of inaction, while socioeconomic impacts reveal the vulnerabilities faced by communities around the world. Ethical imperatives compel us to act with urgency and justice. As Harper Sato emerges as a leading voice for climate justice, her commitment to addressing this global crisis is not just a personal mission; it is a call to action for all of humanity. The time to act is now, for the future of our planet depends on the choices we make today.

Bibliography

[1] Intergovernmental Panel on Climate Change, *Climate Change 2021: The Physical Science Basis*, 2021.

[2] National Oceanic and Atmospheric Administration, *Hurricane Harvey: A Record-Breaking Storm*, 2018.

[3] NASA, *The Effects of Climate Change: Sea Level Rise*, 2020.

[4] Intergovernmental Science-Policy Platform on Biodiversity and Ecosystem Services, *Global Assessment Report on Biodiversity and Ecosystem Services*, 2019.

[5] World Bank, *Climate Change and Poverty: A New Approach*, 2021.

[6] Food and Agriculture Organization, *The State of Food Security and Nutrition in the World*, 2020.

[7] World Health Organization, *Climate Change and Health*, 2018.

[8] National Oceanic and Atmospheric Administration, *Billion-Dollar Weather and Climate Disasters*, 2021.

[9] United Nations Framework Convention on Climate Change, *Climate Change: A Common Concern of Humankind*, 2019.

A Personal Commitment to Environmental Justice

Harper Sato's journey towards becoming a leading advocate for environmental justice was not merely a professional evolution but a deeply personal commitment shaped by her own experiences and observations. This section delves into the multifaceted nature of her dedication to environmental justice, illustrating how her life experiences, societal observations, and theoretical frameworks converged to inform her activism.

Understanding Environmental Justice

Environmental justice is a social movement that seeks to address the disproportionate environmental burdens faced by marginalized communities. It emphasizes the right of all individuals, regardless of race, ethnicity, or socioeconomic status, to live in a clean and healthy environment. The theory of environmental justice is rooted in the recognition that environmental hazards, such as pollution and climate change, often disproportionately affect low-income and minority communities. This inequity is exemplified by the work of scholars like Robert Bullard, who is often referred to as the father of environmental justice. Bullard's research highlighted how communities of color are more likely to be located near hazardous waste sites, leading to significant health disparities.

Personal Experiences Shaping Commitment

Harper's commitment to environmental justice can be traced back to her childhood in a community that faced environmental degradation. Growing up near a factory that emitted toxic waste, she witnessed firsthand the health impacts on her family and neighbors. This experience instilled in her a sense of urgency and responsibility to advocate for those whose voices were often silenced in discussions about environmental policies.

In her formative years, Harper volunteered with local organizations that focused on cleaning up polluted neighborhoods and advocating for cleaner air and water. These experiences reinforced her belief that environmental issues are not just abstract concepts but real challenges that affect people's lives daily. Harper often reflected on her childhood, stating, "I realized that environmental issues are deeply intertwined with social justice. The fight for clean air and water is a fight for human rights."

Theoretical Frameworks Influencing Harper's Activism

Harper's activism was further informed by various theoretical frameworks that emphasize the interconnectedness of social and environmental issues. One such framework is the *intersectionality theory*, which posits that individuals experience overlapping systems of oppression based on their identities, including race, class, gender, and environmental factors. This theory resonated with Harper as she recognized that marginalized communities often face compounded vulnerabilities due to environmental injustices.

Another influential theory was the *precautionary principle*, which advocates for proactive measures to prevent harm to the public and the environment, even in the absence of scientific consensus. This principle became a cornerstone of Harper's advocacy, as she fought against projects that posed potential environmental risks to vulnerable communities. She famously stated, "We cannot afford to gamble with our planet's health. The precautionary principle should guide all decision-making processes."

Mobilizing for Change

Harper's personal commitment to environmental justice propelled her into the forefront of activism. She began organizing community meetings to educate residents about their rights and the environmental issues affecting their neighborhoods. Through these gatherings, she empowered individuals to speak out against pollution and advocate for policy changes.

One notable example of her mobilization efforts was the "Clean Air, Clean Communities" campaign, which aimed to raise awareness about air quality issues in urban areas. Harper collaborated with local schools, community leaders, and environmental organizations to host workshops and rallies. The campaign successfully garnered media attention, leading to increased public pressure on local government officials to implement stricter air quality regulations.

Challenges and Resilience

Despite her dedication, Harper faced numerous challenges in her pursuit of environmental justice. She encountered resistance from powerful corporate interests that sought to maintain the status quo. These entities often dismissed her concerns as radical or unfounded, attempting to undermine her credibility. However, Harper's resilience shone through as she navigated these obstacles with determination and strategic thinking.

In one instance, when a major corporation attempted to build a waste incinerator in a low-income neighborhood, Harper spearheaded a coalition of activists, scientists, and community members to oppose the project. Through extensive research and community engagement, they documented the potential health risks associated with the incinerator, ultimately leading to its cancellation. This victory not only highlighted the power of grassroots activism but also solidified Harper's reputation as a formidable advocate for environmental justice.

Conclusion: A Lifelong Commitment

Harper Sato's personal commitment to environmental justice is a testament to the profound impact of lived experiences on activism. Her journey reflects the understanding that environmental issues are inextricably linked to social justice, necessitating a holistic approach to advocacy. Through her work, Harper has not only raised awareness of environmental injustices but has also inspired a new generation of activists to carry the torch for a sustainable and equitable future. Her story serves as a reminder that true change begins at the personal level, where individuals can transform their experiences into powerful movements for justice.

In summary, Harper's commitment to environmental justice is characterized by a deep understanding of the theoretical frameworks that inform the movement, a personal connection to the issues at hand, and an unwavering determination to mobilize communities for change. As she often reminds her supporters, "Our fight for the planet is also a fight for each other."

The Intersection of Media and Climate Activism

In recent years, the intersection of media and climate activism has become increasingly significant, as the urgency of the climate crisis demands innovative communication strategies to engage the public and inspire action. This section explores how media serves as a powerful tool for climate activism, shaping narratives, amplifying marginalized voices, and mobilizing communities around the globe.

The Role of Media in Shaping Climate Narratives

Media plays a crucial role in framing the discourse surrounding climate change. According to framing theory, the way information is presented influences public perception and understanding of issues. For instance, a study by [Entman(1993)] suggests that framing can lead to different interpretations of the same event, highlighting the power of media in constructing reality.

In the context of climate activism, media outlets can frame climate change either as an urgent crisis requiring immediate action or as a distant problem that can be addressed later. The framing of climate narratives significantly impacts public engagement and policy responses. For example, the portrayal of climate activists as "eco-terrorists" versus "environmental heroes" can sway public opinion and influence political action.

Amplifying Marginalized Voices

One of the most pressing issues in climate activism is the disproportionate impact of climate change on marginalized communities, including Indigenous peoples and low-income populations. Media serves as a platform to amplify these voices, ensuring that their stories and experiences are heard.

Harper Sato, through her show "The Voice of Tomorrow," exemplifies this approach by featuring stories from those directly affected by environmental degradation. By prioritizing these narratives, media can challenge dominant discourses that often overlook the experiences of marginalized communities. This practice aligns with the principles of participatory media, which advocate for inclusive storytelling and representation in media production.

Mobilizing Communities through Social Media

The rise of social media has transformed the landscape of climate activism, enabling rapid dissemination of information and facilitating grassroots organizing. Platforms like Twitter, Instagram, and Facebook allow activists to share real-time updates, mobilize supporters, and create viral campaigns.

For example, the #FridaysForFuture movement, initiated by youth climate activist Greta Thunberg, gained global traction through social media. The movement encouraged students worldwide to strike for climate action, demonstrating the power of digital media in mobilizing communities and fostering collective action. Research by [Bennett(2012)] indicates that social media can enhance civic engagement by providing accessible platforms for political expression and activism.

Challenges in Media and Climate Activism

Despite the potential of media to drive climate action, several challenges persist. Misinformation and climate denialism often infiltrate media narratives, undermining public trust in scientific consensus. The phenomenon of "false balance," where media outlets present opposing views on climate change as equally valid, can mislead the public and create confusion.

Moreover, corporate interests can influence media coverage of climate issues, resulting in biased reporting that favors economic growth over environmental sustainability. This issue is particularly evident in the fossil fuel industry's attempts to downplay climate risks and promote greenwashing initiatives.

To combat these challenges, climate activists and media professionals must work collaboratively to promote accurate and responsible reporting on climate issues. This includes advocating for journalistic integrity, fact-checking, and transparency in media practices.

Conclusion

The intersection of media and climate activism is a dynamic and evolving landscape, with the potential to drive significant change in public perception and policy. By effectively framing climate narratives, amplifying marginalized voices, and leveraging social media for mobilization, media can play a pivotal role in the fight against climate change. However, addressing challenges such as misinformation and corporate influence is essential to ensure that media serves as a force for positive change in the realm of climate activism.

Bibliography

[Entman(1993)] Entman, R. M. (1993). Framing: Toward clarification of a fractured paradigm. *Journal of Communication*, 43(4), 51-58.

[Bennett(2012)] Bennett, W. L. (2012). The personalization of politics: Political identity, social media, and changing patterns of participation. *The ANNALS of the American Academy of Political and Social Science*, 644(1), 20-39.

Harper Becomes a Leading Voice for Climate Justice

Harper Sato's journey into climate justice is not merely a personal crusade; it represents a pivotal shift in how media can serve as a catalyst for environmental activism. In an era defined by climate emergencies, Harper emerged as a leading voice by leveraging her platform to amplify urgent calls for action and foster a collective response to the climate crisis.

The urgency of climate change is encapsulated in the scientific consensus articulated by the Intergovernmental Panel on Climate Change (IPCC), which states that global temperatures must not rise more than 1.5 degrees Celsius above pre-industrial levels to avoid catastrophic consequences. This goal requires a drastic reduction in greenhouse gas emissions, necessitating immediate and concerted efforts across all sectors of society. Harper understood that the media's role in this context is not just to report on climate issues but to engage and mobilize the public.

One of the primary problems Harper confronted was the pervasive misinformation surrounding climate science. Media outlets often perpetuated false equivalences between credible scientific evidence and fringe opinions, leading to public confusion and apathy. To combat this, Harper adopted a strategy grounded in the principles of *evidence-based reporting*, ensuring that her narratives were rooted in verifiable data and expert testimony. For instance, during a segment on her show, she highlighted the findings of a 2021 study published in *Nature*, which revealed that the world is on track for a temperature rise of 2.7 degrees Celsius if current policies remain unchanged. By presenting such stark realities, Harper aimed to awaken her audience to the urgency of climate action.

Moreover, Harper utilized the concept of *intersectionality* to illustrate how climate change disproportionately affects marginalized communities. Her coverage of the 2020 wildfires in Australia included voices from Indigenous activists, emphasizing their traditional ecological knowledge and the need for inclusive climate policies. This approach not only broadened the narrative but also positioned Harper as a champion for social justice within the climate movement. By highlighting the interconnectedness of environmental degradation and social inequities, she fostered a more holistic understanding of climate justice.

Harper's influence extended beyond her own platform. She became a key figure in the global climate movement, participating in international conferences such as COP26, where she advocated for stronger commitments to carbon neutrality. Her presence at these events underscored the importance of media representation in climate discussions, as she used her platform to challenge world leaders on their pledges and accountability. For example, during a live broadcast from the conference, she confronted a delegate from a major industrial nation about their failure to meet emissions targets, a moment that resonated widely and sparked discussions on social media.

To further her impact, Harper collaborated with youth-led climate organizations, recognizing that the next generation would bear the brunt of climate inaction. By featuring young activists on her show, she not only amplified their voices but also encouraged civic engagement among her audience. This collaboration culminated in a campaign that mobilized over a million young people for climate strikes across the globe, demonstrating the power of collective action in the face of systemic challenges.

In conclusion, Harper Sato's emergence as a leading voice for climate justice exemplifies the transformative potential of media in shaping public discourse and mobilizing action. By grounding her advocacy in scientific evidence, embracing intersectionality, and fostering youth engagement, she has not only raised awareness but also inspired a movement that demands accountability and systemic change. Her legacy is a testament to the idea that informed media can be a powerful ally in the fight for a sustainable and equitable future. As we face the realities of climate change, Harper's approach serves as a blueprint for how media can contribute to a more just and resilient world.

Climate Action = Informed Public+Collective Engagement+Policy Accountability
(29)

Building a Coalition for Change

Collaborating with Environmental Organizations

In her quest for climate justice, Harper Sato recognized early on that collaboration with established environmental organizations was crucial for amplifying her message and effecting meaningful change. This synergy allowed her to leverage existing networks, resources, and expertise, which significantly enhanced the impact of her advocacy efforts.

Theoretical Framework

The collaboration between individual activists and larger organizations can be understood through the lens of *network theory*. According to Granovetter (1973), the strength of weak ties plays a critical role in the dissemination of information and mobilization of resources. By collaborating with environmental organizations, Harper effectively created a network of strong and weak ties that facilitated the flow of information and resources necessary for impactful climate activism.

Identifying Common Goals

One of the primary challenges in collaborating with environmental organizations is aligning goals and objectives. Harper approached this by conducting thorough research on various organizations, such as the *Sierra Club* and *Greenpeace*, identifying their missions, ongoing projects, and areas of expertise. For instance, while the Sierra Club focused on grassroots activism and policy advocacy, Greenpeace emphasized direct action and public awareness campaigns. By finding common ground, Harper was able to foster partnerships that complemented her vision for climate justice.

Case Study: The Coalition for Climate Action

A notable example of Harper's successful collaboration with environmental organizations was the formation of the *Coalition for Climate Action*. This coalition brought together over 50 environmental groups, community organizations, and grassroots activists to tackle specific climate issues, such as deforestation and fossil fuel dependency. The coalition's first major campaign, "*Save Our Forests*," aimed to halt illegal logging practices in critical habitats.

The campaign utilized a multi-faceted approach, employing social media outreach, public demonstrations, and policy advocacy. Harper's role as a media reform advocate allowed her to secure significant media coverage, which in turn attracted more supporters and resources to the campaign. This highlights the importance of media in environmental activism, as it can serve as a powerful tool for raising awareness and mobilizing action.

Challenges in Collaboration

Despite the benefits of collaboration, Harper faced several challenges. One significant issue was the potential for conflicting priorities among partner organizations. For example, while some organizations prioritized immediate action against fossil fuel companies, others focused on long-term systemic change. To address this, Harper facilitated regular meetings and open dialogues among coalition members, ensuring that all voices were heard and that strategies were aligned with the coalition's overarching goals.

Another challenge was the issue of funding. Many environmental organizations rely on grants and donations, which can create competition for limited resources. Harper advocated for a shared funding model, where coalition members pooled resources for joint campaigns, thereby reducing competition and increasing overall impact.

Measuring Impact and Success

To evaluate the effectiveness of her collaborations, Harper employed a variety of metrics, including:

$$\text{Impact Score} = \frac{\text{Number of New Supporters}}{\text{Total Campaign Cost}} \times 100 \qquad (30)$$

This formula allowed her to quantify the return on investment for each collaborative campaign, providing valuable insights into which strategies were most effective. For instance, the *"Save Our Forests"* campaign resulted in a 30% increase in supporters for the coalition within six months, demonstrating the power of collaborative efforts in driving public engagement.

Conclusion

Harper Sato's collaboration with environmental organizations exemplifies the potential of collective action in the fight for climate justice. By leveraging the strengths of established organizations, aligning goals, and navigating challenges, she was able to amplify her message and create a more significant impact on environmental issues. This collaborative approach not only enhanced her advocacy efforts but also set a precedent for future activists seeking to foster change through partnership and solidarity.

In summary, the collaboration with environmental organizations was not merely a strategy but a fundamental aspect of Harper's approach to climate activism. It underscores the importance of unity in addressing complex global challenges, demonstrating that together, diverse voices can create a powerful force for change.

Partnerships with Indigenous Climate Activists

In the quest for climate justice, Harper Sato recognized the indispensable role of Indigenous communities in advocating for environmental stewardship and sustainable practices. Indigenous peoples, often the first to experience the adverse effects of climate change, possess invaluable knowledge and perspectives that are crucial in addressing the climate crisis. This section explores the partnerships Harper fostered with Indigenous climate activists, the theoretical frameworks that underpin these collaborations, and the challenges faced in integrating Indigenous voices into broader climate movements.

Theoretical Framework: Indigenous Knowledge Systems

At the heart of Harper's partnerships with Indigenous climate activists lies the recognition of Indigenous Knowledge Systems (IKS). IKS encompasses the traditional ecological knowledge (TEK) that Indigenous communities have accumulated over generations, informed by their deep connection to the land. This knowledge is often holistic, integrating spiritual, cultural, and ecological dimensions, which contrasts sharply with the reductionist approaches prevalent in Western scientific paradigms.

The incorporation of IKS into climate activism aligns with the principles of decolonization, which seeks to dismantle the colonial structures that have historically marginalized Indigenous voices. By valuing IKS, Harper aimed to promote a more inclusive and equitable approach to environmental advocacy. The integration of Indigenous perspectives not only enriches the discourse surrounding climate change but also empowers Indigenous communities to reclaim their agency in shaping climate policies.

Building Alliances: Key Partnerships

Harper's commitment to collaboration with Indigenous climate activists led to the formation of several key partnerships that exemplified effective coalition-building. One notable example is her collaboration with the Indigenous Environmental Network (IEN), an organization that amplifies Indigenous voices in the fight against environmental degradation. Through joint campaigns, such as the "Protect Our Sacred Water" initiative, Harper and IEN mobilized communities to resist harmful extraction projects that threatened water sources vital to both Indigenous and non-Indigenous populations.

Another significant partnership emerged with the Assembly of First Nations (AFN) in Canada. Together, they organized the "Indigenous Climate Action Summit," which brought together Indigenous leaders, scientists, and activists to share knowledge and strategize collective action against climate change. This summit not only highlighted Indigenous resilience but also underscored the importance of Indigenous governance in environmental decision-making.

Challenges and Barriers

Despite the progress made through these partnerships, numerous challenges persisted. One of the primary obstacles was the ongoing legacy of colonialism, which manifested in systemic inequalities and a lack of recognition for Indigenous rights. Many Indigenous activists faced pushback from governmental and corporate entities resistant to acknowledging their sovereignty and expertise in environmental matters.

Furthermore, the intersectionality of climate justice and social justice issues often complicated these partnerships. Indigenous communities frequently grappled with additional challenges, such as poverty, lack of access to resources, and historical trauma, which could hinder their capacity to engage fully in climate activism. Harper recognized the necessity of addressing these underlying issues to foster genuine collaboration and solidarity.

Case Studies: Successful Collaborations

Several case studies exemplify the success of Harper's partnerships with Indigenous climate activists. One such case is the "Standing Rock Sioux Tribe's" resistance against the Dakota Access Pipeline (DAPL). Harper's media platform

BUILDING A COALITION FOR CHANGE

played a crucial role in amplifying the voices of the Standing Rock protestors, bringing global attention to their struggle. By highlighting the cultural significance of the land and water to the Sioux people, Harper helped frame the DAPL issue not merely as a local environmental concern but as a matter of Indigenous rights and sovereignty.

Another successful collaboration occurred during the "Fridays for Future" climate strikes, where Indigenous youth activists joined forces with students worldwide to demand climate action. Harper's support for Indigenous youth leaders, such as Autumn Peltier, who advocated for water protection, exemplified the intersection of youth activism and Indigenous rights. This partnership not only elevated Indigenous voices within the broader climate movement but also inspired a new generation of climate activists committed to justice and equity.

Conclusion: A Path Forward

Harper Sato's partnerships with Indigenous climate activists serve as a model for fostering inclusive and equitable climate movements. By valuing Indigenous Knowledge Systems, building meaningful alliances, and addressing systemic challenges, Harper demonstrated the importance of collaboration in the fight for climate justice. Moving forward, it is essential to continue amplifying Indigenous voices and integrating their perspectives into climate policies and practices. Only through such partnerships can we hope to achieve a sustainable and equitable future for all.

$$\text{Climate Justice} = \text{Social Justice} + \text{Environmental Justice} \qquad (31)$$

This equation encapsulates the essence of Harper's approach: that true climate justice can only be achieved when both social and environmental injustices are addressed in tandem. The partnerships forged with Indigenous climate activists not only enriched the climate movement but also laid the groundwork for a more just and sustainable world.

The Power of Global Solidarity

In the face of an escalating climate crisis, the concept of global solidarity emerges as a crucial mechanism for driving effective action and fostering resilience. Global solidarity refers to the unity and collective action among individuals, communities, and nations across the globe, aimed at addressing shared challenges such as climate change, social injustice, and economic inequality. This section delves into the theoretical underpinnings of global solidarity, the problems it seeks to address, and real-world examples that illustrate its transformative power.

Theoretical Foundations of Global Solidarity

The theoretical framework for global solidarity can be traced back to various disciplines, including sociology, political science, and environmental studies. At its core, global solidarity is rooted in the principles of interdependence and shared responsibility. Scholars like [?] emphasize the need for a holistic understanding of global issues, where the actions of one entity can significantly impact others. This interconnectedness underscores the importance of collective action in addressing climate change, as its effects are not confined by borders.

One prominent theory that supports the notion of global solidarity is the *Global Justice Theory*. This theory posits that justice should not be limited to national boundaries; rather, it should encompass global dimensions. The works of philosophers such as [?] argue that affluent nations have a moral obligation to assist those suffering from the adverse effects of climate change, which they often contribute to disproportionately. This ethical framework serves as a call to action for individuals and governments alike to engage in solidarity efforts.

Problems Addressed by Global Solidarity

The climate crisis presents multifaceted problems that global solidarity seeks to address:

- **Disproportionate Impact:** Developing countries often bear the brunt of climate change, despite contributing the least to greenhouse gas emissions. For instance, small island nations are facing existential threats from rising sea levels, while industrialized nations continue to emit large quantities of carbon dioxide.

- **Resource Inequity:** The unequal distribution of resources exacerbates vulnerabilities. Wealthier nations have more capacity to adapt to climate change, leaving poorer nations struggling to cope with its impacts. This disparity calls for global solidarity to ensure fair resource allocation and support for adaptation efforts.

- **Political Fragmentation:** Political divisions hinder cohesive climate action. Nations often prioritize national interests over global commitments, resulting in a fragmented approach to climate policy. Global solidarity encourages collaboration and unity in pursuing common goals.

Examples of Global Solidarity in Action

Numerous instances illustrate the power of global solidarity in combating climate change:

1. The Paris Agreement: The Paris Agreement, adopted in 2015, exemplifies global solidarity in action. Countries from around the world came together to commit to limiting global warming to well below 2 degrees Celsius. This historic accord reflects a collective acknowledgment of the climate crisis and a shared commitment to address it. Importantly, the agreement recognizes the principle of "common but differentiated responsibilities," emphasizing that wealthier nations should take the lead in reducing emissions and supporting developing countries.

2. Youth Climate Strikes: The global youth climate strikes, inspired by activists like Greta Thunberg, demonstrate the power of solidarity among young people worldwide. Millions of students have mobilized to demand action from their governments, transcending national boundaries and uniting under a common cause. This movement highlights how collective action can amplify voices and influence policy changes.

3. Climate Justice Alliances: Various alliances, such as the Climate Justice Alliance, bring together grassroots organizations, indigenous groups, and environmental activists to advocate for equitable climate solutions. These coalitions emphasize the need for marginalized voices to be heard in climate discussions, reinforcing the idea that solidarity must include those most affected by climate change.

Challenges to Global Solidarity

While the potential for global solidarity is immense, several challenges persist:

- **Nationalism and Isolationism:** Rising nationalism and isolationist policies threaten the collaborative spirit required for global solidarity. Countries may prioritize their interests over global commitments, undermining collective efforts to address climate change.

- **Misinformation and Polarization:** The spread of misinformation regarding climate science can create divisions and hinder solidarity. Polarized narratives can lead to inaction and skepticism, making it difficult to build consensus on climate solutions.

- **Resource Constraints:** Limited financial and technical resources pose significant barriers to solidarity efforts. Developing nations often lack the capacity to engage fully in global initiatives, necessitating support from wealthier nations.

Conclusion

Global solidarity stands as a powerful tool in the fight against climate change, offering a pathway for collective action and shared responsibility. By recognizing our interconnectedness and the moral imperative to support one another, individuals and nations can work together to address the pressing challenges posed by climate change. As Harper Sato exemplifies through her advocacy, fostering global solidarity is not just a noble ideal; it is a practical necessity for achieving meaningful and lasting change in the pursuit of climate justice.

Amplifying Youth Climate Activism

In recent years, the urgency of the climate crisis has galvanized a new generation of activists, particularly among youth. Harper Sato recognized the potential of this demographic not only to advocate for climate justice but also to reshape the discourse around environmental issues. This section explores how Harper amplified youth climate activism, the theoretical frameworks underpinning this movement, the challenges faced, and the notable examples of youth-led initiatives that emerged during this period.

Theoretical Frameworks

Youth climate activism can be understood through several theoretical lenses, including *social movement theory*, *collective efficacy*, and *intergenerational justice*. Social movement theory posits that collective action arises from shared grievances and the mobilization of resources. Youth activists often share a common grievance: the existential threat posed by climate change. This shared concern fosters a sense of community and urgency, leading to organized efforts to advocate for change.

Collective efficacy refers to the shared belief in a group's ability to achieve desired outcomes. Research indicates that when young people perceive their actions as impactful, they are more likely to engage in activism. Harper's role in providing platforms and visibility to youth activists reinforced their belief in their collective efficacy, leading to increased participation and activism.

Intergenerational justice emphasizes the ethical responsibility of current generations to protect the rights and well-being of future generations. This concept resonates deeply with youth activists, who often frame their advocacy as a fight for their future. Harper's media reforms highlighted these ethical dimensions, encouraging a broader societal recognition of the stakes involved.

Challenges Faced by Youth Activists

Despite their passion and commitment, youth climate activists encounter numerous challenges, including:

- **Marginalization:** Youth voices are often sidelined in discussions about climate policy, with decision-makers prioritizing the perspectives of older, more established figures. This marginalization can lead to feelings of frustration and disillusionment among young activists.

- **Access to Resources:** Many youth-led initiatives struggle with limited access to funding and resources, hindering their ability to organize events, conduct research, and amplify their messages. The lack of institutional support can stifle innovation and limit the reach of their activism.

- **Digital Divide:** While social media has become a powerful tool for mobilization, disparities in access to technology can exclude marginalized youth from participating fully in digital activism. This digital divide can perpetuate existing inequalities within the climate movement.

- **Psychological Burden:** The weight of the climate crisis can lead to feelings of anxiety and helplessness among young activists. The phenomenon known as *eco-anxiety* reflects the emotional toll of grappling with such a monumental issue, which can affect motivation and mental health.

Harper's Role in Amplifying Youth Voices

Harper Sato played a pivotal role in amplifying youth climate activism through several key strategies:

- **Media Representation:** By featuring young activists on her show, "The Voice of Tomorrow," Harper provided a platform for their voices to be heard. This representation not only validated their experiences but also inspired other young people to engage in activism. The show highlighted the stories of youth leaders, showcasing their innovative solutions and the urgency of their calls for action.

- **Collaborative Campaigns:** Harper collaborated with youth-led organizations to launch campaigns that resonated with younger audiences. These campaigns utilized social media to spread messages quickly and effectively, leveraging hashtags and viral challenges to engage a broader public. For instance, campaigns such as *#FridaysForFuture* gained momentum through strategic partnerships and media coverage, drawing attention to the climate crisis and mobilizing millions of young people worldwide.

- **Educational Initiatives:** Understanding the importance of education in fostering activism, Harper supported initiatives that aimed to educate young people about climate science, policy, and advocacy. Workshops, webinars, and educational content produced by her media team equipped youth with the knowledge and skills necessary to engage effectively in climate activism.

- **Intergenerational Dialogue:** Harper facilitated conversations between youth activists and seasoned environmental leaders, fostering mentorship and collaboration. These dialogues not only empowered young activists but also ensured that their perspectives were integrated into broader climate strategies. By bridging generational gaps, Harper cultivated a culture of inclusivity and shared responsibility.

- **Highlighting Local Actions:** Harper emphasized the importance of local actions in the fight against climate change, showcasing grassroots efforts led by youth in various communities. By spotlighting these initiatives, she demonstrated that impactful change can occur at the local level, inspiring others to take action within their own communities.

Notable Examples of Youth-Led Initiatives

Several youth-led initiatives exemplify the impact of amplified activism in the climate movement:

- **Greta Thunberg and Fridays for Future:** Perhaps the most recognizable figure in youth climate activism, Greta Thunberg's solitary protest outside the Swedish parliament sparked a global movement. The *Fridays for Future* strikes mobilized millions of students around the world, demanding urgent action on climate change. Harper's coverage of these strikes brought further attention to the movement, highlighting the voices of young activists leading the charge.

- **Sunrise Movement:** This youth-led organization focuses on political advocacy for climate justice, particularly through the lens of the Green New Deal. The Sunrise Movement has successfully mobilized young people to engage in grassroots organizing, exemplifying the power of collective action. Harper's support for their initiatives amplified their message and helped garner national attention.

- **Youth Climate Summit:** In collaboration with various organizations, Harper helped organize a summit that brought together young climate leaders from around the globe. This event facilitated knowledge sharing, networking, and strategic planning, empowering participants to return to their communities with actionable plans. The summit exemplified the potential of youth collaboration in driving systemic change.

- **Local Climate Action Groups:** Across the globe, young people have formed local climate action groups that focus on community-specific issues. These groups often engage in direct action, such as tree planting, clean-up drives, and advocacy for local environmental policies. Harper's media coverage of these initiatives showcased the diverse ways in which youth can make a difference, inspiring others to take similar actions.

Conclusion

Harper Sato's commitment to amplifying youth climate activism has had a profound impact on the movement, fostering a new generation of leaders equipped to tackle the climate crisis. By leveraging media, providing platforms, and facilitating collaboration, Harper not only elevated youth voices but also reinforced the importance of intergenerational solidarity in the fight for climate justice. As youth activists continue to lead the charge, their influence will undoubtedly shape the future of environmental advocacy, ensuring that the fight for a sustainable and equitable world remains at the forefront of public consciousness.

Harper's Vision for a Sustainable Future

Harper Sato's vision for a sustainable future is rooted in a holistic understanding of environmental, social, and economic systems. She advocates for an integrated approach that recognizes the interdependence of these systems and the need for systemic change to address the pressing challenges of climate change, resource depletion, and social inequality.

Theoretical Framework

At the core of Harper's vision is the concept of **sustainability**, defined by the Brundtland Commission in 1987 as "development that meets the needs of the present without compromising the ability of future generations to meet their own needs." This idea encompasses three pillars: environmental stewardship, social equity, and economic viability.

$$\text{Sustainability} = \text{Environmental Health} + \text{Social Equity} + \text{Economic Viability} \tag{32}$$

Harper emphasizes the necessity of balancing these pillars to create a resilient and thriving society. She draws on theories such as **Ecological Economics**, which integrates ecological and economic thinking to address the limitations of traditional economic models that often overlook environmental costs.

Key Problems Addressed

Harper's vision confronts several critical problems, including:

- **Climate Change:** The urgent need for global action to reduce greenhouse gas emissions and transition to renewable energy sources.

- **Resource Depletion:** The unsustainable consumption of natural resources, leading to biodiversity loss and habitat destruction.

- **Social Inequality:** The disproportionate impact of environmental degradation on marginalized communities, necessitating a focus on environmental justice.

- **Corporate Influence:** The role of corporate interests in perpetuating unsustainable practices and resisting regulatory measures.

Harper argues that these problems are interconnected and must be addressed through comprehensive policy solutions that prioritize sustainability.

Examples of Harper's Initiatives

To actualize her vision, Harper has spearheaded several initiatives:

- **Renewable Energy Projects:** Harper advocates for large-scale investments in renewable energy technologies, such as solar and wind power. For instance, her collaboration with local governments has led to the establishment of community solar farms that provide clean energy to underserved populations.

- **Sustainable Agriculture Programs:** Recognizing the impact of industrial agriculture on climate change, Harper promotes sustainable farming practices that enhance soil health and reduce carbon emissions. One successful initiative includes supporting urban agriculture projects that empower communities to grow their own food sustainably.

- **Environmental Education Campaigns:** Harper believes that education is key to fostering a sustainable future. She has developed programs aimed at raising awareness about climate change and sustainability in schools, encouraging students to engage in eco-friendly practices and advocacy.

- **Legislative Advocacy:** Harper actively lobbies for policies that promote sustainability, such as the Green New Deal, which aims to create jobs while addressing climate change. Her work has influenced local and national legislation that prioritizes environmental protection and social equity.

The Role of Technology and Innovation

Harper's vision also embraces the potential of technology and innovation to drive sustainability. She advocates for the development of clean technologies and smart solutions that can enhance efficiency and reduce waste. For example, she supports the use of **blockchain technology** for transparent supply chains that ensure sustainable sourcing of materials.

$$\text{Sustainable Supply Chain} = \text{Transparency} + \text{Traceability} + \text{Ethical Sourcing} \tag{33}$$

By leveraging technology, Harper envisions a future where businesses operate sustainably, consumers make informed choices, and communities thrive.

Inspiring Future Generations

Ultimately, Harper's vision for a sustainable future is about inspiring the next generation of leaders and innovators. She emphasizes the importance of fostering a culture of sustainability in education, encouraging young people to think critically about their impact on the planet and to engage in activism.

Through mentorship programs and youth-led initiatives, Harper empowers young activists to take ownership of their future. She believes that by equipping future generations with the tools and knowledge to address environmental challenges, we can create a more just and sustainable world.

In conclusion, Harper Sato's vision for a sustainable future is a call to action for individuals, communities, and governments. By embracing sustainability as a guiding principle, we can work towards a future that not only meets the needs of the present but also ensures the well-being of generations to come. Her vision is not just a dream; it is a roadmap for transformative change that recognizes the urgent need for collective action in the face of climate change and social injustice.

Challenging the Fossil Fuel Industry

Exposing Corporate Greenwashing

Corporate greenwashing refers to the practice where companies present themselves as environmentally friendly while engaging in practices that are harmful to the environment. This phenomenon has become increasingly prevalent as consumers demand more sustainable practices from businesses, leading to a rise in misleading marketing strategies that exaggerate or fabricate a company's environmental efforts. Harper Sato, through her media platform, has tirelessly worked to expose these deceptive tactics, highlighting the need for transparency and accountability in corporate environmental claims.

Theoretical Framework

To understand corporate greenwashing, we can apply the **Stakeholder Theory**, which posits that businesses must consider the interests of all stakeholders, including customers, employees, suppliers, and the community, rather than solely focusing on shareholder profits. Companies that engage in greenwashing often neglect the genuine interests of their stakeholders in favor of short-term gains.

Furthermore, the **Theory of Planned Behavior** suggests that individuals' behaviors are driven by their intentions, which are influenced by attitudes, subjective norms, and perceived behavioral control. When companies mislead consumers about their environmental practices, they manipulate these factors, leading to a distorted perception of their sustainability efforts.

Identifying Greenwashing Tactics

Harper has identified several common tactics used by corporations to greenwash their image:

1. **Vague Claims:** Companies often make broad statements such as "eco-friendly" or "green" without providing specific evidence or certifications. For instance, a detergent brand may market its product as "biodegradable" without clarifying the timeframe or conditions under which it biodegrades.

2. **Irrelevant Claims:** Some companies highlight minor environmentally friendly features that are not central to the product's overall impact. For example, a car manufacturer might promote a vehicle's recyclable floor mats while ignoring its overall emissions and fuel efficiency.

3. **Misleading Labels:** The use of labels that imply a product is certified by a recognized environmental standard can mislead consumers. For instance, a product may carry a label that resembles an official certification but is actually created by the company itself.

4. **Hidden Trade-offs:** Corporations may focus on one positive environmental aspect while ignoring significant negative impacts. For example, a company might advertise its use of recycled materials while failing to disclose harmful production processes.

Case Studies of Greenwashing

Several high-profile cases have illustrated the extent of corporate greenwashing:

- **Volkswagen's Emissions Scandal:** In 2015, Volkswagen was found to have installed software in diesel vehicles to cheat emissions tests, falsely advertising them as low-emission vehicles. This scandal not only damaged Volkswagen's reputation but also raised questions about the validity of corporate claims regarding environmental performance.

- **BP's "Beyond Petroleum" Campaign:** British Petroleum rebranded itself as "Beyond Petroleum" in an effort to position itself as a leader in renewable energy. However, the company continued to invest heavily in fossil fuels, leading to criticism for its failure to align its marketing with actual practices.

- **H&M's Conscious Collection:** H&M launched its "Conscious Collection," promoting sustainable fashion. However, investigations revealed that the fast-fashion retailer's overall practices contributed significantly to environmental degradation, raising concerns about the sincerity of its sustainability claims.

The Role of Media in Exposing Greenwashing

Harper Sato's media platform has played a crucial role in uncovering instances of greenwashing. By employing investigative journalism, she has brought attention to misleading corporate claims, urging consumers to demand greater transparency.

$$\text{Transparency Index} = \frac{\text{Number of Verified Claims}}{\text{Total Claims Made}} \times 100 \tag{34}$$

This equation can serve as a guideline for assessing a company's transparency regarding its environmental practices. A higher Transparency Index indicates a greater commitment to genuine sustainability efforts.

Challenges in Addressing Greenwashing

Despite the efforts to expose corporate greenwashing, several challenges remain:

- **Consumer Awareness:** Many consumers are unaware of greenwashing tactics, making it difficult for them to distinguish between genuine and misleading claims.

- **Regulatory Gaps:** Current regulations regarding environmental claims are often insufficient, allowing companies to exploit loopholes. For instance, the Federal Trade Commission (FTC) in the United States has guidelines for environmental marketing, but enforcement can be inconsistent.

- **Corporate Resistance:** Companies that engage in greenwashing may push back against scrutiny, using legal threats or public relations campaigns to protect their image.

Conclusion

Exposing corporate greenwashing is essential for fostering a more sustainable future. Harper Sato's commitment to investigative journalism highlights the need for accountability in corporate environmental claims. By raising awareness and demanding transparency, consumers can hold corporations accountable for their practices, ultimately driving meaningful change in the pursuit of environmental justice. The continued collaboration between media, activists, and the public will be crucial in dismantling the facade of greenwashing and promoting authentic sustainability efforts.

Investigating the Effects of Extraction Industries

The extraction industries, encompassing oil, gas, and mining, play a significant role in the global economy. However, their impact on the environment, local communities, and public health is profound and often detrimental. This section delves into the multifaceted effects of extraction industries, highlighting the environmental degradation, social injustices, and economic implications associated with these operations.

Environmental Degradation

The extraction of natural resources is notorious for causing extensive environmental damage. One of the primary concerns is the disruption of ecosystems. For instance, deforestation associated with mining operations leads to habitat loss for countless species. According to the *World Wildlife Fund*, approximately 80% of terrestrial biodiversity is found in forests, making their preservation critical for maintaining ecological balance.

Furthermore, extraction processes often result in soil and water contamination. The use of toxic chemicals in mining, such as cyanide and mercury, poses significant risks. A notable example is the 2015 Samarco disaster in Brazil, where a dam collapse released millions of cubic meters of toxic waste into the Doce River, devastating local ecosystems and communities. The long-term effects of such contamination can render land uninhabitable and water sources unsafe for consumption.

Public Health Concerns

The health implications of extraction industries are alarming. Communities located near extraction sites frequently experience higher rates of respiratory diseases, cancers, and other health issues. The *American Public Health Association* has documented numerous cases where air pollution from oil and gas extraction has led to increased hospitalizations for respiratory ailments.

Moreover, the mental health of residents in extraction regions can be adversely affected due to the constant threat of environmental disasters and the disruption of their way of life. A study published in the *Journal of Environmental Psychology* found that individuals living near fracking sites reported higher levels of anxiety and depression compared to those in non-extraction areas.

Social Injustices and Displacement

Extraction industries often exacerbate social inequalities. Indigenous communities are particularly vulnerable, as their lands are frequently targeted for resource extraction without proper consent or compensation. The *United Nations Declaration on the Rights of Indigenous Peoples* emphasizes the need for free, prior, and informed consent for any development on indigenous lands, yet this principle is often ignored.

For example, the Dakota Access Pipeline project faced widespread opposition from the Standing Rock Sioux Tribe, who argued that the pipeline threatened their water supply and sacred lands. Despite protests and legal challenges, the project proceeded, highlighting the systemic disregard for indigenous rights in favor of economic gain.

Economic Implications

While extraction industries can generate significant revenue and employment opportunities, the economic benefits are often short-lived and unevenly distributed. The *Resource Curse* theory posits that countries rich in natural resources may experience slower economic growth and poorer development outcomes due to corruption, mismanagement, and over-reliance on resource extraction.

In many cases, local communities do not see the benefits of extraction. Wealth generated from resource extraction often flows to multinational corporations and government elites, leaving local populations marginalized. For instance, in Nigeria's Niger Delta region, oil extraction has led to environmental degradation and social unrest, yet the local communities remain impoverished despite the country's oil wealth.

Conclusion

Investigating the effects of extraction industries reveals a complex interplay of environmental, health, social, and economic issues. As Harper Sato advocates for climate justice, it is crucial to recognize the detrimental impacts of these industries and push for sustainable alternatives. Transitioning to renewable energy sources not only mitigates environmental harm but also promotes social equity and public health. The responsibility lies with innovators, policymakers, and communities to demand accountability from extraction industries and strive for a more sustainable future.

$$E = mc^2 \tag{35}$$

Where E is energy, m is mass, and c is the speed of light in a vacuum, illustrating the fundamental principle that energy can be derived from matter, a concept that underpins the potential of renewable energy sources as viable alternatives to extraction industries.

Advocating for Renewable Energy Solutions

The urgency of the climate crisis has necessitated a robust advocacy for renewable energy solutions, a cause that Harper Sato championed with fervor. As a media reformer and climate justice advocate, Harper recognized that the transition from fossil fuels to renewable energy sources is not merely a technical challenge but a moral imperative that intersects with social equity, economic stability, and environmental sustainability.

Theoretical Framework

At the core of Harper's advocacy lies the theory of sustainable development, which posits that current generations must meet their needs without compromising the ability of future generations to meet theirs. This concept is encapsulated in the widely recognized definition provided by the Brundtland Commission in 1987, which emphasizes the interdependence of economic growth, social inclusion, and environmental protection.

Mathematically, the sustainability of energy systems can be expressed through the equation:

$$E_s = E_r - E_f \tag{36}$$

where E_s is the sustainable energy output, E_r represents renewable energy generation, and E_f denotes fossil fuel consumption. For a transition to be deemed sustainable, E_s must remain positive, indicating that renewable energy generation must exceed fossil fuel consumption.

Problems with Fossil Fuel Dependency

The reliance on fossil fuels has led to numerous environmental and social problems, including:

- **Climate Change:** The burning of fossil fuels is the primary contributor to greenhouse gas emissions, which have led to global warming and severe climate events. According to the Intergovernmental Panel on Climate Change (IPCC), limiting global warming to 1.5°C requires a reduction of carbon dioxide emissions by approximately 45% from 2010 levels by 2030.

- **Air Pollution:** Fossil fuel combustion releases pollutants that degrade air quality, leading to health issues such as respiratory diseases and premature deaths. The World Health Organization (WHO) estimates that air pollution is responsible for 7 million deaths annually.

- **Economic Inequities:** The fossil fuel industry often exacerbates social inequalities, disproportionately affecting marginalized communities. These populations frequently bear the brunt of environmental degradation while having the least capacity to adapt to its impacts.

Renewable Energy Solutions

Harper advocated for a multi-faceted approach to renewable energy that includes solar, wind, hydroelectric, and geothermal sources. Each of these technologies offers unique advantages and can be tailored to meet local needs.

- **Solar Energy:** Solar photovoltaic (PV) systems convert sunlight directly into electricity. The cost of solar panels has decreased by more than 80% since 2010, making solar energy one of the most accessible renewable sources. Harper highlighted successful community solar projects that empower local residents to invest in solar energy collectively, thus reducing energy costs and promoting energy independence.

- **Wind Energy:** Wind turbines harness kinetic energy from wind to generate electricity. Onshore and offshore wind farms have seen exponential growth, with the Global Wind Energy Council reporting that the cumulative installed capacity reached over 743 GW in 2020. Harper emphasized the importance of policy frameworks that support wind energy development, such as tax incentives and feed-in tariffs.

- **Hydroelectric Power:** This form of renewable energy utilizes the flow of water to generate electricity. While large-scale hydroelectric projects can have significant ecological impacts, smaller-scale projects, such as run-of-the-river systems, can provide sustainable energy with minimal disruption to local ecosystems.

- **Geothermal Energy:** Geothermal systems tap into the Earth's internal heat for power generation and direct heating applications. Harper advocated for increased investment in geothermal technology, particularly in regions with high geothermal potential, such as the Pacific Ring of Fire.

Examples of Advocacy and Impact

Harper's advocacy took many forms, from public awareness campaigns to direct engagement with policymakers. One notable example was her collaboration with the organization *Renewable Future*, which aimed to educate communities about the benefits of renewable energy. Through workshops, webinars, and community forums, they empowered citizens to advocate for local renewable energy initiatives.

Additionally, Harper played a pivotal role in the successful campaign for the passage of the *Green Energy Act*, which provided incentives for renewable energy projects and established ambitious targets for reducing greenhouse gas emissions. This legislation not only spurred investment in clean energy but also created thousands of jobs in the renewable energy sector.

Conclusion

In conclusion, Harper Sato's advocacy for renewable energy solutions represents a crucial component of the broader fight against climate change and environmental injustice. By promoting sustainable energy practices, she not only addressed immediate environmental concerns but also laid the groundwork for a more equitable and sustainable future. As the world grapples with the realities of climate change, Harper's vision for a renewable energy transition remains a beacon of hope and a call to action for current and future generations.

The Fight for Environmental Justice in Marginalized Communities

The fight for environmental justice in marginalized communities is a critical aspect of Harper Sato's activism, as it highlights the intersection of environmental degradation and social inequities. Marginalized communities, often composed of low-income individuals and people of color, disproportionately bear the brunt of environmental hazards. This subsection explores the theoretical frameworks, systemic issues, and real-world examples that underscore the urgency of addressing environmental justice.

Theoretical Frameworks

Environmental justice is grounded in several theoretical frameworks that emphasize the rights of individuals and communities to a healthy environment. One foundational theory is the **Environmental Justice Movement (EJM)**, which emerged in the United States in the 1980s. This movement argues that environmental policies must consider social justice and equity, asserting that no group should bear a disproportionate share of environmental harms.

The **Social Determinants of Health** framework further elucidates how environmental factors contribute to health disparities. According to this framework, the conditions in which people are born, grow, live, work, and age significantly impact their health outcomes. Marginalized communities often face higher exposure to pollutants, limited access to clean water, and inadequate healthcare services, perpetuating a cycle of disadvantage.

Systemic Issues

Several systemic issues contribute to the environmental injustices faced by marginalized communities:

- **Industrial Pollution:** Many marginalized communities are located near industrial sites, leading to higher exposure to toxic substances. For instance, the residents of Flint, Michigan, faced a public health crisis due to lead-contaminated drinking water, a situation exacerbated by systemic neglect and mismanagement.

- **Housing Inequality:** Poor housing conditions often correlate with environmental hazards. Communities in urban areas may live in proximity to landfills or hazardous waste sites, increasing their risk of health problems. The lack of affordable housing options forces many families into these dangerous environments.

- **Limited Political Power:** Marginalized communities frequently lack the political clout to influence environmental policies. Their voices are often sidelined in decision-making processes, resulting in policies that favor corporate interests over community health.

- **Climate Change Vulnerability:** Climate change disproportionately impacts marginalized communities, which often lack the resources to adapt to its effects. Rising sea levels, extreme weather events, and heatwaves can

CHALLENGING THE FOSSIL FUEL INDUSTRY

devastate these communities, leading to displacement and further marginalization.

Examples of Environmental Justice Struggles

Several notable cases illustrate the fight for environmental justice in marginalized communities:

- **The Flint Water Crisis:** The Flint water crisis serves as a poignant example of environmental injustice. The decision to switch the water supply to the Flint River without proper treatment led to widespread lead contamination, affecting predominantly African American residents. Activists, including Harper, highlighted the systemic failures and called for accountability, ultimately leading to national awareness and policy changes.

- **Standing Rock Sioux Tribe:** The Dakota Access Pipeline protests exemplified the struggle for environmental justice among Indigenous communities. The Standing Rock Sioux Tribe opposed the pipeline's construction due to its potential to contaminate their water supply and violate treaty rights. The movement garnered global attention and solidarity, emphasizing the importance of Indigenous voices in environmental decision-making.

- **Cancer Alley:** In Louisiana, a region dubbed "Cancer Alley" is home to numerous petrochemical plants that disproportionately affect African American communities. Residents have reported higher rates of cancer and respiratory illnesses due to industrial pollution. Activists have organized to demand stricter regulations and accountability from corporations, highlighting the need for environmental justice in their fight for health and safety.

Harper's Advocacy and Impact

Harper Sato's advocacy for environmental justice in marginalized communities has been multifaceted. She has worked to amplify the voices of those directly affected by environmental hazards, ensuring that their stories are heard and their needs addressed. Harper has collaborated with grassroots organizations, providing them with media coverage and resources to strengthen their campaigns.

In her groundbreaking documentary series, *Voices of the Voiceless*, Harper highlighted the struggles faced by marginalized communities dealing with environmental injustices. The series not only raised awareness but also mobilized public support for policy changes aimed at protecting vulnerable populations.

Moreover, Harper's efforts to challenge corporate practices and advocate for stricter environmental regulations have led to significant legislative changes. Her work has inspired a new generation of activists, particularly among youth in marginalized communities, who are now leading the charge for environmental justice.

Conclusion

The fight for environmental justice in marginalized communities is essential for achieving a sustainable and equitable future. By addressing the systemic issues that perpetuate environmental harm and amplifying the voices of those most affected, activists like Harper Sato are paving the way for meaningful change. As the movement continues to grow, it is imperative to recognize the interconnectedness of environmental health and social justice, ensuring that all communities have the right to a safe and healthy environment.

Harper's Impact on the Fossil Fuel Industry

Harper Sato's influence on the fossil fuel industry is a testament to her unwavering commitment to environmental justice and sustainable practices. Through her investigative journalism and advocacy, Harper has significantly challenged the status quo of an industry often criticized for its detrimental impact on the planet. This section explores the multifaceted ways in which Harper has reshaped the discourse surrounding fossil fuels, highlighting key theories, problems, and examples that illustrate her impact.

Theoretical Framework: Environmental Justice and Corporate Responsibility

At the heart of Harper's activism is the theory of environmental justice, which posits that all individuals, regardless of race, ethnicity, or socioeconomic status, have the right to a healthy environment. This theory underscores the disproportionate effects of fossil fuel extraction on marginalized communities, often leading to severe health issues and environmental degradation. Harper's work emphasizes the need for corporate responsibility, advocating for transparency and ethical practices within the fossil fuel sector.

The equation that encapsulates the relationship between fossil fuel consumption and environmental degradation can be simplified as:

$$E = f(C, R)$$

where E represents environmental impact, C denotes the level of fossil fuel consumption, and R signifies regulatory measures in place. As consumption increases without adequate regulation, the environmental impact escalates, leading to dire consequences such as climate change, air and water pollution, and biodiversity loss.

Challenges Faced by Harper

Harper's journey has not been without challenges. The fossil fuel industry, characterized by its immense financial power and political influence, has often retaliated against her efforts. This includes attempts to discredit her work, smear campaigns, and even legal threats aimed at silencing her voice. Such actions highlight the broader problem of corporate influence over media narratives, where powerful entities seek to maintain their interests at the expense of public awareness and accountability.

One notable instance of backlash occurred when Harper published a series of exposés on a major oil company's environmental violations. The company responded with aggressive public relations campaigns, attempting to undermine her credibility and divert attention from the issues she raised. This scenario exemplifies the broader struggle between media advocates for transparency and the entrenched interests of the fossil fuel sector.

Examples of Harper's Impact

Despite these challenges, Harper's work has yielded tangible results in reshaping the fossil fuel industry. One of her most significant contributions has been the exposure of corporate greenwashing, a practice where companies exaggerate or fabricate their environmental efforts to appear more sustainable than they truly are. Through rigorous investigative reporting, Harper has unveiled instances of misleading advertisements and false claims, prompting public outcry and regulatory scrutiny.

For instance, her investigation into a prominent energy company revealed that their claims of transitioning to renewable energy were largely superficial, masking continued investments in fossil fuel extraction. This revelation not only damaged the company's reputation but also sparked a broader discussion about the authenticity of corporate sustainability claims across the industry.

Moreover, Harper has been instrumental in advocating for renewable energy solutions as viable alternatives to fossil fuels. By highlighting successful case studies of communities transitioning to solar, wind, and other sustainable energy sources, she has inspired grassroots movements and policy changes aimed at reducing dependence on fossil fuels.

A prime example of this is the partnership she forged with local activists in a town heavily reliant on coal mining. Together, they launched a campaign that successfully advocated for the development of a solar farm, which not only provided clean energy but also created jobs and stimulated the local economy. This initiative serves as a model for other communities seeking to break free from the shackles of fossil fuel dependency.

The Role of Media in Shaping Public Perception

Harper's impact extends beyond direct activism; her work has fundamentally altered public perception of the fossil fuel industry. By utilizing various media platforms to disseminate information about the environmental and social costs of fossil fuel extraction, she has empowered individuals to question the narratives presented by the industry.

The rise of social media has amplified her voice, allowing her to engage with a global audience. Hashtags like #FossilFuelFree and #ClimateJustice have gained traction, fostering a sense of community among activists and concerned citizens. This digital mobilization has played a crucial role in pressuring governments and corporations to adopt more sustainable practices.

Conclusion: A Lasting Legacy

Harper Sato's impact on the fossil fuel industry is profound and multifaceted. Through her investigative journalism, advocacy for environmental justice, and commitment to corporate accountability, she has challenged the industry's harmful practices and inspired a movement towards sustainability. As the world grapples with the urgent need to address climate change, Harper's contributions serve as a beacon of hope and a call to action for future generations.

In summary, Harper's legacy is not merely one of critique but of empowerment, demonstrating that the intersection of media, activism, and corporate responsibility can drive meaningful change in the fossil fuel industry. Her work exemplifies the potential for individuals to influence systemic transformation, reminding us all of the power of informed advocacy in the face of overwhelming odds.

A Global Movement for Climate Action

Climate Strikes and Mass Demonstrations

In the wake of an escalating climate crisis, climate strikes and mass demonstrations have emerged as pivotal forms of grassroots activism, galvanizing public attention and demanding urgent action from governments and corporations alike. These movements are not merely spontaneous gatherings; they are deeply rooted in a collective consciousness that recognizes the existential threat posed by climate change.

The Rise of Climate Strikes

The phenomenon of climate strikes gained significant momentum in 2018, catalyzed by the actions of young activists like Greta Thunberg, who famously initiated a weekly protest outside the Swedish Parliament. Thunberg's solitary act of defiance quickly transformed into a global movement, known as *Fridays for Future*, inspiring millions of students worldwide to participate in climate strikes. This movement exemplifies the power of individual action to spark collective mobilization, illustrating the concept of *social contagion* in activism, where the actions of one individual can influence the behaviors of many.

Theoretical Framework

The theoretical underpinnings of climate strikes can be analyzed through the lens of *collective action theory*. This framework posits that individuals are more likely to engage in protest when they perceive a shared grievance and believe that their actions can lead to tangible change. In the context of climate strikes, participants often articulate a shared frustration over governmental inaction and corporate irresponsibility regarding environmental degradation.

Mathematically, the likelihood of participation in a climate strike can be modeled using the following equation:

$$P(A) = \frac{N \cdot G \cdot C}{R} \tag{37}$$

where: - $P(A)$ is the probability of individual participation, - N is the number of individuals aware of the strike, - G represents the perceived gravity of the climate crisis, - C denotes the level of collective identity among participants, and - R is the perceived risk of participating (e.g., potential for legal repercussions).

As awareness of climate issues grows and collective identity strengthens, the probability of participation increases, leading to larger and more impactful demonstrations.

Mass Demonstrations: A Platform for Change

Mass demonstrations serve as a powerful platform for raising awareness and pressuring policymakers. Events such as the *Global Climate Strike* on September 20, 2019, saw millions of people across 150 countries take to the streets, demanding immediate action to combat climate change. The sheer scale of these demonstrations underscores the urgency of the climate crisis and the public's demand for accountability.

The effectiveness of mass demonstrations can also be understood through the concept of *political opportunity structures*, which refers to the external factors that influence the likelihood of successful mobilization. For instance, the alignment of public sentiment with climate action, along with the visibility of climate-related disasters, creates a favorable environment for protest.

Challenges Faced by Climate Strikes

Despite their potential for impact, climate strikes face several challenges. One significant issue is the backlash from political and corporate entities that view these movements as threats to their interests. For instance, in some regions, activists have faced legal repercussions, including arrests and charges of trespassing during protests. Furthermore, the media's portrayal of climate strikes can shape public perception, either amplifying the movement's message or trivializing it as mere youthful exuberance.

Additionally, the effectiveness of climate strikes can be undermined by the phenomenon known as *protest fatigue*, where repeated demonstrations lead to diminishing returns in public engagement. To combat this, organizers must innovate strategies to maintain momentum and keep the public engaged, such as integrating educational components or collaborating with local communities to address specific environmental issues.

Examples of Successful Climate Strikes

Several climate strikes have demonstrated the potential for mass mobilization to effect change. The *Youth Climate Strike* on March 15, 2019, mobilized over 1.4 million participants globally, leading to increased media coverage and political discourse surrounding climate policies. In response to these pressures, several governments announced new commitments to reduce carbon emissions and transition to renewable energy sources.

Moreover, the *March for Our Lives* movement, initially focused on gun control, has also intersected with climate activism, highlighting the interconnectedness of social justice issues. This coalition-building illustrates the potential for climate strikes to serve as a catalyst for broader societal change, uniting diverse groups under a common goal of sustainability and justice.

Conclusion

In conclusion, climate strikes and mass demonstrations represent a vital component of the global climate movement, harnessing the collective power of individuals to demand systemic change. While challenges remain, the ongoing mobilization of activists illustrates the resilience and determination of communities worldwide to confront the climate crisis. As Harper Sato exemplifies in her activism, the future of climate justice relies on the ability of individuals to unite, raise their voices, and advocate for a sustainable and equitable world.

Influencing International Climate Agreements

In the face of an escalating climate crisis, Harper Sato emerged as a pivotal figure in advocating for international climate agreements. Her approach was rooted in a combination of scientific evidence, grassroots mobilization, and strategic diplomacy. This section explores how Harper influenced international climate agreements and the complexities involved in this process.

The Role of Scientific Evidence

Harper understood that effective climate action must be grounded in robust scientific research. She frequently collaborated with climate scientists to disseminate data that highlighted the urgency of the situation. For instance, her team utilized the *Intergovernmental Panel on Climate Change (IPCC)* reports, which provide comprehensive assessments of climate change, its impacts, and potential adaptation and mitigation strategies. The key equation often referenced in these discussions is the climate sensitivity equation, which estimates the temperature increase resulting from a doubling of carbon dioxide concentrations:

$$\Delta T = \lambda \cdot \Delta F \tag{38}$$

where ΔT is the change in temperature, λ is the climate sensitivity parameter, and ΔF is the radiative forcing. This equation underscores the scientific basis for limiting greenhouse gas emissions to avoid catastrophic climate impacts.

Mobilizing Grassroots Movements

Recognizing the power of public opinion, Harper effectively mobilized grassroots movements that demanded action from global leaders. She organized international climate strikes, drawing inspiration from youth activists like Greta Thunberg. These strikes not only raised awareness but also pressured governments to commit to international agreements, such as the Paris Agreement of 2015. The Paris Agreement aims to limit global warming to well below 2 degrees Celsius above pre-industrial levels, with efforts to limit the temperature increase to 1.5 degrees Celsius.

Harper's ability to connect with diverse communities was crucial in amplifying the voices of those most affected by climate change, including indigenous populations and low-income communities. By highlighting their struggles, she reinforced the moral imperative for international cooperation.

Strategic Diplomacy

Harper's influence extended to the diplomatic arena, where she engaged with world leaders and negotiators during climate summits. Her approach was characterized by a commitment to transparency and accountability, advocating for binding commitments rather than voluntary pledges. At the COP26 summit in Glasgow, she presented a detailed analysis of the gaps in countries' emissions reduction targets and called for a mechanism to hold nations accountable.

One of the key frameworks she promoted was the *Green Climate Fund*, which aims to assist developing countries in their climate change efforts. By emphasizing the importance of financial support for vulnerable nations, Harper sought to create a more equitable approach to climate action.

Challenges and Resistance

Despite her successes, Harper faced significant challenges in influencing international climate agreements. One major obstacle was the resistance from fossil fuel-dependent nations, which often prioritized economic interests over environmental sustainability. For example, during negotiations at COP meetings, countries like the United States and Saudi Arabia have historically pushed back against stringent climate measures, citing potential economic repercussions.

A GLOBAL MOVEMENT FOR CLIMATE ACTION

Moreover, the phenomenon known as "climate finance" became a contentious issue. Many developed nations promised to provide $100 billion annually to support developing countries in their climate efforts but frequently failed to meet these commitments. Harper tirelessly advocated for accountability in climate finance, arguing that without adequate funding, the goals of international agreements would remain unattainable.

Success Stories and Impact

Despite the hurdles, Harper's efforts bore fruit in several instances. The adoption of the *Glasgow Climate Pact* in 2021, which urged countries to accelerate their efforts to limit temperature rise, was a testament to the collective pressure from activists and civil society. Harper's influence was evident as she played a crucial role in shaping the narrative around climate justice, emphasizing that the burden of climate change should not disproportionately fall on marginalized communities.

Furthermore, her advocacy led to the establishment of a global carbon pricing mechanism, which incentivizes countries to reduce emissions. The equation for carbon pricing can be represented as:

$$P = E \cdot C \tag{39}$$

where P is the price of carbon, E is the emissions level, and C is the carbon price per ton. This market-based approach has gained traction among nations seeking to meet their climate targets while fostering economic growth.

Conclusion

In summary, Harper Sato's influence on international climate agreements exemplifies the intersection of science, activism, and diplomacy. By leveraging scientific evidence, mobilizing grassroots movements, and engaging in strategic diplomacy, she has played a pivotal role in shaping global climate policy. Despite facing significant challenges, her legacy is one of resilience and determination, inspiring future generations to continue the fight for a sustainable and equitable future.

Climate Consciousness in Popular Culture

The intersection of climate change and popular culture has become increasingly significant in shaping public perception and action regarding environmental issues. As society grapples with the realities of climate change, various forms of media—ranging from film and music to social media and literature—have played a crucial role in amplifying climate consciousness. This subsection explores the evolution of climate consciousness within popular culture, its implications, and specific examples that illustrate its impact.

Theoretical Framework

To understand the role of popular culture in climate consciousness, we can reference the **Cultural Studies** approach, which emphasizes how cultural artifacts reflect and shape societal values. According to Stuart Hall's encoding/decoding model, media messages are encoded by producers with specific meanings but can be interpreted differently by audiences based on their cultural contexts. This theory suggests that popular culture can serve as a powerful vehicle for promoting environmental awareness, provided that the messages resonate with the audience's experiences and values.

The Problem of Climate Change Representation

Despite its potential, the representation of climate change in popular culture is fraught with challenges. Many narratives tend to focus on dystopian futures, which can lead to feelings of hopelessness and apathy among audiences. As noted by researchers such as [?], the framing of climate change as an abstract and distant problem often results in disengagement. Moreover, the overwhelming scale of climate issues can create a sense of paralysis, where individuals feel their actions are inconsequential.

Positive Examples of Climate Consciousness

Despite these challenges, there have been numerous positive examples of how popular culture has successfully raised climate consciousness:

1. **Documentaries**: Films like *An Inconvenient Truth* and *Chasing Ice* have provided compelling visual narratives that highlight the urgency of climate action. These documentaries not only educate viewers about the science of climate change but also humanize the issue by showcasing the real-world impacts on communities and ecosystems.

2. **Music**: Artists such as Billie Eilish and Coldplay have incorporated climate themes into their music and public personas. Eilish's song *All the Good Girls Go to Hell* addresses the consequences of environmental neglect, while Coldplay has committed to making their tours more sustainable, directly engaging fans in climate action.

3. **Social Media Campaigns**: Platforms like Instagram and TikTok have become arenas for climate activism, with influencers and activists using hashtags like #FridaysForFuture and #ClimateStrike to mobilize young people. These campaigns often blend entertainment with activism, making climate issues more relatable and urgent.

4. **Literature**: Novels such as *The Overstory* by Richard Powers weave narratives that connect personal stories with environmental themes. This literary approach fosters empathy and a deeper understanding of the interconnectedness of life and the environment.

Challenges and Critiques

While popular culture has made strides in raising climate consciousness, it is not without its critiques. The phenomenon of **Greenwashing**, where brands superficially promote eco-friendly initiatives without substantive action, can undermine genuine climate activism. Additionally, the risk of commodifying climate action—turning activism into a marketable trend—can dilute the urgency of the message.

Moreover, the representation of climate change in popular culture often lacks diversity. Marginalized communities, who are disproportionately affected by climate change, are frequently underrepresented in mainstream narratives. This gap highlights the need for more inclusive storytelling that amplifies diverse voices and experiences in the climate movement.

Conclusion

In summary, climate consciousness in popular culture serves as a double-edged sword. While it has the potential to inspire and mobilize action, it also faces significant challenges that can hinder its effectiveness. The evolution of climate narratives within popular culture reflects broader societal changes and underscores the importance of engaging diverse perspectives to foster a more inclusive and effective climate movement. As we move forward, it is essential for creators, activists, and audiences alike to critically engage with popular culture, ensuring that it serves as a catalyst for meaningful change in the fight against climate change.

The Role of Media in Climate Activism

The role of media in climate activism is multifaceted and critical, serving as both a platform for raising awareness and a tool for mobilizing action. As climate change becomes an increasingly pressing issue, the media's influence in shaping public perception and policy cannot be overstated. This section delves into the theoretical frameworks that underpin the media's role in climate activism, the challenges it faces, and notable examples of its impact.

Theoretical Frameworks

Media theory provides essential insights into how information is disseminated and received. The **Agenda-Setting Theory** posits that the media doesn't tell us what to think, but rather what to think about. This is particularly relevant in the context of climate activism, where media coverage can elevate environmental issues to the forefront of public discourse. For instance, when major news outlets cover climate change extensively, it signals to the public and policymakers that this is a critical issue deserving of attention.

Furthermore, the **Framing Theory** illustrates how the presentation of information influences audience interpretation. In climate activism, how stories are framed—whether as a dire crisis, an economic opportunity, or a moral imperative—can significantly affect public engagement. For example, framing climate change as a threat to national security may resonate more with certain audiences than framing it solely as an environmental issue.

Challenges Faced by Media in Climate Activism

Despite its potential, media engagement in climate activism faces several challenges:

- **Misinformation and Disinformation:** The prevalence of misinformation regarding climate science complicates media efforts. Climate denialism, often propagated through social media and certain traditional outlets, can undermine credible reporting and confuse public understanding.

- **Corporate Influence:** Media outlets that rely on advertising revenue from fossil fuel companies may hesitate to cover climate issues critically. This conflict of interest can lead to biased reporting or downplaying the urgency of climate action.

- **Audience Fatigue:** Continuous coverage of climate disasters can lead to audience desensitization. When viewers are inundated with negative news, they may disengage rather than mobilize for action.

Examples of Media Impact in Climate Activism

Numerous examples illustrate the powerful role media plays in climate activism:

- **The Guardian's Climate Campaign:** In 2019, The Guardian launched a campaign titled "Climate Crisis," committing to comprehensive coverage of climate issues. This initiative not only raised awareness but also set a standard for other media outlets, effectively reframing climate change as a crisis rather than a mere environmental issue.

- **Documentaries and Films:** Documentaries such as *An Inconvenient Truth* and *Before the Flood* have played pivotal roles in educating the public about climate change. These films utilize emotional storytelling and compelling visuals to engage audiences and spur action, showing how media can transcend traditional reporting to inspire activism.

- **Social Media Movements:** Platforms like Twitter, Instagram, and TikTok have become arenas for climate activism. Hashtags such as #FridaysForFuture and #ClimateStrike have mobilized millions globally, demonstrating how social media can amplify grassroots movements and connect activists across borders.

- **Youth Activism and Media:** The rise of youth climate activists, such as Greta Thunberg, exemplifies the intersection of media and activism. Thunberg's speeches and social media presence have garnered global attention, illustrating how individual voices can leverage media platforms to effect change.

Conclusion

In conclusion, the role of media in climate activism is indispensable. It serves not only as a conduit for information but also as a catalyst for social change. By effectively utilizing media strategies grounded in theory, activists can overcome challenges and mobilize public action. As Harper Sato demonstrated, the media's power to inform, engage, and inspire is crucial in the ongoing fight for climate justice. The legacy of media in climate activism will undoubtedly shape the future of environmental movements, highlighting the necessity of responsible and impactful reporting in an era of climate crisis.

$$\text{Impact}_{\text{media}} = \text{Awareness} \times \text{Engagement} \times \text{Action} \qquad (40)$$

Harper's Role in Inspiring Climate Warriors

Harper Sato's influence on the global climate movement cannot be overstated. Through her innovative approach to media and activism, she has ignited a passion for environmental justice in a generation of young people, collectively referred to as "climate warriors." These individuals, motivated by Harper's example, have taken to the streets, classrooms, and digital platforms to advocate for urgent climate action. This section delves into the mechanisms through which Harper has inspired these warriors, the theoretical frameworks underpinning her approach, and the broader implications of her legacy.

Theoretical Frameworks of Inspiration

To understand Harper's impact, we can draw upon motivational theory, particularly the Self-Determination Theory (SDT) proposed by Deci and Ryan (1985). This theory posits that individuals are most motivated when they experience autonomy, competence, and relatedness. Harper's media initiatives provided young activists with a platform to express their concerns and solutions, fostering a sense of autonomy. By showcasing their stories and struggles, she demonstrated their competence, validating their efforts in a world often dismissive of youth activism. Finally, her emphasis on community and collaboration cultivated a sense of relatedness, allowing these warriors to feel connected to a larger movement.

Mobilizing Through Media

Harper's show, *The Voice of Tomorrow*, became a critical tool for mobilizing climate warriors. By featuring young activists, she not only amplified their voices but also educated a broader audience about the climate crisis. For example, episodes highlighting the work of Greta Thunberg and the Fridays for Future movement provided a blueprint for effective activism. The show's format encouraged viewers to engage with the material, leading to increased participation in climate strikes and local initiatives.

The impact of social media cannot be overlooked. Harper utilized platforms such as Twitter, Instagram, and TikTok to reach younger audiences. By creating shareable content that resonated with the values and concerns of youth, she effectively transformed passive viewers into active participants. For instance, hashtags like #ClimateJustice and #YouthForClimate gained traction, becoming rallying cries for a generation eager to demand change.

Creating a Culture of Activism

Harper's influence extends beyond individual actions; she has played a pivotal role in shaping a culture of activism. By promoting stories of resilience and success, she instilled hope in young people disillusioned by the enormity of the climate crisis. This cultural shift is exemplified by the rise of youth-led organizations, such as Zero Hour and Sunrise Movement, which have gained momentum through grassroots mobilization. Harper's media presence legitimized these movements, encouraging young leaders to step forward and take action.

Moreover, her emphasis on intersectionality has broadened the scope of climate activism. Harper consistently highlighted the interconnectedness of climate issues with social justice, emphasizing that marginalized communities are disproportionately affected by environmental degradation. This approach inspired climate warriors to adopt a holistic view of activism, recognizing that fighting for climate justice also means advocating for racial, economic, and gender equality.

Challenges and Resilience

Despite her successes, Harper's journey has not been without challenges. The backlash from powerful interests seeking to maintain the status quo has been fierce. However, her resilience in the face of adversity serves as a powerful lesson for aspiring climate warriors. Her ability to confront threats—ranging from online harassment to legal challenges—demonstrates the importance of perseverance in activism. As she often states, "Change is not easy, but it is necessary." This message resonates deeply with young activists, encouraging them to remain steadfast in their pursuits despite obstacles.

Legacy of Inspiration

Harper's legacy as a catalyst for climate action is evident in the continued engagement of youth in environmental issues. The recent surge in participation in global climate strikes, particularly those organized by young leaders, reflects the enduring impact of her work. For instance, the 2021 Global Climate Strike mobilized millions worldwide, with many participants citing Harper's influence as a motivating factor.

Furthermore, Harper's mentorship of emerging activists has created a ripple effect. By providing resources, guidance, and visibility to young leaders, she has empowered a new generation to take charge of the climate narrative. This mentorship is crucial in sustaining the momentum of the climate movement, ensuring that the voices of youth remain at the forefront of discussions surrounding environmental policy.

In conclusion, Harper Sato's role in inspiring climate warriors is multifaceted, rooted in theoretical frameworks of motivation, media mobilization, cultural shifts, and resilience. Her ability to connect with young people and amplify their voices has transformed the landscape of climate activism, creating a legacy that will continue to inspire future generations. As we face the challenges of climate change, the movement Harper has helped cultivate stands as a testament to the power of youth activism in shaping a sustainable and equitable future.

The Legacy of Harper's Climate Activism

Policies and Legislation Influenced by Harper's Advocacy

Harper Sato's advocacy for climate justice has not only reshaped public discourse but has also led to significant changes in policies and legislation aimed at addressing the climate crisis. Her influence can be traced through various legislative milestones that reflect her commitment to environmental sustainability, social equity, and transparency in governance.

The Green New Deal

One of the most notable pieces of legislation influenced by Harper's advocacy is the Green New Deal (GND), which emerged as a comprehensive framework for addressing climate change while simultaneously promoting economic justice. The GND proposes a bold agenda that combines aggressive climate action with initiatives designed to create millions of jobs, particularly in renewable energy sectors.

The theoretical underpinning of the GND is rooted in the concept of *just transition*, which seeks to ensure that the shift towards a sustainable economy does not disproportionately affect vulnerable communities. This idea aligns with Harper's mission to amplify marginalized voices and prioritize equity in environmental policies. The GND calls for:

$$\text{Investment in Renewable Energy} + \text{Job Creation} + \text{Social Equity} = \text{Sustainable Future} \tag{41}$$

Climate Action Plans

In numerous jurisdictions, local and state governments have implemented Climate Action Plans (CAPs) that reflect the principles championed by Harper. These plans typically outline specific strategies for reducing greenhouse gas emissions, enhancing energy efficiency, and promoting sustainable practices across various sectors.

For example, the City of San Francisco adopted a CAP that aims for carbon neutrality by 2030. This ambitious goal is achieved through:

- **Renewable Energy Initiatives:** Transitioning city operations to 100% renewable energy sources.

- **Building Efficiency Standards:** Implementing strict energy efficiency standards for new constructions and retrofits.

- **Public Transportation Investments:** Expanding public transit options to reduce reliance on fossil fuel-powered vehicles.

Harper's influence is evident in the emphasis on community engagement and the inclusion of vulnerable populations in the planning process, ensuring that the benefits of climate action are equitably distributed.

Environmental Justice Legislation

Harper has also played a pivotal role in advocating for Environmental Justice (EJ) legislation, which seeks to address the disproportionate impact of environmental hazards on marginalized communities. One prominent example is the introduction of the Environmental Justice for All Act, which aims to strengthen protections for communities facing pollution and environmental degradation.

The act incorporates several key provisions:

- **Health Impact Assessments:** Requiring health assessments for projects that may disproportionately affect low-income and minority communities.

- **Community Participation:** Mandating the involvement of affected communities in the decision-making processes regarding environmental policies.

- **Funding for EJ Initiatives:** Allocating federal funding for projects that aim to remediate environmental hazards in vulnerable communities.

This legislation embodies Harper's commitment to ensuring that all individuals, regardless of their socioeconomic status, have the right to a healthy environment.

International Climate Agreements

Harper's advocacy has also extended beyond national borders, influencing international climate agreements such as the Paris Agreement. Her emphasis on global solidarity and the interconnectedness of climate issues has been instrumental in shaping discussions around climate finance and adaptation strategies for developing nations.

The Paris Agreement, which aims to limit global warming to well below 2 degrees Celsius, incorporates elements that align with Harper's vision:

$$\text{Global Temperature Goal} \leq 2°C \implies \text{Collective National Contributions} \quad (42)$$

Harper's work has highlighted the importance of developed nations fulfilling their financial obligations to support climate action in developing countries, emphasizing that climate justice cannot be achieved without addressing historical inequalities.

Local Policy Innovations

At the local level, Harper's influence has spurred innovative policy approaches aimed at fostering sustainability and resilience. Cities across the globe have adopted initiatives inspired by her advocacy, such as:

- **Urban Green Spaces:** Policies promoting the creation of parks and green roofs to enhance urban biodiversity and improve air quality.

- **Zero Waste Initiatives:** Programs aimed at reducing waste through recycling, composting, and the promotion of a circular economy.

- **Sustainable Transportation Policies:** Implementation of bike lanes, pedestrian-friendly infrastructure, and electric vehicle charging stations.

These local innovations reflect Harper's belief in the power of grassroots movements to effect meaningful change and demonstrate the potential for cities to lead the way in climate action.

Conclusion

In summary, Harper Sato's advocacy has profoundly influenced a range of policies and legislation aimed at addressing the climate crisis. Through her efforts, she has championed initiatives that promote environmental justice, foster sustainable economic growth, and advocate for transparency in governance. The legacy of her work continues to inspire future generations of activists and policymakers, ensuring that the fight for climate justice remains at the forefront of public discourse and action.

The Shift Towards a Greener Economy

The transition towards a greener economy is not merely a trend; it is an urgent necessity driven by the realities of climate change and the unsustainable practices of the past. This shift encompasses a wide range of economic activities that prioritize environmental sustainability, social equity, and long-term economic resilience. Harper Sato's advocacy for climate justice has significantly influenced this transition, pushing for policies and practices that align with sustainable development goals.

Understanding the Green Economy

A green economy is defined as one that results in improved human well-being and social equity while significantly reducing environmental risks and ecological scarcities. According to the United Nations Environment Programme (UNEP), a green economy can be understood through the following equation:

$$\text{Green Economy} = \text{Sustainable Development} + \text{Environmental Protection} \quad (43)$$

This equation emphasizes the integration of economic growth with ecological sustainability. The shift towards a greener economy involves rethinking how we produce, consume, and manage resources. It requires a systemic change across all sectors, including energy, transportation, agriculture, and manufacturing.

Key Drivers of the Shift

Several key drivers have propelled the shift towards a greener economy:

- **Policy Initiatives:** Governments worldwide are implementing policies that promote renewable energy, energy efficiency, and sustainable practices. For instance, the European Union's Green Deal aims to make Europe the first climate-neutral continent by 2050, setting ambitious targets for reducing greenhouse gas emissions.

- **Corporate Responsibility:** Many corporations are recognizing the importance of sustainability in their operations. Companies like Unilever and Tesla are leading the way by integrating sustainability into their business models, demonstrating that profitability and environmental stewardship can coexist.

- **Public Awareness:** Increased public awareness of climate change and environmental issues has fueled demand for sustainable products and practices. This shift in consumer behavior pressures businesses to adopt greener practices to remain competitive.

- **Technological Innovation:** Advances in technology are facilitating the transition to a green economy. Innovations in renewable energy, such as solar and wind power, as well as improvements in energy storage and efficiency, are making sustainable options more accessible and affordable.

Challenges in the Transition

Despite the momentum towards a greener economy, several challenges remain:

- **Economic Disparities:** The transition must be equitable, ensuring that marginalized communities are not left behind. Economic disparities can hinder access to green technologies and job opportunities in sustainable sectors.

- **Resistance from Established Industries:** Fossil fuel industries and other established sectors may resist the shift due to the potential loss of profits. This resistance can manifest in lobbying against environmental regulations and promoting misinformation about climate change.

- **Investment Gaps:** Transitioning to a green economy requires significant investments in infrastructure, technology, and education. However, funding for sustainable initiatives often falls short, particularly in developing countries.

- **Policy Inconsistencies:** Inconsistent policies and regulations can create uncertainty for businesses and investors. A lack of clear guidelines can impede progress and slow down the transition.

Examples of Successful Transitions

Several countries and regions have made significant strides in transitioning to greener economies, serving as models for others to follow:

- **Denmark:** Denmark has become a leader in renewable energy, generating over 47% of its electricity from wind power in 2019. The country's commitment to sustainability is reflected in its ambitious goal to be carbon neutral by 2050.

- **Costa Rica:** Known for its rich biodiversity, Costa Rica has invested heavily in renewable energy and conservation. In 2020, the country achieved 99% of its electricity from renewable sources, primarily hydropower.

- **Germany:** Germany's Energiewende (energy transition) policy aims to shift from fossil fuels to renewable energy sources. The country has successfully increased the share of renewables in its energy mix while reducing carbon emissions.

Harper's Influence on the Green Economy

Harper Sato's work has been instrumental in advocating for a greener economy. Through her media platform, she has highlighted the importance of sustainable practices and the need for systemic change. Her efforts have included:

- **Raising Awareness:** Harper has used her platform to educate the public about climate change and the benefits of a green economy. By amplifying the voices of environmental activists and experts, she has fostered a greater understanding of sustainability issues.

- **Promoting Policy Change:** Harper has actively campaigned for policies that support renewable energy and environmental justice. Her investigative reporting has exposed corporate malfeasance and government inaction, holding powerful interests accountable.

- **Encouraging Grassroots Movements:** By inspiring grassroots activism, Harper has mobilized communities to advocate for local sustainability initiatives. Her work has empowered individuals to take action and demand change from their leaders.

Conclusion

The shift towards a greener economy is a complex yet essential process that requires collaboration across all sectors of society. Harper Sato's advocacy has played a crucial role in this transition, highlighting the interconnectedness of economic, social, and environmental issues. As we move forward, it is imperative to embrace sustainable practices and policies that not only address the climate crisis but also promote equity and resilience for future generations.

Future Generations Continuing the Fight for Climate Justice

The fight for climate justice is not merely a struggle of the present; it is an ongoing legacy that future generations must inherit, adapt, and expand. As the impacts of climate change become more pronounced, the role of youth in advocating for sustainable practices and policies is pivotal. This subsection explores the theoretical frameworks, challenges, and examples of how future generations are poised to continue the fight for climate justice.

Theoretical Frameworks

One of the foundational theories relevant to this discourse is the **Intergenerational Justice Theory**. This theory posits that current generations have a moral obligation to ensure that future generations inherit a planet that is not only habitable but thriving. According to [?], principles of justice must be extended to those who will live in the future, thereby fostering a sense of responsibility among today's decision-makers.

Additionally, the **Sustainability Transition Theory** emphasizes the importance of systemic change in socio-technical systems. It suggests that for future generations to effectively combat climate change, they must not only advocate for policy changes but also engage in innovative practices that promote sustainable living. This involves a transformation in energy systems, urban planning, and consumption patterns, which can be achieved through grassroots movements and technological advancements.

Challenges Faced by Future Generations

Despite the momentum generated by current climate activists, future generations will encounter numerous challenges in their pursuit of climate justice. One significant issue is the **political inertia** that often characterizes governmental responses to climate change. As noted by [?], entrenched interests and lobbying from fossil fuel industries can create significant barriers to enacting meaningful legislation.

Moreover, the **psychological burden** of climate anxiety can hinder youth engagement. According to research by [?], many young people experience feelings of helplessness and despair regarding climate change, which can lead to disengagement from activism. This highlights the need for supportive frameworks that empower youth rather than overwhelm them.

Empowerment Through Education and Activism

To combat these challenges, educational initiatives play a crucial role in empowering future generations. Programs that promote **environmental literacy** can equip young people with the knowledge and skills necessary to advocate for climate justice effectively. For example, the *Eco-Schools* program has successfully engaged students worldwide in sustainability practices, fostering a sense of agency among young activists.

Moreover, movements like **Fridays for Future**, initiated by Greta Thunberg, demonstrate the power of youth activism in shaping public discourse around climate issues. This movement has mobilized millions of young people globally, highlighting the urgency of climate action and demanding accountability from political leaders. The success of such grassroots movements illustrates that when youth unite for a common cause, they can influence policy and public perception significantly.

Examples of Youth-Led Initiatives

Numerous examples showcase how future generations are already making strides in the fight for climate justice. One notable initiative is the **Sunrise Movement** in the United States, which focuses on advocating for the Green New Deal. This movement emphasizes the intersectionality of climate justice, linking environmental sustainability with social equity and economic justice. By engaging diverse communities, the Sunrise Movement exemplifies how youth can lead inclusive conversations around climate action.

Additionally, the **Youth Climate Summit**, held annually, serves as a platform for young leaders to collaborate, share ideas, and strategize on climate action. These summits foster international solidarity and empower youth to take actionable steps within their communities, ensuring that the fight for climate justice remains vibrant and persistent.

Conclusion

In conclusion, future generations are not merely passive observers in the fight for climate justice; they are active participants who will shape the trajectory of environmental advocacy. By leveraging theoretical frameworks, overcoming challenges, and drawing inspiration from successful initiatives, they can build upon the legacy of leaders like Harper Sato. As they continue to advocate for sustainable practices and policies, the collective efforts of youth will be essential in addressing the climate crisis and ensuring a just and equitable future for all.

Harper's Lasting Impact on the Climate Movement

Harper Sato's contributions to the climate movement have been profound and multifaceted, leaving a legacy that continues to inspire activists, policymakers, and citizens across the globe. Her approach combined rigorous investigative journalism with passionate advocacy, effectively bridging the gap between information dissemination and grassroots mobilization. This section explores her lasting impact on the climate movement through three primary lenses: policy influence, public engagement, and the cultivation of a new generation of activists.

Policy Influence

Harper's relentless pursuit of environmental justice led to significant changes in policy at both national and international levels. By exposing corporate malfeasance and the detrimental effects of fossil fuel extraction, she played a crucial role in shaping legislation aimed at combating climate change. Her investigative work, particularly in the documentary series *Unmasking the Greenwash*, highlighted how major corporations misled the public about their environmental practices. This series not only garnered millions of views but also prompted legislative reviews and calls for stricter regulations on corporate environmental claims.

For example, the *Green Transparency Act*, which was passed following her exposés, mandated corporations to disclose their environmental impact assessments. The mathematical model used to evaluate corporate emissions, which can be expressed as:

$$E = \sum_{i=1}^{n}(I_i \times F_i)$$

where E represents total emissions, I_i is the intensity of emissions for each activity i, and F_i is the frequency of that activity, became a standard for environmental reporting. This law has since inspired similar legislation in other countries, showcasing Harper's influence beyond her own borders.

Public Engagement

Harper's ability to engage the public was pivotal in mobilizing grassroots movements. Her media platforms served as a conduit for climate activism, transforming complex scientific data into compelling narratives that resonated with everyday people. By utilizing social media strategically, she amplified the voices of marginalized communities disproportionately affected by climate change, such as indigenous populations and low-income neighborhoods.

One notable campaign was the *Climate Justice Now!* initiative, which encouraged citizens to participate in local climate actions. The campaign utilized a formula for calculating individual carbon footprints, which empowered participants to understand their impact and take actionable steps. The equation used was:

$$CF = (A \times B) + (C \times D) + (E \times F)$$

where CF represents the carbon footprint, A is the average miles driven per year, B is the emissions per mile, C is the energy used in the household, D is the emissions per unit of energy, E is the waste generated, and F is the emissions per unit of waste. This engagement strategy not only educated the public but also fostered a sense of community and collective responsibility.

Cultivating Future Activists

Perhaps Harper's most enduring legacy lies in her mentorship of young activists. Through workshops, speaking engagements, and her online platform, she inspired a new generation to take up the mantle of climate advocacy. Her emphasis on critical thinking and innovative solutions encouraged youth to challenge the status quo and seek creative approaches to climate issues.

Programs like *Youth for Climate Action*, which Harper co-founded, provided training in advocacy, media literacy, and environmental science. Participants learned how to effectively communicate their messages, organize protests, and engage with policymakers. The program's success is evidenced by the numerous youth-led initiatives that have emerged, addressing local climate issues with global implications.

One example of this is the *Green Schools Initiative*, where students lobbied for sustainable practices in their educational institutions. The initiative's impact can be quantified through a survey conducted at participating schools, which showed a 40% increase in recycling rates and a 30% reduction in energy consumption within the first year of implementation.

Conclusion

In summary, Harper Sato's lasting impact on the climate movement is characterized by her ability to influence policy, engage the public, and cultivate future activists. Her legacy is not merely one of past achievements but a living testament to the power of informed advocacy and community action. As the climate crisis continues to escalate, the frameworks and movements she established will undoubtedly serve as a foundation for ongoing efforts toward a sustainable and equitable future. Harper's vision of a world where climate justice is prioritized remains an aspiration that inspires countless individuals to take action, ensuring that her influence will echo through generations to come.

Harper's Vision for a Sustainable, Equitable Future

Harper Sato's vision for a sustainable and equitable future is rooted in the belief that environmental justice and social equity are inseparable. She understands that the climate crisis disproportionately affects marginalized communities, and thus, her approach is multifaceted, integrating ecological sustainability with social justice. This section explores her vision through the lens of relevant theories, the problems she aims to address, and practical examples of initiatives that embody her ideals.

Theoretical Framework

At the core of Harper's vision is the concept of *sustainable development*, which, as defined by the Brundtland Commission in 1987, is development that meets the needs of the present without compromising the ability of future generations to meet their own needs. This theory emphasizes the balance between economic growth, environmental protection, and social equity.

Harper also draws from the principles of *environmental justice*, which advocate for the fair treatment and involvement of all people, regardless of race, color, national origin, or income, in environmental policies. This framework highlights the need for inclusive decision-making processes that consider the voices of those most affected by environmental degradation.

Identifying Problems

Harper's vision confronts several critical problems, including:

- **Climate Inequality:** Vulnerable populations often bear the brunt of climate change impacts, such as extreme weather events, pollution, and resource scarcity. For instance, low-income communities are more likely to live in areas with high pollution levels, leading to health disparities.

- **Access to Resources:** Many marginalized communities lack access to clean water, nutritious food, and renewable energy sources. This inequity perpetuates cycles of poverty and hinders community resilience.

- **Corporate Influence:** The fossil fuel industry and other corporate interests often undermine environmental regulations, prioritizing profit over people. This dynamic can stifle grassroots movements and hinder meaningful reform.

Practical Examples of Initiatives

To realize her vision, Harper advocates for and participates in various initiatives that exemplify sustainable and equitable practices:

- **Community-Led Renewable Energy Projects:** Harper supports initiatives that empower communities to develop their own renewable energy sources, such as solar and wind farms. These projects not only reduce reliance on fossil fuels but also create local jobs and promote energy independence. For example, the *Solarize* program in several U.S. states has successfully facilitated community solar installations, making clean energy accessible to low-income households.

- **Urban Green Spaces:** Recognizing the importance of green spaces in urban areas, Harper champions the creation of parks and community gardens in underserved neighborhoods. These spaces improve air quality, provide fresh produce, and foster community engagement. The *Greening the Concrete* initiative in cities like Detroit has transformed vacant lots into vibrant community gardens, offering both food security and a sense of community ownership.

- **Education and Advocacy:** Harper emphasizes the importance of education in fostering a culture of sustainability. She collaborates with schools to integrate environmental education into the curriculum, ensuring that the next generation understands the principles of sustainability and social justice. Programs like *Eco-Schools* engage students in hands-on projects that promote environmental stewardship and critical thinking.

- **Policy Advocacy for Climate Justice:** Harper actively engages in policy advocacy to push for legislation that addresses climate change while prioritizing social equity. She has been instrumental in campaigns for the Green New Deal, which aims to create millions of jobs in renewable energy and infrastructure while ensuring that marginalized communities receive the support they need to thrive.

The Role of Collaboration

Harper's vision is not limited to individual initiatives; she recognizes the power of collaboration among diverse stakeholders. By forming coalitions with environmental organizations, social justice groups, and indigenous communities, Harper amplifies the collective voice advocating for systemic change. This collaborative approach is essential for addressing the interconnected challenges of climate change and social inequality.

Conclusion

In conclusion, Harper Sato's vision for a sustainable and equitable future is a comprehensive framework that seeks to address the root causes of environmental degradation and social injustice. By integrating sustainable development principles with environmental justice, she champions a holistic approach that empowers communities, promotes resilience, and fosters a more equitable society. Her legacy will inspire future generations to continue the fight for a world where both people and the planet can thrive together, paving the way for a sustainable future that is truly inclusive and just.

$$\text{Sustainable Future} = \text{Environmental Health} + \text{Social Equity} + \text{Economic Viability} \tag{44}$$

Harper's Lasting Contribution to Society

The Evolution of Media in Harper's Wake

New Standards for Journalism and Reporting

In the wake of Harper Sato's transformative influence on the media landscape, new standards for journalism and reporting emerged, redefining the profession's ethical framework and operational methodologies. These standards were not merely reactions to the challenges of the day; they were proactive measures aimed at restoring public trust in media institutions.

Theoretical Foundations

The evolution of journalism standards can be traced back to several theoretical frameworks, including the *Social Responsibility Theory* and the *Public Sphere Theory*. The Social Responsibility Theory posits that the media has an obligation to serve the public good, balancing the need for freedom with the responsibility to provide accurate and fair information. This theory emphasizes that journalists should act as watchdogs, ensuring that power is held accountable and that diverse viewpoints are represented.

The Public Sphere Theory, articulated by Jürgen Habermas, underscores the role of media as a facilitator of public discourse. It argues that a healthy democracy relies on an informed citizenry engaged in rational-critical debate. Harper's reforms aimed to rejuvenate this public sphere by promoting transparency and fostering dialogue between the media and the community.

Problems Addressed

Harper's initiatives directly addressed several pervasive problems in journalism, including:

- **Misinformation and Disinformation:** The rise of social media platforms and the rapid dissemination of information have led to an increase in false narratives. Harper advocated for rigorous fact-checking protocols and the development of media literacy programs to equip audiences with the tools to discern credible sources.

- **Lack of Diversity:** Traditional media often failed to represent marginalized voices. Harper's standards emphasized the importance of inclusivity, urging news organizations to diversify their staff and coverage to reflect the multifaceted nature of society.

- **Corporate Influence:** The entanglement of corporate interests with journalistic integrity posed a significant challenge. Harper championed the separation of newsrooms from advertising and corporate influence, promoting independent journalism as a means to uphold editorial integrity.

Examples of New Standards

To operationalize these theoretical foundations and address the identified problems, Harper introduced several new standards that became benchmarks for journalistic practice:

1. **Transparency in Reporting:** Journalists were encouraged to disclose their sources and methodologies. This transparency allowed audiences to understand the context of the news and the rationale behind editorial decisions. For example, news outlets began publishing "behind-the-scenes" articles detailing how stories were researched and reported.

2. **Ethical Guidelines for Social Media Use:** Recognizing the power of social media, new guidelines were established to govern how journalists engage with these platforms. This included policies on verifying information before sharing and maintaining professional boundaries in online interactions.

3. **Community Engagement Initiatives:** Harper promoted the idea of community journalism, where local reporters actively engaged with their audiences to understand their needs and perspectives. This led to initiatives

such as town hall meetings and public forums where journalists could solicit feedback and input from the community.

4. **Diversity and Inclusion Training:** News organizations were encouraged to implement training programs focused on diversity and inclusion. These programs aimed to sensitize journalists to biases and equip them with the skills necessary to report on issues affecting underrepresented communities.

Impact on the Media Landscape

The impact of these new standards was profound. Media outlets that adopted Harper's principles saw a resurgence in public trust and engagement. For instance, a study conducted by the Media Trust Institute revealed that news organizations implementing transparency measures experienced a 30% increase in audience trust ratings within two years.

Furthermore, the emphasis on community engagement led to a revitalization of local journalism. Many newspapers reported increased subscription rates and higher attendance at community events, demonstrating that when the media prioritizes the needs and voices of the public, it fosters a more informed and engaged citizenry.

Conclusion

Harper Sato's legacy in establishing new standards for journalism and reporting serves as a blueprint for the future of the media industry. By addressing the critical issues of misinformation, diversity, and corporate influence, these standards not only enhanced journalistic integrity but also reinforced the media's role as a pillar of democracy. As the landscape continues to evolve, the principles laid down by Harper will undoubtedly guide future generations of journalists in their quest to inform, engage, and empower the public.

The Expansion of Independent Media Outlets

The landscape of media has undergone a seismic shift in the wake of Harper Sato's reforms, particularly in the realm of independent media outlets. These platforms have emerged as vital players in the dissemination of information, challenging the traditional narratives propagated by corporate media conglomerates. The expansion of independent media is not merely a trend; it represents a fundamental transformation in how news is produced, consumed, and understood.

Theoretical Framework

The rise of independent media can be contextualized within the framework of media pluralism, which posits that a diverse media ecosystem is essential for a healthy democracy. According to McQuail's Mass Communication Theory, a variety of media sources is crucial for the representation of multiple viewpoints, fostering informed public discourse. This pluralism is threatened when a few corporations dominate the media landscape, leading to what is termed the "market failure" of information, where the public is deprived of diverse perspectives.

The concept of "disintermediation," where consumers bypass traditional media gatekeepers, has also played a significant role in the rise of independent outlets. With the advent of digital technology, individuals can now create and share content without the need for traditional media institutions. This democratization of information aligns with Habermas's Public Sphere theory, which emphasizes the importance of open dialogue and participation in democratic societies.

Problems with Traditional Media

Before Harper's reforms, traditional media was often criticized for its lack of transparency, bias, and corporate influence. The concentration of media ownership led to a homogenization of content, where critical issues were frequently overlooked or misrepresented. This was particularly evident in the coverage of marginalized communities, whose voices were often silenced or mischaracterized.

Moreover, the reliance on advertising revenue created a conflict of interest, where sensationalism and clickbait often took precedence over journalistic integrity. As noted by media scholars, this "advertising-driven model" compromises the quality of reporting, resulting in a public that is poorly informed and disengaged from crucial societal issues.

The Role of Technology

The technological revolution has been a catalyst for the expansion of independent media outlets. The internet has enabled individuals and small organizations to publish their content, reaching global audiences without the constraints of traditional media. Platforms such as social media, blogs, and podcasts have provided alternative avenues for news dissemination, allowing independent journalists to circumvent established media gatekeepers.

For instance, the rise of platforms like Medium and Substack has empowered writers to share their insights and analyses directly with readers, fostering a culture of independent thought. These platforms often prioritize quality content over sensationalism, appealing to audiences seeking in-depth reporting and diverse perspectives.

Examples of Successful Independent Media Outlets

Several independent media outlets have gained prominence in recent years, showcasing the viability of this model. For example, *ProPublica* has established itself as a leader in investigative journalism, focusing on stories that matter to the public but are often neglected by mainstream media. Their commitment to transparency and accountability has garnered significant support, demonstrating that audiences value integrity over sensationalism.

Another notable example is *The Intercept*, which has gained recognition for its fearless reporting on issues such as government surveillance and corporate malfeasance. By prioritizing investigative journalism and ethical reporting, these outlets have built trust with their audiences, creating a loyal following that values their commitment to truth.

Challenges Faced by Independent Media

Despite the growth of independent media, challenges remain. Funding is a significant obstacle, as many independent outlets struggle to secure sustainable revenue streams. Unlike corporate media, which can rely on extensive advertising budgets, independent media often depend on donations, subscriptions, and crowdfunding. This financial vulnerability can compromise their ability to maintain independence and produce high-quality journalism.

Moreover, independent media outlets often face hostility from powerful interests threatened by their reporting. Legal challenges, harassment, and online attacks are common tactics used to silence dissenting voices. As highlighted by the Committee to Protect Journalists, the risks associated with independent journalism can be substantial, particularly in politically charged environments.

The Future of Independent Media

Looking forward, the future of independent media appears promising, albeit fraught with challenges. The increasing demand for transparency and accountability in journalism suggests that audiences are more inclined to support independent outlets that align with their values. As Harper Sato's legacy continues to inspire a new generation of journalists and activists, the expansion of independent media will likely play a crucial role in shaping the future of public discourse.

In conclusion, the expansion of independent media outlets represents a significant shift in the media landscape, driven by technological advancements and a growing demand for diverse perspectives. While challenges persist, the resilience and innovation demonstrated by these outlets signal a hopeful future for journalism, one that prioritizes integrity, accountability, and the voices of the marginalized.

$$\text{Media Pluralism} \Rightarrow \text{Diverse Perspectives} \Rightarrow \text{Informed Public Discourse} \quad (45)$$

$$\text{Disintermediation} + \text{Digital Technology} \Rightarrow \text{Independent Media Expansion} \quad (46)$$

Media Accountability and Public Trust

In the landscape of modern journalism, media accountability and public trust have emerged as cornerstones for a healthy democracy. The work of Harper Sato exemplifies the pivotal role that accountability plays in ensuring that media serves the public interest rather than corporate or political agendas. This section delves into the theoretical frameworks surrounding media accountability, the challenges that exist in achieving it, and the significant examples that illustrate its importance in contemporary society.

Theoretical Frameworks

Media accountability can be understood through several theoretical lenses, including the **Social Responsibility Theory**, which posits that the media has an obligation to serve the public good, and the **Public Interest Theory**, which emphasizes the need for media to act in the best interests of society. According to McQuail (2010), "the media must be accountable to the public and must operate in a way that fosters a democratic society." This accountability can manifest in various forms, such as transparency in reporting, adherence to ethical standards, and responsiveness to audience concerns.

$$\text{Media Accountability} = \text{Transparency} + \text{Ethical Standards} + \text{Audience Engagement} \quad (47)$$

This equation illustrates the multifaceted nature of media accountability, where each component contributes to the overall trustworthiness of the media.

Transparency involves disclosing sources and methodologies, ethical standards encompass adherence to truthfulness and fairness, and audience engagement refers to the media's responsiveness to public feedback.

Challenges to Media Accountability

Despite the clear theoretical foundations, achieving media accountability is fraught with challenges. One major issue is the **concentration of media ownership**, which often leads to conflicts of interest. When a small number of corporations control a vast majority of media outlets, the diversity of viewpoints diminishes, and the potential for biased reporting increases. This concentration can result in a lack of accountability, as corporate interests may take precedence over journalistic integrity.

Another significant challenge is the rise of **misinformation** and **disinformation**. The proliferation of social media platforms has enabled the rapid spread of false information, eroding public trust in traditional news sources. A study by the Pew Research Center (2021) found that 64% of Americans believe that misinformation has a significant impact on their confidence in the news media. This distrust can lead to a vicious cycle where the public becomes skeptical of all media, even reputable sources.

Examples of Media Accountability in Action

Harper Sato's initiatives serve as a beacon of hope in the quest for media accountability. One notable example is her establishment of the **Truth in Reporting Initiative**, which aimed to create a framework for media organizations to adhere to ethical standards and practices. This initiative included a certification process for news outlets that demonstrated a commitment to transparency and accountability. Outlets that received certification were required to disclose their funding sources, editorial processes, and any potential conflicts of interest.

Another example is Harper's response to the rise of misinformation during the COVID-19 pandemic. She spearheaded a campaign called **Fact Check First**, which encouraged media outlets to prioritize fact-checking before disseminating information. This initiative not only improved the accuracy of reporting but also restored some level of public trust in the media. According to a survey conducted by the Media Trust Alliance (2022), news organizations that participated in the campaign saw a 35% increase in public trust ratings.

The Role of the Public in Media Accountability

Public engagement is crucial for fostering media accountability. Harper emphasized the importance of audience feedback, encouraging viewers to hold media organizations accountable for their reporting. By creating platforms for public discourse, such as community forums and social media discussions, she empowered citizens to voice their concerns and demand higher standards from the media.

The concept of **media literacy** also plays a vital role in promoting accountability. Educating the public about how to critically evaluate news sources and identify misinformation is essential for rebuilding trust in the media. Programs aimed at enhancing media literacy have shown promise in helping individuals discern credible information from falsehoods, thereby fostering a more informed citizenry.

Conclusion

In conclusion, media accountability and public trust are intertwined elements that are essential for a functioning democracy. Harper Sato's contributions to the field of media reform highlight the importance of transparency, ethical standards, and public engagement in building trust between the media and society. As challenges such as media concentration and misinformation continue to threaten journalistic integrity, the ongoing efforts to enhance accountability will be critical in ensuring that the media fulfills its role as a watchdog of democracy. The future of journalism depends on a collective commitment to uphold these principles, ensuring that the media remains a trusted source of information for all.

The Role of Social Media in Shaping Public Opinion

Social media has fundamentally transformed the landscape of public discourse and opinion formation in the 21st century. Platforms such as Twitter, Facebook, Instagram, and TikTok serve as both amplifiers and battlegrounds for ideas, influencing everything from political campaigns to social movements. Harper Sato, as a media reformer, recognized the potential and pitfalls of social media in shaping public opinion and sought to harness its power for positive change.

Theoretical Framework

The influence of social media on public opinion can be understood through several theoretical lenses:

- **Agenda-Setting Theory:** This theory posits that media does not tell people what to think, but rather what to think about. Social media platforms, through algorithms and trending topics, can prioritize certain issues, shaping the public agenda. For instance, during the Black Lives Matter movement, hashtags such as #BlackLivesMatter and #SayHerName brought issues of racial injustice to the forefront, compelling mainstream media to cover them more extensively.

- **Framing Theory:** This theory examines how the presentation of information influences perceptions. On social media, the way issues are framed can significantly impact public understanding. Harper utilized framing to highlight marginalized voices, ensuring that narratives surrounding social justice were not only heard but also understood in their broader contexts.

- **Spiral of Silence Theory:** This theory suggests that individuals may remain silent when they perceive their views to be in the minority. Social media can counteract this by creating echo chambers where like-minded individuals reinforce each other's beliefs, leading to a false sense of consensus. Harper's initiatives aimed to break these echo chambers by promoting diverse viewpoints and encouraging constructive dialogue.

Problems and Challenges

While social media has the potential to democratize information dissemination, it also presents significant challenges:

- **Misinformation and Disinformation:** The rapid spread of false information can distort public perception and undermine trust in legitimate sources. During significant events, such as the COVID-19 pandemic, misinformation about the virus and vaccines proliferated on social media, leading to public confusion and hesitancy.

- **Polarization:** Social media can exacerbate societal divisions by creating echo chambers where users are exposed primarily to views that align with their own. This polarization can hinder constructive dialogue and compromise, as individuals become entrenched in their beliefs.

- **Manipulation and Exploitation:** The use of social media for targeted political advertising and manipulation raises ethical concerns. The Cambridge Analytica scandal highlighted how personal data could be weaponized to influence voter behavior, prompting calls for greater transparency and regulation.

Examples of Social Media's Impact

Harper Sato's media reforms exemplified the effective use of social media to shape public opinion positively:

- **#MeToo Movement:** Social media played a crucial role in the #MeToo movement, allowing survivors of sexual harassment and assault to share their stories and connect with others. Harper leveraged this momentum to advocate for changes in media representation and accountability, fostering a culture of support and empowerment.

- **Climate Activism:** Harper utilized platforms like Instagram and TikTok to engage younger audiences in climate activism. By creating visually compelling content that highlighted the urgency of climate change, she mobilized a generation to participate in protests and advocate for policy changes. The viral nature of social media campaigns, such as the climate strikes initiated by Greta Thunberg, showcased how digital platforms could galvanize mass movements.

- **Political Campaigns:** Harper's approach to media reform included training aspiring journalists and activists on the effective use of social media for political engagement. By emphasizing the importance of authenticity and transparency, she helped candidates connect with constituents in meaningful ways, as seen in the success of grassroots campaigns that utilized social media to build community support.

Conclusion

The role of social media in shaping public opinion is multifaceted, encompassing both opportunities and challenges. Harper Sato's recognition of this dynamic allowed her to navigate the complexities of modern media effectively. By advocating for ethical practices and promoting diverse voices, she contributed to a more informed and engaged public. As social media continues to evolve, its influence on public opinion will remain a critical area of focus for future innovators and reformers seeking to foster positive societal change.

$$\text{Public Opinion} = f(\text{Media Influence, Social Dynamics, Individual Perceptions}) \tag{48}$$

Harper's Enduring Legacy in Media Reform

Harper Sato's impact on media reform is not merely a chapter in history but a lasting legacy that reshapes how journalism is perceived and practiced in the modern world. Her vision and tireless advocacy have led to significant changes in the media landscape, establishing a new paradigm rooted in transparency, accountability, and ethical reporting.

Theoretical Framework of Media Reform

At the core of Harper's approach to media reform lies the theory of *Participatory Journalism*, which emphasizes the role of the audience as active participants rather than passive consumers of news. This theory posits that media should serve as a platform for dialogue, enabling diverse voices to be heard. Harper's initiatives have demonstrated that when citizens engage with media, they can challenge the dominant narratives perpetuated by established outlets.

Furthermore, Harper's work aligns with the principles of *Media Literacy*, which advocates for the ability to critically analyze media content. By promoting media literacy, Harper empowered individuals to discern credible information from misinformation, thereby fostering a more informed public.

Addressing Media Consolidation

One of the most pressing issues Harper confronted was media consolidation, where a handful of corporations control the majority of news outlets. This concentration of power often leads to homogenized content that fails to reflect the diversity of society. Through her advocacy for independent media, Harper championed the idea that a plurality of voices is essential for a healthy democracy.

For example, her campaign to support local news outlets resulted in the establishment of community-funded journalism initiatives, which not only provided employment opportunities for journalists but also ensured that local issues received the attention they deserved. This movement towards decentralization of media ownership is a critical aspect of Harper's legacy, as it encourages a more democratic media landscape.

Promoting Ethical Reporting Standards

Harper's influence extended to redefining ethical standards in journalism. She was a vocal advocate for the *SPJ Code of Ethics*, which emphasizes the importance of accuracy, fairness, and accountability in reporting. Under her guidance, numerous media organizations adopted stricter ethical guidelines, leading to increased trust in journalistic practices.

In a notable instance, Harper's investigative team exposed a significant case of misinformation propagated by a major news outlet. By holding the outlet accountable, she not only restored public trust in the media but also set a precedent for future reporting practices. This incident highlighted the importance of ethical reporting in maintaining the integrity of journalism.

Challenging Misinformation

In an era marked by the rampant spread of misinformation, Harper's legacy is particularly relevant. She spearheaded initiatives aimed at fact-checking and debunking false narratives, which have become essential tools in the fight against misinformation.

For instance, the establishment of the *Truth Initiative*, a collaborative effort between various media organizations and fact-checkers, has significantly reduced the spread of false information online. By empowering journalists and citizens alike to identify and challenge misinformation, Harper's efforts have fostered a more informed public discourse.

Amplifying Marginalized Voices

A cornerstone of Harper's media reform efforts has been her commitment to amplifying marginalized voices. She recognized that traditional media often overlooks the stories of underrepresented communities. Through her platform, she provided a space for these voices, ensuring that their narratives were not only heard but celebrated.

Harper's partnership with grassroots organizations led to the production of documentaries and news segments that highlighted issues faced by marginalized groups. This approach not only diversified the media landscape but also inspired a new generation of journalists from these communities to tell their own stories.

The Future of Media Reform

Harper's enduring legacy in media reform continues to inspire current and future generations of journalists and media advocates. Her emphasis on ethical reporting, the importance of diversity in media ownership, and the necessity of challenging misinformation remain crucial in today's media environment.

As we look to the future, the principles championed by Harper serve as a guiding framework for emerging media reform movements. The ongoing struggle for media accountability, transparency, and representation reflects her vision of a media landscape that is not only informative but also equitable and just.

Conclusion

In conclusion, Harper Sato's contributions to media reform have left an indelible mark on the industry. By advocating for participatory journalism, ethical standards, and the amplification of marginalized voices, she has transformed the media landscape into one that prioritizes truth, diversity, and accountability. Her legacy serves as a reminder that the fight for a better media is ongoing, and that each generation must continue to push for reform to ensure that journalism fulfills its vital role in democracy.

$$\text{Media Reform} = \text{Ethics} + \text{Diversity} + \text{Accountability} \tag{49}$$

This equation encapsulates the essence of Harper's legacy and the foundational elements necessary for a thriving media ecosystem. As we move forward, it is imperative that we honor her legacy by continuing to advocate for these principles in our own media practices.

Political Transparency and Accountability

Grassroots Movements for Political Reform

Grassroots movements for political reform have emerged as a powerful force in contemporary society, driven by ordinary citizens who seek to influence policy and challenge entrenched systems of power. These movements are characterized by their bottom-up approach, where individuals and communities mobilize to address issues that directly affect their lives, often in response to perceived injustices or failures of government.

Theoretical Framework

The theoretical underpinning of grassroots movements can be found in social movement theory, which posits that collective action arises when individuals perceive a discrepancy between their current situation and their desired state. This is often articulated through the lens of relative deprivation theory, which suggests that people are motivated to act when they feel deprived of something they believe they are entitled to. As articulated by [Tilly(2004)], social movements are a form of contentious politics that can lead to significant social change.

The dynamics of grassroots movements are often analyzed using the resource mobilization theory, which emphasizes the importance of resources—such as time, money, and social connections—in facilitating collective action. This theory posits that successful movements are those that can effectively mobilize these resources to achieve their goals. Additionally, framing theory plays a crucial role, as movements must construct narratives that resonate with potential supporters and the broader public.

Key Problems Addressed

Grassroots movements for political reform often address a myriad of issues, including:

- **Corruption and Lack of Transparency:** Many grassroots movements arise in response to corruption scandals or lack of transparency in government operations. Activists seek to hold elected officials accountable and demand greater openness in political processes.

- **Voter Suppression:** Movements have emerged to combat practices that disenfranchise voters, particularly marginalized communities. These efforts often focus on advocating for legislation that protects voting rights and ensures equitable access to the ballot.

- **Campaign Finance Reform:** The influence of money in politics is a significant concern for many grassroots activists. Movements advocating for campaign finance reform seek to limit the power of corporate donations and establish fairer systems for political funding.

- **Social Justice Issues:** Many grassroots movements are also rooted in broader social justice concerns, such as racial equality, gender rights, and economic justice, which intersect with political reform efforts.

Notable Examples

Several grassroots movements have successfully influenced political reform in recent years:

- **The Tea Party Movement:** Emerging in the United States in the late 2000s, the Tea Party was a grassroots movement that advocated for reduced government spending, lower taxes, and a strict interpretation of the U.S. Constitution. The movement significantly impacted the Republican Party and led to the election of numerous candidates who espoused its values.

- **Black Lives Matter (BLM):** Founded in 2013, BLM is a grassroots movement that addresses systemic racism and police brutality against Black individuals. Through protests, social media campaigns, and policy advocacy, BLM has brought national attention to issues of racial injustice and has influenced local and national policy discussions on policing and criminal justice reform.

- **March for Our Lives:** Following the tragic shooting at Marjory Stoneman Douglas High School in 2018, students organized the March for Our Lives movement to advocate for gun control reform. The movement successfully mobilized millions of young people and has led to increased discussions around gun legislation at both state and federal levels.

- **The Women's March:** Initiated in 2017, the Women's March brought together millions of participants advocating for women's rights, gender equality, and social justice. This grassroots movement has inspired ongoing activism around issues such as reproductive rights, workplace equality, and combating sexual harassment.

Challenges Faced by Grassroots Movements

Despite their potential for impact, grassroots movements often encounter significant challenges:

- **Opposition from Established Powers:** Grassroots movements frequently face pushback from established political entities and corporate interests that may feel threatened by calls for reform. This can manifest in attempts to discredit the movement or suppress its activities.

- **Resource Limitations:** Many grassroots organizations operate with limited financial and human resources, which can hinder their ability to mobilize effectively or sustain long-term campaigns.

- **Internal Divisions:** As movements grow, they may experience internal divisions over strategy, priorities, and leadership, which can weaken their overall effectiveness and coherence.

- **Media Representation:** The portrayal of grassroots movements in the media can significantly influence public perception. Movements may struggle to gain media attention or may be misrepresented, complicating their efforts to garner support.

Conclusion

Grassroots movements for political reform represent a vital expression of democratic engagement and civic responsibility. They harness the collective power of individuals to challenge systemic injustices and advocate for meaningful change. As demonstrated by various successful movements, the ability to mobilize communities, engage in strategic advocacy, and build coalitions is essential for effecting political reform. The legacy of these movements not only influences current policy discussions but also paves the way for future generations to continue the fight for a more equitable and just society.

Increased Government Transparency and Openness

The concept of government transparency and openness has gained prominence in the political discourse of the 21st century, particularly in the wake of numerous scandals and the erosion of public trust in governmental institutions. At its core, government transparency refers to the accessibility of information held by public authorities, allowing citizens to understand the decision-making processes that affect their lives. Openness, on the other hand, encompasses the willingness of governments to engage with citizens and stakeholders, fostering an environment where feedback and participation are encouraged.

Theoretical Framework

The theoretical underpinnings of government transparency can be traced back to democratic theory, particularly the notion of informed citizenry as a pillar of democracy. According to [?], transparency is essential for accountability, as it

POLITICAL TRANSPARENCY AND ACCOUNTABILITY

enables citizens to scrutinize government actions and hold public officials responsible for their decisions. Furthermore, [?] highlights that transparency can enhance trust in government by reducing information asymmetry between the state and its citizens.

Mathematically, the relationship between transparency, accountability, and trust can be represented as:

$$T = f(A, C) \qquad (50)$$

where T is trust, A is accountability, and C is the level of citizen engagement. This equation illustrates that trust increases as accountability and citizen engagement rise, suggesting that transparency is a critical factor in fostering a healthy democratic environment.

Challenges to Transparency

Despite the theoretical benefits of government transparency, various obstacles hinder its implementation. One significant challenge is the entrenched culture of secrecy within many governmental institutions. Bureaucratic inertia often prioritizes the protection of sensitive information over public access, leading to a lack of transparency. Moreover, the fear of backlash from powerful interests can deter officials from disclosing information that may expose corruption or mismanagement.

Additionally, the digital divide poses a challenge to transparency efforts. While technology has the potential to enhance access to information, disparities in internet access and digital literacy can exacerbate inequalities in civic engagement. As noted by [?], marginalized communities may lack the resources to participate fully in the democratic process, undermining the goal of inclusive transparency.

Examples of Increased Transparency

In recent years, several initiatives have emerged to promote government transparency and openness. One notable example is the implementation of Freedom of Information (FOI) laws in various countries, which allow citizens to request information from public authorities. For instance, the United States' Freedom of Information Act (FOIA), enacted in 1966, has been instrumental in uncovering government misconduct and enhancing accountability.

Another example is the rise of open data initiatives, where governments proactively release datasets to the public. The City of New York's Open Data initiative, launched in 2012, provides access to a wealth of information on city operations, enabling citizens to analyze and engage with their local government. This initiative has not only increased transparency but has also spurred civic innovation, as developers create applications that utilize the data to address community needs.

Furthermore, the role of civil society organizations in advocating for transparency cannot be overstated. Organizations such as Transparency International and Open Government Partnership have been pivotal in pushing for reforms and holding governments accountable. Their efforts have resulted in the establishment of global standards for transparency and the promotion of best practices.

The Impact of Increased Transparency

The impact of increased government transparency and openness is multifaceted. Research indicates that transparency can lead to better governance outcomes, as it encourages public participation and informed decision-making. A study by [?] found that higher levels of transparency are associated with reduced corruption and increased public trust in government institutions.

Moreover, increased transparency can empower citizens to advocate for their rights and hold their governments accountable. As illustrated by the Arab Spring, social media platforms have played a crucial role in mobilizing citizens and demanding government accountability. The ability to share information quickly and widely has transformed the landscape of civic engagement, making it more difficult for governments to operate without scrutiny.

In conclusion, the push for increased government transparency and openness represents a critical component of contemporary democratic governance. While challenges remain, the theoretical benefits and real-world examples of successful transparency initiatives underscore the importance of fostering a culture of openness. As Harper Sato's legacy continues to inspire future innovators, the ongoing fight for transparency will be essential in shaping a more accountable and equitable society.

The Fight Against Corruption and Special Interests

In the contemporary political landscape, corruption and the influence of special interests pose significant challenges to democratic governance. Harper Sato, through her media platform and advocacy, has emerged as a formidable force in the fight against these pervasive issues. This section explores the theoretical underpinnings of corruption, the problems it engenders, and the impactful examples of Harper's efforts to combat these challenges.

Theoretical Framework

Corruption can be understood through various theoretical lenses, including institutional theory, public choice theory, and social capital theory. Institutional theory posits that corruption arises from weak institutions that fail to enforce rules and regulations effectively. Public choice theory suggests that individuals in power may act in their self-interest rather than the public interest, leading to corrupt practices. Social capital theory emphasizes the role of trust and networks in fostering accountability and transparency within governance structures.

Mathematically, the relationship between corruption and governance can be expressed as:

$$C = f(I, T, R) \tag{51}$$

where C represents the level of corruption, I is the integrity of institutions, T denotes transparency, and R signifies the robustness of regulations. A decrease in any of these variables typically results in an increase in corruption levels.

Problems Associated with Corruption

Corruption undermines public trust in government, distorts economic development, and exacerbates social inequalities. It often leads to the misallocation of resources, where funds intended for public services are siphoned off for personal gain. This phenomenon can be illustrated through the following consequences:

- **Erosion of Public Trust:** Citizens lose faith in government institutions when corruption is prevalent, leading to apathy and disengagement from civic duties.

- **Economic Inefficiencies:** Corruption creates a barrier to fair competition, stifling innovation and entrepreneurship. Businesses may be forced to engage in corrupt practices to survive, perpetuating a cycle of unethical behavior.

- **Social Inequality:** Vulnerable populations are disproportionately affected by corruption, as resources meant for poverty alleviation and social services are diverted. This exacerbates existing inequalities and hinders social mobility.

Harper's Approach to Combatting Corruption

Harper Sato's strategy to fight corruption and special interests is multifaceted, combining investigative journalism, public advocacy, and grassroots mobilization. Her approach can be categorized into several key components:

- **Investigative Reporting:** Harper's team employs rigorous investigative techniques to uncover corrupt practices within both public and private sectors. By exposing the ties between politicians and corporate interests, they bring transparency to the political process.

- **Public Awareness Campaigns:** Utilizing social media and traditional platforms, Harper raises awareness about the detrimental effects of corruption. Her campaigns educate the public on how to recognize and report corrupt practices, empowering citizens to take action.

- **Collaborations with Whistleblowers:** Harper actively collaborates with whistleblowers who provide insider information about corrupt activities. This partnership not only protects the whistleblowers but also amplifies their voices, ensuring their stories reach a wider audience.

- **Advocacy for Legislative Reforms:** Harper advocates for stronger anti-corruption laws and policies. She pushes for measures such as campaign finance reform, lobbying regulations, and increased transparency in government contracts.

Examples of Impact

One notable example of Harper's impact in the fight against corruption is her exposé on a high-profile bribery scandal involving a multinational corporation and government officials. Through meticulous research and investigative journalism, Harper's team uncovered a network of illicit payments that aimed to secure favorable contracts for the corporation. The revelations led to public outrage, resulting in:

- **Legal Action:** The scandal prompted investigations by law enforcement agencies, leading to the prosecution of several officials and corporate executives involved in the bribery scheme.

- **Policy Changes:** In response to the public outcry, lawmakers introduced legislation aimed at increasing transparency in government contracting processes and limiting the influence of corporate donations in political campaigns.

- **Public Mobilization:** Harper's reporting galvanized grassroots movements demanding accountability and reform, leading to increased civic engagement and participation in local governance.

Conclusion

The fight against corruption and special interests is an ongoing battle that requires vigilance, transparency, and active participation from both the media and the public. Harper Sato's innovative approach combines investigative journalism with grassroots activism, creating a powerful movement for change. By challenging the status quo and holding powerful interests accountable, Harper has not only reshaped the media landscape but has also laid the groundwork for a more transparent and equitable political system. Her legacy serves as a reminder that the fight against corruption is essential for the health of democracy and the well-being of society as a whole.

A New Era of Civic Engagement and Accountability

In the wake of Harper Sato's transformative influence on media and politics, a new era of civic engagement and accountability has emerged, characterized by heightened public participation in democratic processes and a demand for transparency from those in power. This shift can be attributed to a combination of grassroots activism, technological advancements, and a growing awareness of the importance of accountability in governance.

Theoretical Framework

Civic engagement refers to the ways in which individuals participate in the political and civic life of their communities. According to Putnam's theory of social capital, active participation in civic activities strengthens communities and fosters trust among citizens [?]. This theory posits that social networks and the norms of reciprocity and trustworthiness are essential for a healthy democracy. In the context of Harper's legacy, the revitalization of civic engagement can be seen as a response to the erosion of trust in traditional political institutions and media outlets.

Emerging Problems

Despite the positive trends in civic engagement, several challenges persist. The increasing polarization of political discourse often leads to disengagement among citizens who feel that their voices are drowned out by extremist viewpoints. Additionally, misinformation campaigns, particularly on social media platforms, can undermine public trust in legitimate sources of information, further complicating the landscape of civic participation.

Mathematically, we can describe the relationship between civic engagement (CE) and public trust (PT) as follows:

$$CE = f(PT, E, C) \tag{52}$$

Where:

- CE = Civic Engagement

- PT = Public Trust

- E = Education Level

- C = Community Involvement

This equation suggests that civic engagement is positively correlated with public trust, education levels, and community involvement. Therefore, addressing misinformation and promoting education are crucial for fostering a more engaged citizenry.

Examples of Civic Engagement

Harper's advocacy for transparency and accountability has inspired various grassroots movements across the globe. One notable example is the rise of community-led initiatives aimed at monitoring local government actions. These initiatives often utilize technology to collect data and disseminate information to the public, empowering citizens to hold their representatives accountable.

For instance, the "OpenGov" movement has seen citizens using platforms like SeeClickFix and OpenStreetMap to report issues in their communities, ranging from potholes to unresponsive local officials. Such platforms not only facilitate communication between citizens and government but also foster a sense of ownership and responsibility among community members.

Case Study: Youth Engagement

The involvement of youth in civic engagement has been particularly noteworthy. Inspired by Harper's commitment to social justice, young activists have taken to the streets to demand action on issues such as climate change and racial equality. The global climate strikes, led by figures like Greta Thunberg, exemplify how young people are mobilizing to demand accountability from their governments. These strikes have not only raised awareness but have also pressured policymakers to take meaningful action on climate issues.

Impact on Accountability

The rise of civic engagement has led to increased accountability among public officials. Citizens are now more equipped to demand transparency and question decisions made by their leaders. This is evident in movements advocating for campaign finance reform, where organizations like Common Cause have mobilized citizens to push for legislation that limits the influence of money in politics.

Furthermore, the use of social media as a tool for civic engagement has revolutionized how information is shared and how citizens interact with their governments. Hashtags such as #TransparencyNow and #AccountabilityMatters have gained traction, galvanizing public support for various causes and holding officials accountable in real-time.

Conclusion

In conclusion, the new era of civic engagement and accountability catalyzed by Harper Sato's influence is reshaping the political landscape. While challenges remain, the increased participation of citizens in democratic processes signifies a robust response to the call for transparency and ethical governance. As civic engagement continues to evolve, it is imperative for individuals and communities to remain vigilant, informed, and active in their pursuit of a more accountable and just society.

Harper's Lasting Influence on Political Culture

Harper Sato's impact on political culture transcends her immediate achievements in media reform and activism; it resonates through the very fabric of democratic engagement and civic responsibility. Her influence can be understood through several theoretical frameworks, including the Public Sphere theory by Jürgen Habermas, which posits that a healthy public discourse is essential for democracy.

This section will explore how Harper's initiatives have reshaped political culture, the problems she addressed, and the examples that illustrate her enduring legacy.

Theoretical Foundations

The Public Sphere theory emphasizes the role of communication in fostering democratic participation. Habermas argues that an informed citizenry, engaged in rational-critical debate, is fundamental for a functioning democracy. Harper's work embodies this theory by advocating for transparency, ethical journalism, and the empowerment of marginalized voices. By creating platforms that encourage open discourse, she has redefined the parameters of public engagement.

Challenges to Political Culture

Harper's journey was not without challenges. The political landscape she navigated was rife with issues such as misinformation, corporate influence, and voter apathy. These problems are highlighted by the following equations that represent the dynamics of political engagement:

$$P = \frac{C}{I + D} \tag{53}$$

Where P is political engagement, C is civic knowledge, I is misinformation, and D represents disillusionment. This equation illustrates that as misinformation and disillusionment increase, civic knowledge must also rise to maintain political engagement. Harper's efforts aimed to bolster C while combating I and D.

Examples of Influence

Harper's influence on political culture can be illustrated through several key initiatives:

- **The Launch of "The Voice of Tomorrow":** This groundbreaking media platform not only provided a space for ethical journalism but also prioritized stories that highlighted systemic injustices and political corruption. By focusing on these issues, Harper challenged the status quo and encouraged audiences to engage critically with news content.

- **Grassroots Mobilization:** Harper's investigations into political corruption inspired grassroots movements across the globe. For example, her exposé on corporate lobbying practices led to the formation of local advocacy groups that demanded greater transparency and accountability from elected officials. This ripple effect demonstrated how one individual's commitment to truth could galvanize collective action.

- **Collaboration with Whistleblowers:** By collaborating with whistleblowers, Harper shed light on clandestine governmental operations and corporate malfeasance. Her work not only protected these individuals but also set a precedent for the protection of whistleblowers, thereby reinforcing a culture of accountability and ethical governance.

- **Youth Engagement Initiatives:** Recognizing the power of youth in shaping the future, Harper launched educational programs that emphasized critical thinking and civic engagement. These initiatives empowered young people to become informed citizens, fostering a new generation of activists dedicated to political reform.

Long-term Impact on Political Culture

The long-term impact of Harper's work on political culture is evident in the following areas:

- **Increased Civic Engagement:** Harper's advocacy for transparency and accountability has resulted in a more politically aware and active citizenry. Voter turnout in regions where her influence has been felt has seen significant increases, indicating a shift towards greater public participation in the democratic process.

- **Redefining Political Norms:** Harper's emphasis on ethical reporting and the importance of independent media has redefined the norms within political culture. Politicians are now more accountable to the public, as the demand for transparency has grown. The expectation that leaders must operate with integrity has become a cornerstone of contemporary political discourse.

- **Resilience Against Authoritarianism:** In an era where authoritarianism threatens democratic institutions, Harper's legacy serves as a bulwark against such trends. Her commitment to freedom of the press and the protection of civil liberties has inspired movements worldwide, reinforcing the idea that democracy requires constant vigilance and active participation.

- **The Rise of Social Movements:** Harper's influence has catalyzed the emergence of social movements that prioritize justice, equity, and environmental sustainability. These movements, rooted in the principles she championed, continue to challenge entrenched power structures and advocate for systemic change.

Conclusion

In conclusion, Harper Sato's lasting influence on political culture is profound and multifaceted. By fostering a culture of transparency, accountability, and civic engagement, she has not only transformed the media landscape but also redefined the expectations of political participation. Her legacy serves as a reminder of the power of one individual to inspire change and the importance of an informed citizenry in the preservation of democracy. As we look to the future, Harper's vision for a more equitable and just society continues to resonate, reminding us that the fight for political reform is an ongoing journey, one that requires the collective effort of all citizens.

The Fight for Environmental Justice

The Transition to Renewable Energy Sources

The transition to renewable energy sources represents one of the most critical shifts in the global energy landscape. As the world grapples with the consequences of climate change, the need for sustainable energy solutions has never been more pressing. This section explores the theoretical foundations, challenges, and real-world examples of this transition.

Theoretical Foundations of Renewable Energy Transition

The transition to renewable energy can be understood through various theoretical frameworks, including the *Energy Transition Theory* and the *Sustainability Transition Theory*.

Energy Transition Theory posits that societies evolve through distinct phases of energy sources, moving from traditional biomass to fossil fuels, and eventually to renewable energy. This theory suggests that technological, economic, and social factors interplay to facilitate this transition.

Mathematically, we can represent the relationship between energy consumption and carbon emissions using the Kaya Identity:

$$E = P \times G \times \frac{C}{E} \qquad (54)$$

Where: - E = total CO2 emissions - P = population - G = GDP per capita - C = energy consumption - E = energy intensity (energy per unit of GDP)

This identity illustrates that reducing carbon emissions requires a multifaceted approach, including improving energy efficiency and transitioning to cleaner energy sources.

Problems and Challenges in Transitioning

Despite the theoretical frameworks supporting the transition to renewable energy, several challenges hinder progress:

- **Infrastructure Limitations:** Many countries lack the necessary infrastructure to support renewable energy technologies. For instance, the integration of solar and wind energy into existing grids often requires significant upgrades.

- **Economic Barriers:** The initial investment costs for renewable energy projects can be prohibitively high. For example, while the cost of solar panels has decreased dramatically, the upfront costs still present a barrier for many consumers and businesses.

- **Political and Regulatory Hurdles:** Policymaking can be slow to adapt to the fast-paced developments in renewable energy technologies. Additionally, lobbying from fossil fuel industries can impede legislative progress towards renewable energy initiatives.

- **Intermittency Issues:** Renewable energy sources like solar and wind are inherently intermittent. This variability necessitates the development of energy storage solutions or backup systems to ensure a reliable energy supply.

Real-World Examples of Successful Transitions

Several countries have made significant strides in transitioning to renewable energy sources, serving as models for others:

- **Germany:** The *Energiewende* (energy transition) policy has led Germany to become a leader in renewable energy, with over 40% of its electricity generated from renewable sources as of 2020. This transition involved substantial investments in wind and solar energy, as well as energy efficiency measures.

- **Denmark:** Denmark has successfully integrated wind energy into its grid, with wind turbines generating approximately 47% of the country's electricity in 2019. This achievement was made possible through a combination of government incentives, technological innovation, and public acceptance of renewable energy.

- **Costa Rica:** Costa Rica has become a beacon of renewable energy, running on over 99% renewable sources since 2015. The country primarily relies on hydroelectric power, supplemented by wind and solar energy, showcasing the potential for small nations to lead in sustainability.

Conclusion

The transition to renewable energy sources is not merely an environmental imperative but also a socio-economic opportunity. By overcoming the challenges of infrastructure, economic barriers, political resistance, and intermittency, societies can harness the benefits of renewable energy. The examples of Germany, Denmark, and Costa Rica illustrate that a successful transition is possible, paving the way for a sustainable future. As Harper Sato championed media reforms, the narrative around renewable energy must evolve to inspire collective action and commitment to this vital transition.

Sustainable Practices in Both Public and Private Sectors

Sustainable practices are essential for achieving long-term environmental goals and ensuring that both public and private sectors contribute positively to the planet's health. The integration of sustainability into organizational practices is not merely a trend; it is a necessary evolution in response to the climate crisis. This subsection explores the theoretical frameworks underpinning sustainable practices, the challenges faced in their implementation, and notable examples that illustrate successful integration in various sectors.

Theoretical Frameworks

The concept of sustainability is often anchored in the *Triple Bottom Line* (TBL) framework, which posits that businesses should focus on three key areas: social, environmental, and economic performance. This approach encourages organizations to measure their success not just by financial profit, but also by their impact on people and the planet. The TBL is mathematically represented as:

$$TBL = P + E + S \qquad (55)$$

where P represents profit, E represents environmental stewardship, and S represents social responsibility. This holistic view of success encourages organizations to adopt practices that are beneficial across all three dimensions.

Another important theory is the *Circular Economy* model, which advocates for the redesign of production and consumption systems to minimize waste and make the most of resources. The circular economy contrasts with the traditional linear economy, which follows a take-make-dispose pattern. In a circular economy, resources are reused, recycled, and repurposed, creating a closed-loop system that enhances sustainability.

Challenges in Implementation

Despite the theoretical frameworks supporting sustainable practices, organizations often face significant challenges in their implementation. These challenges can be broadly categorized into:

- **Financial Constraints:** Many organizations perceive the upfront costs of implementing sustainable practices as prohibitive. The initial investment in green technologies, sustainable materials, or training can deter businesses, especially small and medium-sized enterprises (SMEs).

- **Resistance to Change:** Organizational culture plays a critical role in the adoption of sustainable practices. Employees and management may resist changes to established processes, fearing disruption or uncertainty about the benefits of new practices.

- **Lack of Knowledge and Expertise:** Many organizations lack the necessary knowledge or expertise to implement sustainable practices effectively. This gap can lead to ineffective strategies that fail to achieve the desired outcomes.

- **Regulatory Barriers:** In some regions, regulatory frameworks may not support or incentivize sustainable practices, creating a disincentive for organizations to adopt environmentally friendly policies.

Examples of Successful Integration

Despite these challenges, there are numerous examples of organizations in both public and private sectors that have successfully integrated sustainable practices:

Public Sector Example: Government Initiatives Many governments have recognized the importance of sustainability and have initiated programs to promote sustainable practices. For instance, the *Green New Deal* in various countries aims to address climate change while promoting economic growth and job creation. This initiative includes investments in renewable energy, infrastructure improvements, and sustainable agriculture, demonstrating how public policy can drive significant change.

Private Sector Example: Corporate Sustainability In the private sector, companies like *Unilever* and *Patagonia* have become leaders in sustainability. Unilever's Sustainable Living Plan focuses on reducing the company's environmental footprint while increasing its positive social impact. The plan includes specific targets, such as halving the environmental impact of products by 2030. Patagonia, on the other hand, is renowned for its commitment to environmental activism, using sustainable materials in its products and donating a percentage of profits to environmental causes.

The Role of Innovation

Innovation plays a crucial role in advancing sustainable practices across sectors. Technological advancements enable organizations to develop new processes and products that minimize environmental impact. For example, the rise of renewable energy technologies, such as solar and wind power, has revolutionized energy production, allowing for cleaner alternatives to fossil fuels.

Moreover, the integration of digital technologies, such as the Internet of Things (IoT), can enhance resource efficiency in both public and private sectors. Smart grids, for instance, optimize energy distribution and reduce waste, contributing to sustainability goals.

Conclusion

In conclusion, sustainable practices in both public and private sectors are vital for addressing the pressing challenges of climate change and environmental degradation. By leveraging theoretical frameworks like the Triple Bottom Line and Circular Economy, organizations can navigate the complexities of sustainability. Despite facing financial, cultural, and regulatory challenges, successful examples from various sectors illustrate that sustainable practices are not only feasible but also beneficial for long-term success. As innovation continues to drive

Climate Adaptation and Resilience Efforts

Climate adaptation refers to the process of adjusting to current or expected changes in climate and its effects. This is crucial in mitigating the adverse impacts of climate change, especially for vulnerable communities. Resilience, on the other hand, is the capacity of a system, community, or society to resist, absorb, and recover from the effects of climate-related hazards. Together, adaptation and resilience are essential components of a comprehensive climate strategy.

Theoretical Framework

The concept of climate adaptation is grounded in several theoretical frameworks, including the vulnerability framework, resilience theory, and the socio-ecological systems approach. The vulnerability framework emphasizes the susceptibility of communities to climate impacts and their capacity to cope with these changes. Resilience theory focuses on the ability of systems to maintain functionality in the face of disturbances. The socio-ecological systems approach integrates human and ecological systems, highlighting the interdependencies between them.

Mathematically, the adaptation and resilience of a community can be expressed through various models. For instance, the adaptive capacity (AC) can be defined as:

$$AC = f(S, R, E)$$

where S represents social capital, R represents resource availability, and E signifies environmental conditions. A higher adaptive capacity indicates a greater ability to adjust to climate impacts.

Current Problems in Climate Adaptation

Despite the theoretical frameworks guiding climate adaptation efforts, several challenges persist:

- **Lack of Funding:** Many adaptation projects suffer from inadequate funding, limiting their scope and effectiveness. According to the Global Commission on Adaptation, an estimated $1.8 trillion is needed globally for climate adaptation by 2030.

- **Insufficient Data:** A lack of localized climate data hinders effective planning and implementation of adaptation strategies. Many regions, particularly in developing countries, lack the necessary climate monitoring systems.

- **Political and Institutional Barriers:** Political will is often lacking, with many governments prioritizing short-term economic gains over long-term sustainability. Institutional fragmentation can also impede coordinated adaptation efforts.

- **Social Inequities:** Vulnerable populations, including low-income communities and marginalized groups, often face greater risks from climate impacts and have fewer resources to adapt. This exacerbates existing social inequities.

Examples of Successful Adaptation and Resilience Initiatives

1. **The Netherlands' Delta Works:** This engineering marvel is a series of dams, sluices, locks, dikes, and storm surge barriers designed to protect the Dutch coastline from rising sea levels and storm surges. The project is a prime example of proactive adaptation, combining engineering with natural systems to enhance resilience.

2. **The 100 Resilient Cities Initiative:** Launched by the Rockefeller Foundation, this initiative supports cities worldwide in developing resilience strategies against climate change and other shocks. Cities like New Orleans and Cape Town have implemented comprehensive plans to address vulnerabilities and enhance community resilience.

3. **Community-Based Adaptation in Bangladesh:** In response to increasing flooding and cyclones, local communities in Bangladesh have developed adaptive strategies, such as constructing raised homes and using salt-resistant crops. These initiatives empower communities to take ownership of their adaptation processes.

4. **Urban Green Infrastructure:** Cities like Melbourne and Singapore have integrated green infrastructure into urban planning to enhance resilience against climate impacts. Green roofs, urban forests, and permeable pavements help manage stormwater, reduce urban heat, and improve air quality.

The Role of Policy in Climate Adaptation

Effective climate adaptation requires strong policy frameworks at local, national, and international levels. Policies must prioritize funding for adaptation initiatives, enhance data collection and sharing, and promote collaboration across sectors.

The Paris Agreement emphasizes the need for countries to develop National Adaptation Plans (NAPs) to address climate vulnerabilities. These plans should incorporate stakeholder engagement, particularly from marginalized communities, to ensure that adaptation strategies are equitable and effective.

Conclusion

In conclusion, climate adaptation and resilience efforts are critical in addressing the challenges posed by climate change. By understanding the theoretical frameworks, acknowledging current problems, and learning from successful examples, we can develop more effective strategies to enhance community resilience. Policymakers must prioritize adaptation initiatives, ensuring that vulnerable populations are supported and that resources are allocated effectively to build a sustainable future for all.

Harper's Vision of a Thriving, Equitable Planet

In an era marked by unprecedented environmental challenges and social inequities, Harper Sato's vision for a thriving, equitable planet stands as a beacon of hope and a blueprint for sustainable development. Her approach integrates environmental sustainability with social justice, emphasizing that the two are inextricably linked. This section explores Harper's holistic vision, the theoretical foundations that support it, the pressing problems it addresses, and the real-world examples that illustrate its potential.

Theoretical Foundations

Harper's vision draws from several key theories that advocate for an integrative approach to sustainability. One of the primary frameworks is the **Triple Bottom Line (TBL)** theory, which posits that businesses and organizations should focus on three pillars: People, Planet, and Profit. This model encourages decision-makers to consider social equity and environmental health alongside economic growth.

$$TBL = \text{Social Equity} + \text{Environmental Stewardship} + \text{Economic Viability} \quad (56)$$

Additionally, Harper is influenced by **Ecological Economics**, which emphasizes the economy as a subsystem of the environment. This perspective advocates for the valuation of natural resources and ecosystem services, recognizing that the depletion of these resources ultimately undermines economic stability and social welfare.

Addressing Pressing Problems

Harper's vision confronts several urgent global issues:

1. **Climate Change**: The increasing frequency and severity of climate-related disasters necessitate immediate action. Harper advocates for a transition to renewable energy sources, arguing that sustainable energy infrastructure can mitigate climate impacts while creating jobs.

2. **Social Inequality**: Economic disparities exacerbate environmental degradation, as marginalized communities often bear the brunt of pollution and resource exploitation. Harper's vision emphasizes equitable access to resources and decision-making processes, ensuring that all voices are heard.

3. **Biodiversity Loss**: The rapid decline of species and ecosystems threatens the planet's health. Harper promotes conservation efforts and sustainable land-use practices, recognizing that biodiversity is crucial for ecosystem resilience and human well-being.

4. **Resource Depletion**: Unsustainable consumption patterns lead to the overexploitation of natural resources. Harper calls for circular economy practices, which prioritize recycling, reusing, and reducing waste.

Real-World Examples

Harper's vision is not merely theoretical; it is grounded in practical applications that demonstrate its feasibility:

- **The Green New Deal**: This comprehensive policy proposal aims to address climate change and economic inequality simultaneously. By investing in renewable energy infrastructure and creating millions of jobs, it embodies Harper's commitment to a sustainable and equitable future.

- **Community-Led Initiatives**: Harper has championed grassroots movements that empower local communities to take charge of their environmental futures. For instance, the **Transition Towns** movement encourages communities to develop localized solutions to energy and food security, fostering resilience and self-sufficiency.

- **Corporate Social Responsibility (CSR)**: Many companies are now adopting CSR practices that align with Harper's vision. Businesses like **Patagonia** not only prioritize environmental sustainability but also engage in social justice initiatives, demonstrating that profit and purpose can coexist.

The Path Forward

To realize Harper's vision of a thriving, equitable planet, several strategies must be implemented:

1. **Education and Awareness**: Enhancing public understanding of sustainability issues is crucial. Educational programs that focus on environmental literacy can empower individuals to make informed choices.

2. **Policy Advocacy**: Harper emphasizes the importance of advocating for policies that promote sustainability and social equity. This includes supporting legislation that addresses climate change, protects natural resources, and fosters economic justice.

3. **Collaboration Across Sectors**: Harper's vision calls for collaboration among governments, businesses, and civil society. Multi-stakeholder partnerships can leverage diverse resources and expertise to tackle complex challenges.

4. **Innovative Technologies**: Embracing technological advancements can facilitate the transition to a sustainable future. Innovations in renewable energy, waste management, and sustainable agriculture are essential components of Harper's vision.

In conclusion, Harper Sato's vision of a thriving, equitable planet is a call to action that transcends traditional boundaries. By integrating environmental sustainability with social justice, her approach offers a comprehensive framework for addressing the pressing challenges of our time. As we move forward, it is imperative to embrace this vision, fostering a world where both people and the planet can flourish together.

Harper's Enduring Legacy in the Climate Justice Movement

Harper Sato's contributions to the climate justice movement have not only reshaped public discourse around environmental issues but have also established a framework for future activists and policymakers. Her legacy is characterized by a multifaceted approach that combines advocacy, education, and grassroots mobilization, creating a ripple effect that continues to influence the movement today.

Theoretical Foundations of Harper's Legacy

At the core of Harper's impact is the recognition that climate justice is inherently linked to social justice. Drawing from the theories of environmental justice, Harper emphasized that marginalized communities disproportionately bear the brunt of climate change impacts. This intersectional approach aligns with the work of scholars such as [?] who argue that environmental hazards are often sited in low-income neighborhoods, exacerbating existing inequalities. Harper's advocacy for policies that prioritize these communities has been pivotal in framing climate action as a moral imperative.

Addressing Systemic Inequities

One of the significant problems that Harper addressed was the systemic inequities within climate policy frameworks. For instance, while many climate initiatives focused on reducing carbon emissions, they often overlooked the needs of vulnerable populations. Harper's insistence on inclusive policy-making led to the incorporation of community voices in environmental discussions. This shift is evident in the success of initiatives like the Green New Deal, which integrates economic revitalization with environmental sustainability, as highlighted by [?].

Case Studies of Harper's Influence

Harper's legacy can be illustrated through various case studies that highlight her effectiveness in mobilizing communities and influencing policy. One notable example is the **Youth Climate Strike**, where Harper collaborated with young activists to organize global demonstrations. This movement, which gained momentum in 2019, saw millions of young people demand urgent climate action, demonstrating the power of collective action. Harper's role in amplifying youth voices has inspired a new generation of climate activists, as evidenced by the emergence of organizations like *Fridays for Future*.

Another example is Harper's involvement in the **Paris Agreement** negotiations. By advocating for stronger commitments to limit global warming to 1.5 degrees Celsius, she played a crucial role in pushing for accountability mechanisms that hold nations responsible for their climate pledges. The incorporation of transparency measures in the agreement reflects Harper's influence on international climate policy, emphasizing the need for equitable solutions that consider the most affected populations.

Innovative Approaches to Climate Activism

Harper's enduring legacy is also marked by her innovative approaches to climate activism. She recognized the importance of integrating technology and social media into her campaigns. By leveraging platforms like Twitter and Instagram, Harper effectively mobilized support and raised awareness about climate issues. Her viral campaigns, such as **#ClimateJusticeNow**, have sparked conversations across demographics, demonstrating the power of digital activism in the modern age.

Additionally, Harper's commitment to education and outreach has established a framework for climate literacy. Through initiatives like the *Climate Justice Curriculum*, she provided resources for educators to teach students about the intersections of climate change and social justice. This educational approach ensures that future generations are equipped with the knowledge and tools necessary to advocate for sustainable practices and policies.

Challenges and Resilience

Despite her significant contributions, Harper faced numerous challenges in her advocacy work. The fossil fuel industry, with its substantial financial resources and political influence, often attempted to undermine her efforts. However, Harper's resilience in the face of adversity is a testament to her commitment to climate justice. She famously stated, "The fight for our planet is a marathon, not a sprint," emphasizing the importance of perseverance in the pursuit of long-term change.

Conclusion: A Lasting Impact on Future Generations

Harper Sato's legacy in the climate justice movement is profound and far-reaching. By intertwining environmental advocacy with social justice, she has not only addressed immediate climate challenges but has also laid the groundwork for a more equitable future. Her innovative strategies, commitment to inclusivity, and resilience in the face of opposition serve as an enduring inspiration for activists around the globe.

As future generations continue to confront the climate crisis, they will undoubtedly draw upon Harper's principles and strategies. Her legacy will live on through the countless individuals she has inspired to take action, ensuring that the fight for climate justice remains a central focus in the broader struggle for a sustainable and equitable world.

Inspiring Future Innovators

Harper as a Mentor and Role Model

Harper Sato has emerged as a beacon of inspiration and guidance for a generation of aspiring innovators and activists. Her unique journey through the tumultuous landscape of media reform, political accountability, and climate justice has positioned her as a mentor whose impact extends far beyond her immediate achievements. This section explores the multifaceted role Harper plays as a mentor and role model, highlighting the theories of mentorship, the challenges she faced, and the tangible examples of her influence on young activists.

Theoretical Framework of Mentorship

Mentorship is a critical component in the development of future leaders and innovators. According to Kram's (1985) theory of mentoring, there are two primary functions of mentorship: career development and psychosocial support. Career development encompasses sponsorship, exposure, and coaching, while psychosocial support includes role modeling, acceptance, and friendship. Harper embodies both dimensions in her interactions with young activists and journalists.

Challenges and Opportunities

Despite her successes, Harper faced numerous challenges that tested her resilience and commitment to mentorship. The media landscape is notoriously competitive, and many young journalists struggle to find their voice amid the cacophony of misinformation and corporate influence. Harper's own experiences navigating these challenges have equipped her with the tools to guide others through similar obstacles.

For instance, during her early career, Harper encountered significant pushback from established media institutions resistant to change. This experience taught her the importance of perseverance and adaptability—qualities she emphasizes to her mentees. By sharing her personal stories of overcoming adversity, Harper instills a sense of hope and determination in those she mentors.

Practical Examples of Mentorship

Harper's mentorship is not limited to one-on-one interactions; she has also established programs aimed at fostering the next generation of innovators. One notable initiative is the "Future Voices" program, which provides training and resources for young journalists from marginalized communities. This program emphasizes the importance of diverse perspectives in media, aligning with Harper's commitment to amplifying underrepresented voices.

Through workshops, mentorship circles, and internships, participants in the "Future Voices" program gain hands-on experience in investigative journalism, ethical reporting, and media literacy. Harper often leads these sessions, sharing her insights and encouraging participants to challenge the status quo. For example, during a workshop on combating misinformation, Harper guided participants through the process of fact-checking and source verification, empowering them to become critical consumers and producers of media.

The Ripple Effect of Harper's Influence

The impact of Harper's mentorship extends beyond individual mentees; it creates a ripple effect within communities. Many of her former mentees have gone on to establish their own initiatives, inspired by Harper's example. For instance, one mentee, Maya Rodriguez, founded a grassroots organization focused on media literacy in schools, ensuring that young students are equipped to navigate the complexities of the digital information age.

This phenomenon aligns with Bandura's (1977) social learning theory, which posits that people learn from one another through observation, imitation, and modeling. By embodying the values of integrity, courage, and social responsibility, Harper serves as a powerful role model for young activists, encouraging them to take initiative and drive change in their own communities.

Conclusion: Harper's Enduring Legacy as a Mentor

In conclusion, Harper Sato's role as a mentor and role model is characterized by her commitment to fostering the next generation of innovators and activists. Through her mentorship, she not only imparts valuable skills and knowledge but also instills a sense of purpose and empowerment in her mentees. The challenges she has faced and the initiatives she has established serve as a testament to her dedication to nurturing future leaders who will continue the fight for media reform, political accountability, and climate justice.

As Harper continues to inspire and guide young activists, her legacy will undoubtedly shape the future of social change, ensuring that the values of integrity, resilience, and inclusivity remain at the forefront of the ongoing struggle for a better world.

The Impact of Harper's Story on Young Activists

Harper Sato's journey from a passionate media reformer to a global symbol of activism has profoundly influenced a new generation of young activists. Her story serves not only as an inspiration but also as a roadmap for effecting change in a world increasingly characterized by complex social, political, and environmental challenges. This section explores the multifaceted impact of Harper's narrative on youth activism, focusing on three key areas: empowerment through representation, the cultivation of critical thinking, and the mobilization of grassroots movements.

Empowerment through Representation

One of the most significant aspects of Harper's story is her role as a representative figure for marginalized communities. By breaking through the glass ceiling in a competitive media industry, Harper has become a beacon of hope for young activists who often feel voiceless in the face of systemic injustices. According to social identity theory, individuals derive a sense of self from their group memberships, which can significantly influence their motivation to engage in activism [Tajfel(1982)].

Harper's visibility as a woman of color in a predominantly male and white media landscape challenges the status quo and encourages young activists to embrace their identities. For instance, the rise of social media platforms has allowed diverse voices to gain traction, echoing Harper's message of inclusivity. Young activists, inspired by her, have begun to champion causes that resonate with their communities, from racial justice to climate action.

Cultivation of Critical Thinking

Harper's commitment to ethical journalism and the promotion of critical thinking has also left a lasting impact on young activists. In an age where misinformation spreads rapidly, her emphasis on fact-checking and accountability encourages the youth to question narratives presented to them. Theories of critical pedagogy, such as those proposed by Paulo Freire, emphasize the importance of dialogue and reflection in education, fostering an environment where learners can critically engage with the world around them [Freire(1970)].

Through initiatives like workshops and mentorship programs, Harper has instilled a sense of responsibility in young activists to seek the truth and challenge dominant narratives. For example, her collaboration with high school journalism programs has empowered students to investigate local issues, fostering a generation that is not only informed but also actively engaged in their communities. This cultivation of critical thinking is essential for sustaining long-term activism, as it equips young people with the tools to analyze and confront the complexities of societal issues.

Mobilization of Grassroots Movements

Harper's story has also catalyzed the mobilization of grassroots movements, demonstrating the power of collective action. Her advocacy for government transparency and accountability has inspired young activists to organize campaigns that demand change at local, national, and global levels. The concept of social movements, as outlined by Charles Tilly, emphasizes the importance of mobilizing resources and creating networks to achieve common goals [Tilly(2004)].

For instance, the youth-led climate strikes inspired by Harper's activism have mobilized millions worldwide, showcasing the effectiveness of grassroots organizing. Movements like Fridays for Future have utilized social media to amplify their message, drawing parallels to Harper's innovative use of media to reach wider audiences. These movements not only highlight the urgency of climate action but also demonstrate the capacity of young activists to effect change, echoing Harper's belief that every voice matters.

Conclusion

In summary, Harper Sato's story has had a profound impact on young activists by empowering them through representation, cultivating critical thinking, and mobilizing grassroots movements. Her legacy serves as a reminder that activism is not just about individual efforts but also about fostering a collective spirit of change. As young activists continue to draw inspiration from Harper's journey, they are equipped to challenge the status quo and advocate for a more just and equitable world.

Bibliography

[Tajfel(1982)] Tajfel, H. (1982). *Social Identity and Intergroup Relations*. Cambridge University Press.

[Freire(1970)] Freire, P. (1970). *Pedagogy of the Oppressed*. Continuum.

[Tilly(2004)] Tilly, C. (2004). *Social Movements, 1768-2004*. Paradigm Publishers.

Fostering Innovation and Critical Thinking in Education

In an era where information is abundant yet often misleading, fostering innovation and critical thinking in education has become paramount. Harper Sato's influence extends beyond media reform into the realm of education, where she champions an approach that encourages students to think critically, question assumptions, and innovate solutions to the pressing challenges of our time.

Theoretical Framework

The foundation of fostering innovation and critical thinking in education can be traced to several educational theories. One prominent theory is **Constructivism**, which posits that learners construct knowledge through experiences and reflections. According to Piaget (1976), children learn best when they engage actively with their environment, allowing them to form their own understanding of concepts. This theory underlines the importance of hands-on learning and real-world problem-solving in education.

Another relevant theory is **Critical Pedagogy**, as articulated by Paulo Freire (1970). Freire emphasizes dialogue and critical consciousness, encouraging students to engage in discussions about societal issues and challenge the status quo. This pedagogical approach aligns with Harper's vision of an educational system that not only imparts knowledge but also empowers students to become active participants in their communities.

Challenges in Education

Despite the recognized importance of fostering innovation and critical thinking, several challenges hinder its implementation in educational settings:

- **Standardized Testing:** The prevalence of standardized testing often prioritizes rote memorization over critical thinking skills. Educators may feel pressured to "teach to the test," stifling creativity and innovation in the classroom.

- **Curriculum Rigidity:** Traditional curricula can be inflexible, leaving little room for exploration and inquiry-based learning. This rigidity can discourage students from pursuing their interests and developing innovative solutions.

- **Resource Disparities:** Schools in underfunded areas may lack the necessary resources to implement innovative teaching methods or provide students with hands-on learning experiences.

Innovative Educational Practices

To combat these challenges, Harper advocates for several innovative educational practices that promote critical thinking and creativity:

Project-Based Learning (PBL) is one such approach that immerses students in real-world challenges, encouraging them to collaborate, research, and develop solutions. PBL not only fosters critical thinking but also helps students to apply their knowledge in practical contexts. For instance, students might work on a project to design a sustainable community garden, requiring them to research environmental science, engage with community members, and present their findings.

Interdisciplinary Learning is another practice that Harper supports. By integrating subjects such as science, technology, engineering, arts, and mathematics (STEAM), educators can create a more holistic learning experience. This approach allows students to draw connections between different disciplines, encouraging them to think critically and innovate across fields. For example, a unit on climate change could incorporate scientific research, artistic expression, and technological solutions, fostering a comprehensive understanding of the issue.

Technology-Enhanced Learning also plays a crucial role in fostering innovation. Digital tools and platforms can facilitate collaborative projects, provide access to a wealth of information, and enable students to engage with global issues. For instance, using virtual reality (VR) technology, students can explore ecosystems affected by climate change, deepening their understanding and inspiring them to think critically about potential solutions.

Examples of Successful Implementation

Several educational institutions and programs exemplify Harper's vision for fostering innovation and critical thinking:

- **High Tech High** in San Diego, California, is a network of charter schools that emphasizes project-based learning and real-world applications. Students engage in interdisciplinary projects that require critical thinking and collaboration, preparing them for future challenges.

- **The International Baccalaureate (IB)** program promotes inquiry-based learning and encourages students to think critically about global issues. The curriculum is designed to foster creativity, communication, and collaboration, equipping students with the skills needed to navigate an increasingly complex world.

- **The Design Thinking Model** has been adopted by various educational institutions to promote innovation. This model encourages students to empathize with users, define problems, ideate solutions, prototype their ideas, and test them in real-world scenarios. This iterative process fosters critical thinking and creativity.

Conclusion

In conclusion, fostering innovation and critical thinking in education is essential for preparing future generations to tackle the complex challenges facing society. Harper Sato's advocacy for educational reform emphasizes the need for a shift away from traditional teaching methods towards more engaging, inquiry-based approaches. By embracing constructivist and critical pedagogical theories, addressing existing challenges, and implementing innovative practices, educators can inspire students to think critically, innovate, and become active contributors to their communities. As Harper demonstrates, the future of education lies in empowering students to question, create, and lead with purpose.

The Next Generation of Future Innovators

The legacy of Harper Sato is not merely a series of accomplishments documented in the annals of media reform, political transparency, and climate justice; it is a living, breathing testament to the power of individual agency in shaping the future. As we delve into the impact of Harper's journey on the next generation of future innovators, it is essential to recognize the multifaceted nature of innovation itself. Innovation is not confined to technological advancements; it encompasses social change, political activism, and environmental stewardship.

The Role of Mentorship

Mentorship plays a crucial role in nurturing the potential of young innovators. Harper's commitment to guiding the next generation is exemplified by her establishment of mentorship programs aimed at empowering aspiring journalists, activists, and environmentalists. According to a study by Allen et al. (2004), mentoring relationships significantly enhance the professional development of mentees, leading to increased job satisfaction and career advancement. Harper's mentorship initiatives have fostered a culture of collaboration and knowledge-sharing, enabling young innovators to cultivate their skills and pursue their passions.

Fostering Innovation through Education

Education is a powerful catalyst for innovation. Harper recognized the need for educational reform that emphasizes critical thinking, creativity, and problem-solving skills. In her advocacy for educational initiatives, she championed project-based learning and interdisciplinary approaches that encourage students to tackle real-world challenges. Research by Hattie (2009) indicates that such educational strategies lead to higher levels of student engagement and improved academic outcomes. For instance, schools that have adopted these methodologies have reported increased student participation in environmental and civic projects, reflecting Harper's vision for a more socially conscious generation.

The Intersection of Technology and Social Change

In the digital age, technology serves as both a tool and a platform for innovation. Harper's influence extends to the integration of technology in activism and journalism. Young innovators are increasingly utilizing social media and digital platforms to amplify their voices and effect change. The Arab Spring, for example, demonstrated how social media could mobilize youth and foster democratic movements (Howard et al., 2011). Harper's emphasis on digital literacy equips the next generation with the skills necessary to navigate and leverage these platforms effectively, ensuring that they can challenge injustices and advocate for their causes.

Challenges Faced by Young Innovators

Despite the potential for innovation, the next generation faces significant challenges. Economic disparities, access to education, and systemic barriers can hinder their ability to realize their aspirations. According to the World Economic Forum (2020), youth unemployment rates remain alarmingly high, particularly in developing regions. Harper's advocacy for equitable access to resources and opportunities is crucial in addressing these issues. By promoting policies that support youth entrepreneurship and vocational training, she has laid the groundwork for a more inclusive environment where young innovators can thrive.

Examples of Emerging Innovators

The impact of Harper's legacy is evident in the stories of emerging innovators who have taken up the mantle of change. For instance, Maya Chen, a young journalist inspired by Harper's work, has launched a digital platform that focuses on environmental justice issues in marginalized communities. Her investigative reporting has uncovered critical information about pollution in low-income neighborhoods, prompting local governments to take action. Similarly, Jamal Rivera, a climate activist, has organized youth-led climate strikes, mobilizing thousands of students to demand policy changes from their governments. These examples illustrate how Harper's influence continues to resonate, empowering young innovators to pursue their passions and drive meaningful change.

Conclusion: A Brighter Future

In conclusion, the next generation of future innovators is poised to carry forward the torch of activism, journalism, and environmental stewardship ignited by Harper Sato. Through mentorship, innovative educational practices, and the effective use of technology, they are equipped to tackle the pressing challenges of our time. While obstacles remain, the legacy of Harper serves as a beacon of hope, inspiring young innovators to envision and create a brighter, more equitable future. As they navigate the complexities of a rapidly changing world, they embody the spirit of resilience and determination that Harper exemplified throughout her career.

Bibliography

[1] Allen, T. D., Eby, L. T., Poteet, M. L., Lentz, E., & Lima, L. (2004). Career Benefits Associated with Mentoring for Mentors: A Meta-Analysis. *Journal of Applied Psychology*, 89(1), 127-136.

[2] Hattie, J. (2009). *Visible Learning: A Synthesis of Over 800 Meta-Analyses Relating to Achievement.* Routledge.

[3] Howard, P. N., Aiden, D., & Hussain, M. (2011). Opening Closed Regimes: What Was the Role of Social Media During the Arab Spring? *Project on Information Technology and Political Islam.*

[4] World Economic Forum. (2020). The Future of Jobs Report 2020. Retrieved from https://www.weforum.org/reports/the-future-of-jobs-report-2020

Harper's Vision for a Brighter Future

Harper Sato's vision for a brighter future is rooted in her unwavering belief that a society can only thrive when its media, politics, and environmental practices are aligned with the principles of transparency, accountability, and sustainability. In this subsection, we will explore her multifaceted approach to creating a better world, which encompasses the realms of education, technology, social justice, and environmental stewardship.

Empowering Future Generations

At the heart of Harper's vision is the empowerment of future generations. She believes that education is the cornerstone of societal progress. By fostering critical thinking, creativity, and a sense of social responsibility among young people, Harper aims to cultivate a generation of innovators who are equipped to tackle the challenges of the future. This philosophy is encapsulated in her advocacy for curricula that emphasize:

- **Media Literacy:** Understanding the dynamics of media consumption and production, enabling students to discern credible information from misinformation.

- **Environmental Education:** Instilling a sense of urgency regarding climate change and environmental degradation, motivating students to engage in sustainable practices.

- **Civic Engagement:** Encouraging active participation in democratic processes, fostering a culture of accountability and transparency in governance.

By integrating these elements into educational frameworks, Harper envisions a society where individuals are not only informed consumers of information but also proactive participants in their communities.

Technological Innovation for Social Good

Harper recognizes the transformative potential of technology in shaping a brighter future. She advocates for the development and deployment of technologies that prioritize social good over profit. This includes:

- **Open Source Initiatives:** Promoting platforms that allow for collaborative development and sharing of resources, thus democratizing access to technology.

- **Sustainable Tech Solutions:** Encouraging innovations that reduce carbon footprints, such as renewable energy technologies, energy-efficient appliances, and sustainable agriculture practices.

- **Digital Platforms for Civic Engagement:** Supporting the creation of online spaces that facilitate dialogue between citizens and their representatives, enhancing governmental accountability.

In this context, Harper's vision aligns with the concept of *technological determinism*, which posits that technology shapes societal structures. By advocating for technology that serves the public interest, she aims to steer society towards a more equitable and sustainable trajectory.

Social Justice as a Pillar of Progress

Harper's vision cannot be separated from her commitment to social justice. She believes that true progress is only possible when all voices are heard, particularly those from marginalized communities. Her initiatives focus on:

- **Inclusive Representation:** Ensuring that media and political institutions reflect the diversity of society, thereby amplifying underrepresented voices.
- **Equitable Access to Resources:** Advocating for policies that dismantle systemic barriers to education, healthcare, and economic opportunities for disadvantaged groups.
- **Community Empowerment:** Supporting grassroots movements that empower local communities to advocate for their rights and interests, fostering a sense of ownership over social change.

This commitment to social justice is informed by the theory of *intersectionality*, which recognizes that individuals experience overlapping systems of oppression. Harper's approach seeks to address these complexities, ensuring that her vision for the future is inclusive and equitable.

Environmental Stewardship as a Moral Imperative

Central to Harper's vision is the belief that humanity has a moral obligation to protect the planet for future generations. She emphasizes the need for:

- **Sustainable Practices:** Encouraging individuals and organizations to adopt practices that minimize environmental impact, such as reducing waste, conserving energy, and supporting local economies.
- **Policy Advocacy:** Pushing for robust environmental regulations that hold corporations accountable for their ecological footprints and incentivize sustainable business practices.
- **Global Cooperation:** Recognizing that climate change is a global issue that requires collective action, Harper supports international agreements aimed at reducing greenhouse gas emissions and promoting sustainable development.

Harper's environmental stewardship is grounded in the concept of *ecological justice*, which posits that environmental issues are intrinsically linked to social issues. By advocating for a holistic approach to environmentalism, she seeks to create a future where both people and the planet can thrive.

Conclusion: A Vision Realized Through Collective Action

Harper Sato's vision for a brighter future is not merely aspirational; it is a call to action for individuals, communities, and institutions to work collaboratively towards meaningful change. By prioritizing education, technological innovation, social justice, and environmental stewardship, she believes that society can overcome the myriad challenges it faces.

The realization of this vision hinges on collective action, where each individual plays a role in shaping the future. As Harper often states, "The voice of tomorrow is not just one voice; it is the chorus of many, harmonizing for a better world." In this spirit, she inspires others to join her in the quest for a future that is not only brighter but also more just and sustainable for generations to come.

Harper's Lasting Impact on Society

The Enduring Importance of Media Reform

The landscape of media has undergone significant transformations over the past few decades, with the advent of digital technology, social media, and the rise of independent journalism. The importance of media reform, as championed by Harper Sato, cannot be overstated. Media reform is essential not only for the integrity of information dissemination but also for the preservation of democratic values and the promotion of social justice.

Theoretical Framework

To understand the significance of media reform, it is crucial to examine several theoretical frameworks that highlight the role of media in society. The **Public Sphere Theory**, proposed by Jürgen Habermas, posits that the media serves as a platform for public discourse and democratic deliberation. In an ideal public sphere, individuals engage in rational-critical debate, leading to informed decision-making. However, the commercialization of media has compromised this ideal, resulting in a landscape dominated by corporate interests and sensationalism.

Furthermore, the **Agenda-Setting Theory** suggests that media doesn't just report the news but actively shapes public perception by prioritizing certain issues over others. This can lead to a distorted understanding of reality, where critical issues such as climate change, political corruption, and social injustices are sidelined in favor of entertainment or trivial matters. Thus, media reform is vital to ensure that a diverse range of voices and issues are represented, fostering a more informed and engaged populace.

Problems in the Current Media Landscape

Despite the advancements in technology and communication, several pressing issues continue to plague the media industry:

- **Consolidation of Media Ownership:** A handful of corporations control a significant portion of media outlets, leading to a homogenization of content. This concentration of power stifles diversity in viewpoints and limits the public's access to varied perspectives. For instance, in the United States, the top six media companies own over 90% of the media, raising concerns about the implications for democracy and public discourse.

- **Misinformation and Disinformation:** The rise of social media has facilitated the rapid spread of false information. Misinformation can undermine public trust in legitimate news sources, leading to apathy or cynicism regarding critical issues. The COVID-19 pandemic exemplified this problem, where misinformation regarding the virus and vaccines proliferated, impacting public health responses.

- **Ethical Standards and Accountability:** Many media organizations prioritize profit over ethical reporting, leading to sensationalism and a lack of accountability. Instances of fabricated stories or unethical journalistic practices can damage the credibility of the entire industry. The 2016 election cycle in the United States saw numerous examples of misleading headlines and clickbait journalism that prioritized engagement over accuracy.

Examples of Successful Media Reform Initiatives

Harper Sato's advocacy for media reform has inspired various initiatives aimed at addressing these issues:

- **Independent Journalism Initiatives:** Organizations such as ProPublica and The Guardian's "The Guardian Foundation" have emerged as models for independent journalism. By focusing on investigative reporting and holding power accountable, these outlets prioritize the public interest over corporate profit. Their work has led to significant revelations regarding political corruption and social injustices, demonstrating the impact of ethical journalism.

- **Media Literacy Programs:** Increasing media literacy among the public is essential for combating misinformation. Initiatives like the News Literacy Project aim to educate individuals on how to critically evaluate news sources and discern credible information from falsehoods. By empowering citizens with the tools to navigate the media landscape, these programs contribute to a more informed and engaged society.

- **Advocacy for Policy Changes:** Harper's influence has also extended to advocating for policy changes that promote media diversity and accountability. For example, the Federal Communications Commission (FCC) has been urged to implement regulations that prevent further media consolidation and promote local journalism, ensuring that communities have access to diverse and relevant news sources.

Conclusion

The enduring importance of media reform is evident in its potential to restore public trust, promote ethical journalism, and ensure that diverse voices are heard in the public discourse. Harper Sato's legacy serves as a reminder that a vibrant democracy relies on a robust and accountable media landscape. By addressing the problems inherent in the current media system and championing initiatives for reform, we can pave the way for a more equitable and informed society.

As we continue to navigate the complexities of the digital age, the call for media reform remains as urgent as ever. It is not merely a matter of improving journalism; it is about safeguarding democracy, promoting social justice, and ensuring that the voices of all citizens are amplified in the public sphere. The future of media, and indeed democracy itself, hinges on our commitment to reforming the systems that govern information dissemination and representation.

Political Transformation and Democratic Renewal

In the wake of Harper Sato's groundbreaking contributions to media reform, a significant transformation in the political landscape emerged, characterized by a renewed commitment to democratic principles and practices. Harper's advocacy for transparency and accountability catalyzed a wave of grassroots movements, fundamentally altering the relationship between citizens and their governments.

Theoretical Framework

The concept of political transformation can be understood through the lens of democratic theory, particularly the ideas of participatory democracy and deliberative democracy. Participatory democracy emphasizes the role of citizens in decision-making processes, while deliberative democracy focuses on the importance of dialogue and reasoned debate among citizens and their representatives. Harper's initiatives exemplified these theories, fostering an environment where public engagement and discourse became paramount.

Challenges to Political Transformation

Despite the progress made, the path to political transformation was fraught with challenges. The entrenched interests of powerful political and corporate entities often resisted change, employing various tactics to undermine reform efforts. For instance, the phenomenon of *astroturfing*—the creation of fake grassroots movements—was used to mislead public opinion and stifle genuine democratic engagement. Additionally, the rise of misinformation campaigns aimed to discredit reform advocates and sow distrust in legitimate democratic processes.

Examples of Political Transformation

Harper's impact can be illustrated through several key examples that highlight the transformation of political culture and practices:

- **The Rise of Grassroots Movements:** Inspired by Harper's work, numerous grassroots organizations emerged, advocating for issues ranging from campaign finance reform to environmental justice. These movements utilized social media to mobilize support and raise awareness, exemplifying the effectiveness of participatory democracy in action. For instance, the *Youth for Change* movement successfully lobbied for legislation aimed at increasing transparency in political donations, resulting in the passage of the *Fair Funding Act*.

- **Increased Government Transparency:** In response to public demand for accountability, several governments enacted reforms to enhance transparency. The introduction of open data initiatives allowed citizens to access government spending and decision-making processes, fostering a culture of openness. For example, the city of New Haven implemented the *Open Government Initiative*, which provided real-time access to municipal budgets and project statuses, empowering citizens to engage with local governance.

- **Legislative Changes:** Harper's influence extended to legislative reforms aimed at curbing corruption and promoting democratic integrity. The *Accountability in Politics Act* was passed in several jurisdictions, mandating stricter regulations on lobbying activities and increasing penalties for unethical conduct among public officials. This legislation was a direct response to the public's demand for greater accountability and served as a testament to the power of collective civic action.

- **Civic Education Programs:** Recognizing the importance of informed citizenry, various organizations launched civic education initiatives aimed at increasing public understanding of democratic processes. These programs, often developed in collaboration with schools and community organizations, emphasized the significance of voting, civic participation, and the role of media in democracy. The *Civic Empowerment Project* successfully educated thousands of young people on their rights and responsibilities as citizens, leading to increased voter turnout in subsequent elections.

The Role of Media in Democratic Renewal

Harper Sato's media reforms played a pivotal role in fostering democratic renewal. By promoting ethical journalism and challenging misinformation, Harper created an informed public capable of engaging in meaningful political discourse. The establishment of independent media outlets, free from corporate influence, allowed for diverse perspectives to be shared, enriching public debate and enhancing democratic engagement.

The equation representing the relationship between media integrity (MI), public engagement (PE), and democratic health (DH) can be expressed as follows:

$$DH = f(MI, PE)$$

Where f denotes a function that indicates that as media integrity and public engagement increase, so too does the health of democracy.

Conclusion

Harper Sato's legacy in political transformation and democratic renewal is marked by a profound shift in how citizens interact with their governments. Through grassroots activism, legislative reforms, and a commitment to transparency, Harper inspired a generation to reclaim their democratic rights. The ongoing struggle for political accountability and civic engagement remains crucial in the pursuit of a more just and equitable society. As future innovators continue to build on Harper's foundation, the principles of participatory and deliberative democracy will guide their efforts in shaping a brighter political future.

Achieving Global Climate Justice

Achieving global climate justice is a multifaceted challenge that requires a comprehensive understanding of the interconnectedness between environmental degradation, social inequalities, and systemic injustices. This section delves into the theoretical frameworks, prevalent issues, and practical examples that illustrate the pursuit of climate justice on a global scale.

Theoretical Frameworks

At its core, climate justice is grounded in the principles of equity, fairness, and the recognition of the rights of marginalized communities. Theories of environmental justice emphasize the disproportionate impacts of climate change on vulnerable populations, particularly in developing nations. According to [?], environmental justice encompasses three key dimensions: recognition, procedural justice, and distributive justice.

$$\text{Environmental Justice} = \text{Recognition} + \text{Procedural Justice} + \text{Distributive Justice} \tag{57}$$

Recognition refers to the acknowledgment of the diverse experiences and needs of different communities affected by climate change. **Procedural justice** entails ensuring that all stakeholders have a voice in decision-making processes, while **distributive justice** focuses on the fair allocation of resources and responsibilities in addressing climate impacts.

Key Problems in Achieving Climate Justice

Despite the theoretical frameworks that support climate justice, several challenges hinder its realization:

- **Inequitable Resource Distribution:** Wealthier nations historically contribute the most to greenhouse gas emissions while poorer nations often bear the brunt of climate impacts. For instance, small island nations face existential threats from rising sea levels, despite contributing minimally to global emissions.

- **Corporate Influence and Lobbying:** Powerful fossil fuel corporations exert significant influence over political processes, often prioritizing profit over environmental sustainability. This corporate capture of policy-making undermines efforts to implement equitable climate solutions.

- **Lack of Global Cooperation:** Climate change is a global issue that requires collective action. However, geopolitical tensions and differing national interests impede international agreements, such as the Paris Agreement, from being fully realized.

- **Systemic Inequalities:** Social, racial, and economic inequalities exacerbate the vulnerabilities of marginalized communities. For example, low-income neighborhoods often lack access to resources that would enable them to adapt to climate impacts, such as green infrastructure or emergency services.

Practical Examples of Climate Justice Initiatives

Numerous initiatives around the world exemplify the pursuit of climate justice. These projects highlight the importance of grassroots movements, community engagement, and international solidarity:

- **The Global Climate Strike Movement:** Initiated by youth activists, including *Greta Thunberg*, the Global Climate Strike has mobilized millions worldwide, demanding urgent action on climate change. This movement emphasizes the need for intergenerational equity, ensuring that future generations inherit a livable planet.

- **The Just Transition Framework:** Advocated by labor unions and environmental groups, the Just Transition framework seeks to create equitable pathways for workers affected by the shift from fossil fuels to renewable energy. This approach ensures that job losses in traditional sectors are met with the creation of new, sustainable jobs, with a focus on training and support for impacted workers.

- **Indigenous Rights and Climate Action:** Indigenous communities play a crucial role in climate justice, as they often possess traditional ecological knowledge that contributes to sustainable land management. Initiatives like the *Indigenous Peoples' Climate Change Assessment* highlight the importance of integrating Indigenous voices in climate policy and recognizing their land rights.

- **Community-Led Renewable Energy Projects:** In various countries, community-led initiatives have emerged to develop renewable energy sources that prioritize local needs. For example, the *Solar Sister* program empowers women in Africa to become solar entrepreneurs, addressing energy poverty while promoting gender equality.

Conclusion

Achieving global climate justice requires a concerted effort to address the systemic inequalities that underpin the climate crisis. By integrating theoretical frameworks that prioritize equity and fairness, tackling the key problems that hinder progress, and drawing inspiration from successful initiatives, we can pave the way for a more just and sustainable future. As [?] aptly states, "Climate justice is not merely an option; it is a necessity for the survival of our planet and the well-being of all its inhabitants."

Index

-up, 76

a, 1–5, 7, 8, 10, 12, 14, 15, 17–19, 21–27, 29–31, 33–35, 37–43, 45, 47, 49–63, 65, 66, 68, 70–73, 75–78, 80–88, 92–99, 104–107, 109, 111–116, 118–121, 124–129, 131–135, 137–144, 146–149, 152, 153, 155, 157, 158, 160–165, 168–171, 173, 175, 177, 179–188, 190–192, 194, 195, 197–200, 202, 204–208, 210–212, 214–218, 220–222, 224, 225, 227, 229, 231–235, 239–241, 243–246, 248, 250, 251
ability, 23, 49, 53, 55, 58, 61, 63, 77, 83, 106, 114, 115, 152, 163, 173, 174, 182, 191, 192, 199, 210, 212, 225
academia, 33
access, 1, 58, 117, 148, 211
accessibility, 77, 210
account, 14
accountability, 4, 18, 27, 31, 41, 42, 45, 47, 56, 58, 68, 70, 72, 73, 75, 78, 80, 86–88, 93, 96, 98, 102–104, 106, 109, 113, 116, 118, 120, 121, 123, 124, 126–128, 144, 158, 160, 163, 169, 170, 199, 200, 202, 207, 211–213, 215–217, 220, 231, 233, 243, 248, 251
accountable, 2, 31, 49, 57, 72, 87, 99, 104, 120–124, 160, 202, 206, 212, 215–217, 248
accuracy, 29–31, 33, 77
achievement, 124
acknowledgment, 86
act, 53, 55, 62, 68, 71, 88, 95, 117, 120, 135, 183, 213
action, 25, 56, 60, 61, 63, 81, 106, 113, 114, 126, 132, 133, 135, 140, 143, 144, 146, 147, 149, 152, 158, 165, 170, 171, 174, 177, 179–181, 183–185, 192, 217, 222, 229, 231, 234, 235, 246
activism, 54–56, 59, 87, 104, 109, 112, 113, 115, 118, 124, 125, 132, 137, 139–143,

146–149, 152–155, 158, 165, 168, 170, 171, 173, 175, 177–182, 191, 215, 217, 233–235, 240, 241, 251
activist, 106
adaptability, 10
adaptation, 24, 29, 184, 225–227
addition, 22, 51, 81, 120
adherence, 26, 29, 30, 201
advancement, 26
advent, 40, 198, 246
adversity, 49, 54, 56, 60, 61, 63, 68, 83, 85, 231
advertising, 22, 42–46, 51, 198, 199
advocacy, 50, 53, 58, 61, 62, 80, 82, 99, 104, 112, 116, 118, 126, 128, 140, 144–147, 152, 153, 155, 163, 165, 167, 168, 170, 175, 182, 184, 185, 188, 190–192, 205, 210, 212, 214, 216, 229, 231, 239, 244, 247, 248
advocate, 42, 60, 78, 81, 104, 108, 113, 116, 132, 137–139, 141, 146, 152, 163, 168, 173, 180, 185, 190, 207, 210, 212, 235
age, 1, 3, 29, 45, 77, 96, 233, 248
agency, 41, 111, 115, 148, 240
agenda, 82
agriculture, 185
air, 139
ally, 144
alternative, 198
America, 115
amplification, 24, 52, 58, 207
analysis, 17

anti, 119
anxiety, 55
apathy, 111, 218
approach, 5, 6, 14, 17, 19, 22, 23, 31, 33, 37, 41, 43, 47, 66, 72, 73, 77, 87, 88, 98, 111, 124, 140, 141, 144, 146, 147, 149, 155, 164, 173, 179–181, 190, 192, 194, 206, 207, 214, 215, 221, 225, 227, 229, 237, 243
area, 204
arena, 86
array, 3
article, 1, 31
ascent, 52
aspect, 31, 41, 68, 147, 165, 205
aspiration, 29, 192
assailant, 55
assembly, 17
attendance, 197
attention, 1, 30, 62, 82, 107, 133, 139, 160, 169, 171, 205
audience, 18, 22–24, 26, 29, 30, 41, 42, 144, 201, 202
authenticity, 14, 169
authority, 71, 122
Autumn Peltier, 149
awakening, 131
awareness, 7, 30, 56, 62, 76, 132, 139, 140, 144, 146, 160, 169, 172, 174, 177, 215, 217

background, 5
backing, 53, 60
backlash, 18, 52–54, 58, 61, 76, 78–80, 125, 169, 172, 211
backroom, 96

Index

balance, 54
ballot, 58
barrage, 55, 81
bastion, 47
battle, 34, 73, 98, 109, 215
battleground, 96
beacon, 14, 29, 37, 56, 61, 68, 83, 165, 170, 227, 231, 241
bedrock, 73
behavior, 114, 115
being, 22, 30, 76, 81, 152, 158, 215
belief, 1, 2, 4, 7, 14, 114, 152, 184, 192, 235, 243, 245
benefit, 97
betrayal, 95
bias, 12, 30, 33, 198
bidding, 92
biography, 54
blueprint, 144, 197, 227
board, 30
box, 58
brainstorming, 18
Brazil, 161
break, 12, 13, 170
bribery, 71–73, 88, 95, 119, 214
broadcast, 144
broadcasting, 4
brunt, 144, 165
building, 2, 18, 60, 75, 76, 106, 149, 202
Bullard, 138

cacophony, 232
call, 51, 88, 135, 158, 165, 170, 217, 229, 246, 248
calling, 3
camaraderie, 18
campaign, 43, 53, 61, 62, 97, 107–109, 115, 119, 139, 144, 146, 170, 205, 217
cancellation, 139
candidness, 38
capacity, 61, 148, 225, 235
capital, 22, 53, 213
car, 81
carbon, 133, 144, 175, 183, 220, 221
career, 2–4, 12, 14, 241
case, 30, 34, 36, 38, 44, 46, 51, 55, 60, 61, 78, 81, 111, 170, 206
cat, 14
catalyst, 85, 106, 124–126, 143, 177, 179, 181, 198
cause, 22, 60–62, 96, 163
ceiling, 11–14
censorship, 62
century, 202, 210
challenge, 1, 2, 4–6, 22, 31, 38, 49, 52, 54, 55, 58, 60–62, 79, 104, 125, 141, 144, 146, 163, 168, 191, 207, 210, 211, 234, 235, 251
champion, 22, 58, 234
change, 2, 4, 5, 14, 19, 25, 31, 40, 47, 52, 54, 56, 60, 63, 70, 76, 78, 87, 88, 98, 106, 107, 109, 112–114, 116, 124–126, 131–133, 138, 140, 142, 144–149, 151, 152, 155, 158, 161, 165, 168, 170, 171, 173, 174, 177, 179, 182, 184, 185, 187, 188, 191, 194, 202, 204, 210, 215, 217, 220, 224, 225, 227, 231, 233, 235, 240, 246

chapter, 54
character, 82
charge, 73, 155, 168, 181
check, 57
checking, 30, 33, 38, 41, 50, 141, 206
childhood, 2, 138
choice, 3, 213
chorus, 246
citizen, 41, 102
citizenry, 58, 87, 195, 197, 216, 218, 220
city, 211
clarion, 88
class, 1
clickbait, 198
climate, 25, 47, 55, 75, 98, 114, 126, 131–135, 138, 140–145, 147–155, 158, 162, 163, 165, 170–185, 188, 190–192, 194, 217, 220, 222, 224–227, 229, 231, 233–235, 240, 251, 252
coal, 170
coalition, 56, 106, 139, 146
cohesion, 18, 31
collaboration, 16–18, 33, 34, 37, 76, 92, 95–97, 126, 144–149, 155, 161, 188, 194, 226, 234
collapse, 161
collection, 226
college, 2, 131
colonialism, 148
color, 2, 16, 138, 165, 234
combat, 32–34, 58, 98, 141, 213, 238
combination, 22, 61, 173, 215
commentary, 83

commitment, 2, 3, 5, 9, 16–18, 24, 29, 31, 34, 35, 37, 39, 41, 42, 45, 50–52, 63, 70, 71, 73–77, 83, 93, 96, 98, 104, 109, 114, 115, 124, 126, 128, 135, 137–139, 153, 155, 160, 168, 170, 182, 183, 202, 206, 217, 222, 231–233, 245, 248, 251
commodity, 45
communication, 18, 140, 218, 247
community, 1, 3, 4, 16, 17, 22, 23, 25, 47, 51, 54, 56, 58–60, 75, 76, 78, 85, 111, 115, 126, 131, 138, 139, 183, 192, 195, 197, 202, 205, 212, 216, 225, 227, 252
company, 158, 160, 169
competition, 146
component, 98, 99, 165, 173, 200, 212
compromise, 199
concentration, 30, 45, 47, 198, 202, 205
concept, 19, 29, 51, 56, 99, 114, 121, 149, 152, 163, 198, 210, 225, 249
concern, 31
conclusion, 5, 7, 23, 39, 42, 52, 56, 58, 60, 63, 78, 85, 87, 104, 120, 126, 128, 144, 158, 165, 173, 179, 181, 190, 194, 200, 202, 207, 212, 217, 220, 224, 227, 229, 233, 239, 241
conduit, 179, 191
conference, 4, 55, 144
confidence, 2, 126
conflict, 18, 30, 54, 198

confrontation, 55
confusion, 47
connection, 54
consciousness, 68, 114, 115, 155, 171, 176, 177
consensus, 47
consideration, 17
consolidation, 7, 205
constant, 29, 55
construction, 71
constructivism, 7
consumption, 4, 41, 161, 168, 220
contamination, 161
content, 23, 30, 33, 42, 198, 205
context, 29, 33, 56, 68, 114, 121
contract, 95
contracting, 92
contrast, 58
contribution, 117
control, 30, 45–47, 49, 58, 205
cooperation, 174
core, 17, 29, 105, 121, 163, 210
cornerstone, 31, 51, 56, 62, 87, 99, 206, 243
corporate, 17, 41, 42, 45–47, 49–54, 56–58, 61, 65, 67, 78, 81, 83, 86, 88, 93, 96, 98, 104, 106, 119, 139, 142, 148, 158–160, 168–170, 172, 197–200, 218, 232, 250
corporation, 53, 55, 61, 81, 95, 97, 139, 214
correlation, 42
corruption, 4, 30, 38, 53, 54, 58, 61, 68, 70–76, 78, 80, 81, 85, 86, 88, 93, 97, 104, 106, 107, 114, 118–120, 124, 211–215
Costa Rica, 222

counter, 41, 53
country, 162
courage, 58, 61–63, 73, 98
cover, 1, 68–70, 76, 119
coverage, 46, 47, 87, 146, 167, 198
creation, 51
creativity, 17, 113, 238, 243
credibility, 22, 30, 31, 33, 41, 53, 77, 82, 94, 139, 169
crisis, 25, 41, 47, 131, 133–135, 140, 143, 147, 149, 150, 152, 155, 163, 171, 173, 179, 181, 182, 184, 188, 190, 192, 222, 231
criticism, 22
critique, 170
crowdfunding, 22, 199
crusade, 143
culmination, 18
cultivation, 85, 190, 234
culture, 12, 18, 30, 31, 60, 70, 87, 88, 93, 96, 104, 125, 126, 158, 176, 177, 180, 198, 211, 212, 217–220, 249
curiosity, 1–3
curricula, 38, 244
cyanide, 161
cycle, 51, 71
cynicism, 86

dam, 161
damage, 53
dark, 70
data, 17, 19, 191, 211, 212, 216, 226
day, 195
debate, 2, 195, 218, 249, 250
decentralization, 205
decision, 2, 30, 52, 71, 210, 249
decline, 50, 119

decolonization, 147
dedication, 37, 51, 73, 137, 139, 233
defamation, 82
defense, 68
defiance, 62
definition, 163
degradation, 131, 138, 141, 161, 162, 165, 168, 181, 194, 224, 251
delegate, 144
demand, 70, 75, 86–88, 93, 109, 129, 149, 158, 160, 163, 173, 199, 200, 202, 215, 217
democracy, 7, 29, 49, 51, 58, 60, 62, 70, 73, 78, 93, 96, 98, 99, 106, 109, 111, 113, 195, 197, 198, 200, 202, 205, 207, 215, 217, 218, 220, 248, 249, 251
democratization, 198
demographic, 152
demonstration, 56
Denmark, 222
denominator, 118
dependence, 170
dependency, 170
depletion, 155
deployment, 244
depth, 19, 51, 199
desire, 2, 3, 107
despair, 131
determination, 12, 14, 58, 139, 173, 175, 241
development, 33, 163, 170, 185, 194, 213, 227, 244
dialogue, 4, 20, 23, 45, 195, 198, 249
difference, 132
dignity, 29

dioxide, 133
diplomacy, 173, 175
disaster, 46, 161
discern, 33
discourse, 33, 40, 47, 74, 86, 87, 108, 115, 144, 147, 152, 168, 182, 185, 195, 198, 199, 202, 210, 216–218, 229, 248–250
discovery, 5, 132
discrediting, 53, 78
discussion, 169
disengagement, 216
disinformation, 50, 77
disintermediation, 198
disregard, 162
disruptor, 22
dissemination, 30, 50, 56, 141, 190, 197, 198, 203, 246, 248
dissent, 53
distrust, 58
diversity, 16–18, 29, 35, 42, 50, 51, 177, 197, 205, 207
document, 120
dominance, 41
dream, 158
drive, 142, 170, 224
duty, 29, 134
dynamic, 17, 18, 23, 142, 204

echo, 192
economy, 161, 170, 185–188
ecosystem, 198, 207
editorial, 30, 50
education, 1, 2, 30, 109–111, 158, 216, 229, 237, 239, 243, 246
effect, 4, 60, 63, 106, 119, 126, 181, 184, 229, 233, 235

Index

effectiveness, 34, 36, 48, 106, 111, 117, 146, 177, 235
efficacy, 114, 115, 152
efficiency, 221
effort, 14, 33, 53, 98, 220
election, 51
electorate, 58, 87, 109, 111
emergence, 113, 144
empathy, 25
emphasis, 41, 120, 181, 183, 184, 191, 197
employee, 95
employment, 205
empower, 33, 115, 197, 212
empowerment, 39, 50, 126, 170, 218, 233, 234, 243
endeavor, 34, 60, 62, 68
energy, 126, 162–165, 169, 170, 185, 220–222, 224
enforcement, 55, 119
engagement, 3, 10, 17, 23, 24, 26, 29, 33, 41, 42, 49, 75, 78, 86, 93, 99, 101, 104, 106, 109–113, 115, 127, 128, 132, 139, 144, 178, 181, 183, 190, 197, 201, 202, 210, 212, 215–218, 220, 249–252
enormity, 181
environment, 2, 3, 35, 54–56, 58, 134, 138, 158, 161, 168, 183, 210, 249
episode, 19, 25
equality, 109, 181, 217
equation, 3, 22, 23, 26, 50, 80, 93, 94, 96, 117, 118, 133, 149, 160, 163, 168, 171, 175, 185, 200, 207, 216
equity, 133, 149, 162, 163, 182, 185, 188, 192
era, 14, 24, 26, 31, 34, 38, 49, 58, 61, 75, 112, 113, 143, 179, 206, 215, 217, 227, 237
erosion, 210
essence, 149, 207
establishment, 30, 50, 51, 62, 175, 205, 212, 250
ethnicity, 138, 168
ethos, 73
event, 4, 19, 55, 56
evidence, 33, 133, 135, 144, 173, 175
evolution, 22, 26, 114, 137, 177, 222
examination, 6
example, 19, 25, 38, 41, 46, 47, 51, 57, 59, 62, 78, 85, 92, 97, 98, 114, 119, 139, 144, 146, 161, 162, 170, 174, 180, 183, 205, 211, 214, 216, 224, 233, 234
exchange, 71
exercise, 68, 131
exit, 55
expansion, 197–200
expense, 30, 97, 169
experience, 1, 2, 4, 23, 38, 60, 62, 131, 138, 147
expert, 33
expertise, 17, 145, 148
exploration, 61
exposure, 1, 2, 55, 68, 72, 95, 98, 169
exposé, 81, 119, 214
exposés, 86, 169
expression, 210
extent, 159
extraction, 161–163, 168–170
exuberance, 172

fabric, 127, 217
facade, 161
face, 4, 38, 49, 54, 56, 58, 60–63, 68, 80, 83, 94, 104, 144, 149, 158, 170, 172, 173, 182, 199, 223, 225, 231
facilitator, 195
fact, 30, 33, 38, 41, 50, 141, 206
factor, 181
factory, 138
failure, 144, 198
fairness, 29, 77, 201
fallout, 95
family, 1, 3, 25, 138
farm, 170
father, 138
favor, 96, 162
fear, 55, 56, 58, 61, 62, 81, 88, 94, 211
feasibility, 228
feat, 9
feedback, 201, 202, 210
fervor, 163
field, 2, 3, 56, 70, 131, 202
fight, 44, 45, 47, 52, 54, 56, 58, 60, 73, 96, 98, 109, 124, 126, 142, 144, 147, 149, 152, 153, 155, 165, 167, 168, 175, 177, 179, 185, 188, 190, 194, 206, 207, 210, 212, 214, 215, 220, 231, 233
fighting, 120, 181
figure, 26, 39, 52, 53, 144, 173
finance, 107–109, 119, 184, 217
financing, 119
fishing, 131
focus, 22, 41, 53, 85, 95, 204, 231, 245

following, 33, 55, 70, 72, 119, 121, 171, 213, 218, 219
force, 31, 96, 109, 113, 142, 147, 207, 212
forefront, 139, 155, 181, 185, 233
formation, 202
forming, 194
fossil, 47, 146, 163, 168–170, 174, 224, 231
foster, 49, 118, 143, 147, 148, 177, 185, 204
foundation, 2, 5, 73, 75, 121, 132, 192, 251
framework, 29, 51, 134, 194, 195, 198, 207, 225, 229
framing, 132, 142
freedom, 56–58, 60, 62, 93, 98
fuel, 47, 146, 168–170, 174, 231
function, 70
functionality, 225
functioning, 58, 73, 106, 202, 218
funding, 22, 24, 47, 146, 226
future, 2–5, 10, 12, 14, 29, 34, 38, 39, 50, 52, 56, 58, 60, 63, 70, 75, 87, 96, 109, 111, 115, 116, 124, 126, 133–135, 140, 144, 147, 149, 152, 153, 155, 157, 158, 160, 163, 165, 168, 170, 173, 175, 179, 182, 185, 188, 190, 192, 194, 197, 199, 200, 202, 204, 206, 207, 210, 212, 220, 222, 225, 227, 229, 231, 233, 239–241, 243–246, 248, 251

gain, 4, 61, 77, 78, 88, 162, 213, 234
gap, 132, 177, 190

Index 263

garden, 29
gas, 161
gender, 35, 181
generation, 7, 31, 39, 42, 45, 52, 61, 73, 85, 93, 98, 106, 111, 113–116, 120, 124, 129, 140, 144, 149, 152, 155, 157, 168, 180, 181, 190, 191, 199, 206, 207, 231, 233, 234, 240, 241, 243, 251
Germany, 222
glass, 11–14
globe, 37, 140, 144, 149, 184, 190, 216, 231
goal, 17, 183
good, 30, 31, 244
Gordon Tullock, 53
governance, 47, 71, 73, 78, 87, 95, 96, 99, 104, 106, 120, 127, 129, 182, 185, 212, 213, 215, 217
governing, 86
government, 56, 57, 61, 68–72, 76, 78, 86, 92, 93, 95, 96, 98–104, 114, 117, 119, 139, 162, 207, 210–214, 216
graduation, 2
greed, 61
greenwashing, 158–161, 169
Greta Thunberg, 174, 217
groundbreaking, 7, 78, 85, 88, 104, 113, 121, 124, 248
groundwork, 3, 29, 34, 50, 87, 93, 111, 149, 165, 215, 231
group, 55, 63, 114, 152
growth, 23, 61, 63, 163, 185, 199
guidance, 4, 126, 181, 231

guideline, 160
gun, 115

Habermas, 218
hallmark, 41
hand, 71, 210, 225
handful, 30, 205
harassment, 54, 55, 62, 81, 82, 199
harm, 162, 168
harness, 202, 210, 222
Harper, 1–7, 9, 12–20, 22–26, 28, 30–42, 44, 45, 50–56, 58, 60–63, 65–70, 72–78, 80–88, 92, 95–98, 103, 104, 109, 111, 118–129, 131–133, 138–140, 143, 144, 146–149, 152, 153, 155–159, 163–165, 167–170, 173, 174, 180, 181, 183, 184, 191–198, 202, 205–207, 213–220, 227–229, 231–235, 238–241, 243–246, 248–251
Harper Sato, 1, 8, 9, 14, 17, 21, 23, 26, 29–31, 34, 42, 43, 47, 49, 52, 60, 65, 66, 68, 71, 73, 80, 81, 83, 93, 94, 96, 102, 109, 110, 115, 135, 141, 145, 147, 152, 153, 158, 162, 163, 168, 173, 179, 190, 200, 202, 212, 222, 231, 240, 241, 246
Harper Sato's, 2, 3, 5, 7, 12, 14, 29, 31, 34, 37, 39, 40, 42, 45, 50, 52, 54, 56, 58, 61, 63, 68, 70, 73, 75, 78, 85, 87, 88, 93, 96, 98, 99, 104, 106, 109, 111–113, 116,

118, 120, 121, 124,
126–128, 131, 137, 139,
143, 144, 147, 149, 155,
158, 160, 165, 167, 168,
170, 175, 179, 181, 182,
184, 185, 187, 188, 190,
192, 194, 195, 197, 199,
202, 204, 207, 212, 214,
215, 217, 220, 227, 229,
231, 233, 235, 237, 239,
243, 246–248, 250
head, 61
health, 29, 33, 55, 97, 124, 132, 138,
139, 161, 162, 168, 215,
222
heart, 73, 168, 243
highlight, 45, 48, 58, 61, 115, 169,
202, 235, 249, 252
hindrance, 118
hiring, 18
home, 81
homogenization, 198
hope, 56, 61, 63, 68, 73, 109, 149,
165, 170, 181, 227, 241
host, 18, 33, 139
hostility, 199
humanity, 135, 245

idea, 73, 126, 144, 205
ideal, 152
identification, 7
identity, 35, 63, 114, 115, 172, 221
image, 159
impact, 4, 21, 30, 40–42, 44, 46,
50–52, 55, 63, 68, 69, 72,
73, 86, 87, 96, 103, 104,
106, 109, 116, 118–120,
124, 126, 139, 140,
144–147, 154, 155, 158,
161, 168, 170, 172, 178,
181, 190, 192, 209, 214,
217, 219, 224, 232, 233,
235, 240, 249
impartiality, 77
imperative, 18, 29, 45, 152, 163,
168, 174, 188, 207, 217,
222, 229
implementation, 211, 222, 223, 238
importance, 1, 3, 4, 10, 18, 29–31,
33, 37, 38, 48, 51, 54,
56–58, 60–62, 69, 76, 78,
80, 85, 96, 104, 106, 118,
126, 144, 146, 147, 149,
155, 157, 177, 184, 187,
198, 200, 202, 206, 212,
215, 220, 231, 238, 246,
248, 249, 252
impunity, 88
in, 1–8, 10, 12–14, 16–19, 22–26,
28–31, 33, 34, 36, 37,
39–43, 45–47, 49–63, 65,
68, 70–78, 80, 82, 83,
85–88, 92–96, 99–102,
104, 106–109, 111,
113–115, 117–126, 128,
129, 131–133, 138–144,
146–149, 151–155, 158,
160–163, 165, 167–175,
177–185, 187, 188,
190–193, 195–200, 202,
204–207, 209–225, 227,
228, 231, 233, 234,
237–240, 243, 244,
246–251
inaction, 133, 135, 144
incident, 55, 61, 62, 81, 131, 206
incinerator, 139
inclusion, 163, 183

Index 265

inclusivity, 18, 27, 37, 39, 231, 233, 234
income, 1, 138, 139, 141, 165, 174, 191
incorporation, 147
increase, 174
independence, 51, 199
individual, 72, 76, 80, 85, 95, 124, 126, 180, 194, 220, 233, 235, 240, 246
industry, 5, 7, 9, 11, 12, 22, 41, 46, 71, 131, 168–170, 197, 207, 231, 247
inequality, 71, 114, 149, 155, 194
inequity, 138
inertia, 211
inflation, 117
influence, 3, 12, 17, 18, 23, 28, 33, 37, 40, 42, 47, 50–54, 61, 65, 68, 71, 72, 81, 86, 104, 106–109, 114, 115, 123, 124, 142, 144, 155, 168–170, 175, 177, 179–184, 190, 192, 195, 197, 198, 202, 204, 207, 212, 215, 217, 218, 220, 229, 231, 232, 237, 250
information, 1, 19, 26, 30, 31, 33, 34, 41, 45, 50, 51, 56, 58, 92–94, 96, 98, 141, 170, 179, 190, 197, 198, 202, 203, 210–212, 216, 233, 237, 244, 246, 248
infrastructure, 71, 222
initiative, 22, 30, 41, 50, 51, 170, 211, 212
injustice, 124, 149, 158, 165, 194
innovation, 23, 34, 200, 212, 224, 237–240, 246

innovator, 5
inquiry, 75, 239
inspiration, 4, 37, 52, 63, 75, 174, 190, 231, 233, 235
instance, 22, 25, 33, 41, 51, 53, 55, 56, 61, 71, 72, 76, 95, 119, 126, 139, 162, 169, 172, 181, 198, 206, 233–235
integration, 23, 147, 185, 222
integrity, 10, 17, 29–31, 40–42, 45, 47, 49, 52, 61, 63, 71, 73, 75, 78, 80, 85, 87, 96, 107, 120, 124, 125, 141, 197, 198, 200, 202, 206, 233, 246
intent, 82
interaction, 23
interconnectedness, 59, 63, 132, 152, 168, 181, 184, 188, 251
interdependence, 155, 163
interest, 30, 51, 53, 54, 56, 58, 75, 77, 94, 198, 200, 213
interference, 56
intermittency, 222
internet, 198
interplay, 54, 80, 162
intersection, 54, 140, 142, 149, 165, 170, 175
intersectionality, 144, 148, 181
intertwining, 45, 65, 86, 88, 231
intervention, 55
intimidation, 54, 62, 81, 82
introduction, 86
invasion, 82
investigation, 68, 71, 76, 92, 169
involvement, 53, 60, 111, 216, 217
isolation, 55
issue, 25, 42, 47, 53, 60, 62, 65, 76, 94, 107, 109, 133, 146,

172, 177

James Buchanan, 53
journalism, 1, 2, 4, 5, 9, 14, 17, 19, 26–31, 33, 34, 37–39, 41, 42, 45, 47, 49–52, 54, 57, 58, 68–70, 73, 75, 78, 83, 87, 93, 96, 104, 112, 118, 126, 160, 168, 170, 190, 195–197, 199, 200, 202, 205–207, 214, 215, 218, 234, 241, 246, 248, 250
journalist, 2, 4, 81
journey, 3–5, 10, 12, 14, 19, 54, 58, 61, 63, 65, 75, 78, 81, 83, 85, 124, 127, 132, 137, 139, 143, 169, 218, 220, 231, 233, 235, 240
justice, 1, 2, 4, 17, 25, 34, 47, 49, 52, 58, 63, 75, 85, 87, 96, 113–115, 120, 125, 126, 131, 133–135, 137–140, 143–145, 147–149, 152, 155, 161–163, 165, 167, 168, 170, 173, 179–182, 184, 185, 188, 190, 192, 194, 217, 227, 229, 231, 233, 234, 240, 243, 245, 246, 248, 251, 252
Jürgen Habermas, 195, 217

Kant, 29
kickback, 71–73
knowledge, 1, 96, 115, 147, 158, 233

labeling, 33
lack, 1, 3, 7, 42, 43, 47, 96, 132, 148, 198, 211
land, 161

landscape, 2–5, 7, 8, 10, 12, 14, 15, 17, 21, 24, 29–31, 34, 35, 37, 39–42, 45, 47, 50–52, 54, 56, 58, 61, 65, 68, 70, 73, 75, 80, 83, 85, 87, 88, 93, 98, 104, 106, 107, 109, 113, 118, 120, 124, 125, 127, 128, 141, 142, 182, 195, 197, 198, 200, 202, 205–207, 212, 215–218, 220, 231, 232, 234, 246, 248
launch, 18, 19, 22, 41
law, 55
lead, 23, 30, 43, 55, 114, 155, 184, 239
leader, 8, 54
leadership, 12
learning, 1, 85, 115, 227
legacy, 14, 29, 37, 39, 42, 45, 50–52, 60, 63, 70, 75, 78, 87, 93, 104, 106, 111, 113, 120, 121, 124, 126–128, 144, 148, 170, 175, 179–182, 185, 188, 190–192, 194, 197, 199, 205–207, 210, 212, 215, 218, 220, 229, 231, 233, 235, 240, 241, 248, 250
legislation, 86, 97, 116, 119, 126, 182–184, 217
lens, 29, 53, 86, 109, 133, 192, 249
level, 25, 55, 93, 140, 184
life, 1, 2, 54, 56, 61, 62, 137
light, 42, 52, 58, 70
likelihood, 171
limit, 117, 174, 184
listening, 18
literacy, 3, 7, 33, 34, 38, 233

litigation, 53
living, 192, 240
lobbying, 86, 96, 98, 119, 126
love, 1

mainstream, 3, 41, 132, 177
majority, 30, 205
making, 30, 41, 71, 118, 210, 212, 249
male, 2, 12, 234
malfeasance, 51, 54, 93
malpractice, 93
management, 25
maneuvering, 71, 83
manipulation, 88
manner, 19
mantle, 191
manufacturing, 185
marathon, 231
mark, 127, 207
market, 198
marketing, 158
mass, 171, 173
matter, 17, 133, 134, 248
Maya, 126
Maya Chen, 126
Maya Rodriguez, 233
McQuail, 198
means, 29, 181
measure, 41
mechanism, 96, 149, 175
media, 1–12, 14–19, 21–26, 29–31, 33–35, 37–42, 45–52, 54–56, 58–62, 70, 75, 77, 78, 80–82, 85, 87, 95, 96, 104, 106, 109, 113, 116, 118, 120, 121, 124, 125, 132, 139–144, 146, 153, 155, 158, 160, 161, 163, 167, 169, 170, 172, 177–179, 181, 187, 191, 195, 197–207, 212, 215–217, 220, 222, 231–235, 237, 240, 243, 246–248, 250
mediation, 18
mentee, 233
mentor, 4, 124, 126, 232, 233
mentorship, 4, 39, 52, 124–126, 158, 181, 191, 232–234, 241
mercury, 161
message, 60, 81, 145, 147, 172, 234, 235
method, 53
microcosm, 1
million, 144
mining, 161, 170
minority, 138
misallocation, 213
misinformation, 7, 14, 17, 19, 29–34, 38, 39, 41, 49, 50, 58, 61, 111, 142, 197, 202, 206, 216, 218, 232, 250
mismanagement, 211
misrepresentation, 132
mission, 38, 85, 98, 132, 135
misuse, 92
mobilization, 54, 104, 106, 114, 139, 142, 173, 181, 190, 214, 229, 234
model, 22, 27, 33, 41, 45, 55, 87, 146, 149, 170, 198, 232, 233
moment, 1, 4, 131, 144
momentum, 115, 181, 186
money, 71, 72, 107, 217
monitoring, 216

motivation, 181
move, 45, 53, 102, 177, 188, 207, 229
movement, 51, 62, 63, 72, 95, 104, 106, 112, 115, 118, 124, 126, 138, 144, 149, 152, 154, 155, 168, 170, 172, 173, 177, 179, 181, 182, 190, 192, 205, 215, 229, 231
myriad, 21, 208, 246

narrative, 25, 41, 83, 133, 181, 222, 233
nation, 88, 107, 144
nature, 3, 7, 52, 65, 78, 79, 133, 137, 200, 240
necessity, 29, 58, 60, 68, 80, 85, 148, 152, 179, 185
need, 33, 34, 50, 56, 70, 86, 104, 107, 109, 134, 155, 158, 160, 168, 170, 177, 187, 198, 220, 239, 245
neighborhood, 3, 139
nepotism, 88
network, 2, 214
neutrality, 26, 144, 183
news, 2–4, 22, 30, 31, 33, 41, 42, 45–47, 49–51, 58, 197, 198, 205, 206
newspaper, 2
nexus, 61
Niger Delta, 162
Nigeria, 162
notion, 60
nuance, 19
number, 52
numerator, 118

objectivity, 26, 46
obligation, 121, 134, 245
obstacle, 18, 174, 199
off, 213
official, 71
oil, 46, 161, 162, 169
on, 1, 2, 4, 5, 18, 21, 22, 25, 28–31, 33, 35, 37, 40–42, 46, 50, 51, 53, 56, 57, 60, 61, 63, 65, 68, 71, 77, 82, 83, 85–87, 92, 95, 96, 98, 103, 104, 107, 109, 111, 117–121, 124–127, 129, 131, 132, 135, 138–141, 144–147, 155, 158, 161, 163, 168–170, 173, 175, 179, 181, 183, 184, 190–192, 195, 197–199, 202, 204, 207, 210, 211, 214–220, 225, 231–235, 240, 245, 246, 248, 249, 251
one, 24, 25, 27, 55, 61–63, 81, 124, 126, 139, 152, 170, 175, 192, 200, 207, 220, 233, 246
online, 2, 23, 33, 54, 55, 120, 191, 199
opacity, 68
openness, 210, 212
opinion, 174, 202, 204
opportunity, 61, 222
opposition, 162, 231
oppression, 60, 63
organization, 30, 31, 233
organizing, 62, 106, 139, 141, 235
other, 11, 16, 31, 33, 35, 62, 71, 170, 210, 225
outcome, 95

outcry, 51, 92, 169
outlet, 33, 51, 206
outpouring, 58, 62
outrage, 30, 214
outreach, 146
overhaul, 88
oversight, 99–102
ownership, 22, 30, 45, 76, 158, 198, 205

pain, 61
panel, 4
paradigm, 27
paradox, 55
part, 54
participation, 99, 102, 109, 111, 119, 152, 171, 172, 181, 198, 210, 215–218, 220
partner, 146
partnership, 147, 149, 170, 206
passion, 1, 2, 4, 5, 37, 39, 131, 153, 179
past, 185, 192, 246
path, 2, 4, 5, 132
pathway, 152
people, 3, 16, 62, 107, 109, 114, 115, 120, 124, 144, 152, 158, 165, 180–182, 191, 194, 217, 229, 234, 243
perception, 1, 3, 86, 87, 132, 142, 170, 172, 178
peril, 54, 81
period, 152
persecution, 62
perseverance, 38, 231
person, 63
perspective, 5–7
phase, 22
phenomenon, 30, 45, 63, 158, 213

philosophy, 244
phone, 81
phrase, 11
picture, 62
pillar, 60, 197
pipeline, 18, 162
place, 94, 123
plan, 55
planet, 134, 135, 158, 168, 194, 222, 227, 229, 231, 245
planning, 18, 183
platform, 5, 23, 33, 40, 41, 47, 87, 94, 96, 132, 141, 143, 144, 158, 160, 177, 187, 191, 206, 212
play, 96, 115, 142, 161, 199
pluralism, 51, 198
plurality, 205
point, 31, 40, 132
polarization, 216
police, 115
policy, 62, 68, 71, 86, 98, 108, 114, 115, 139, 142, 146, 156, 170, 175, 178, 181, 184, 190, 192, 207, 210, 226
politician, 81
politics, 65, 72, 107, 118, 121, 124, 215, 217, 243
pollution, 25, 138, 139
populace, 93
portion, 71, 86
portrayal, 172
position, 71
potential, 17, 18, 22, 55, 60, 68, 107, 108, 116, 139, 142, 144, 146, 147, 151, 152, 170, 172, 174, 177, 178, 184, 202, 203, 209, 225, 227, 244, 248

poverty, 148
power, 1–5, 12, 14, 25, 31, 40, 48, 49, 53, 54, 57, 60–63, 73, 75, 78, 80, 87, 88, 96, 98, 104, 109, 113, 120–124, 139, 144, 150, 151, 169, 170, 173, 174, 179, 182, 184, 192, 194, 202, 205, 207, 210, 213, 215, 220, 224, 240
practicality, 134
practice, 31, 71, 141, 158, 169, 196
praise, 19
precedence, 198
precedent, 31, 34, 147, 206
premise, 53
presence, 12, 23, 144, 181
present, 19, 47, 133, 158, 188
preservation, 49, 220, 246
press, 55–58, 60, 62, 80, 119
pressure, 30, 120, 139
prestige, 2
prevalence, 71
pricing, 175
principle, 45, 134, 158
privacy, 82
probability, 172
problem, 18, 30, 169
process, 17, 41, 45, 73, 77, 102, 109, 111, 119, 173, 183, 188, 225
procurement, 92
produce, 30, 185, 199
production, 141, 206, 224
profession, 29, 73, 195
professional, 85, 137
profile, 30, 38, 55, 67, 69, 74, 79, 119, 159, 214
profit, 22, 30, 51, 244

program, 2, 125
progress, 148, 221, 243, 245
project, 18, 21, 33, 71, 139, 162
proliferation, 26, 32, 120
prominence, 210
promotion, 33, 41, 50, 212, 246
propaganda, 45
protection, 149, 163, 211
protest, 4
protocol, 41
public, 1, 3, 29–31, 33, 34, 40–42, 45, 47, 51–53, 55, 56, 58, 59, 61, 68, 71, 72, 74–78, 80, 86–88, 92–94, 96–102, 108, 112, 115, 117, 119, 120, 122, 125, 132, 139, 140, 142, 144, 146, 155, 161, 162, 169–172, 174, 177, 179, 182, 185, 190–192, 195, 197–202, 204, 206, 210, 211, 213–218, 222–224, 229, 248–250
publication, 50
purpose, 17, 40, 233, 239
pursuit, 29, 54, 56, 63, 68, 73–75, 85, 87, 93, 118, 121, 123, 127, 139, 152, 161, 217, 231, 251, 252
push, 93, 106, 112, 162, 207, 212, 217
pushback, 22, 148

quality, 71, 87, 139, 198, 199
quest, 73, 145, 147, 197, 246
question, 170, 217, 237, 239
quo, 1, 4, 6, 16, 22, 42, 49, 52, 53, 55, 60, 61, 79, 87, 98, 109,

125, 139, 168, 191, 215, 234, 235

race, 35, 138, 168
radio, 4
range, 96, 116, 184, 185
reach, 17, 23, 76, 235
reaction, 41
reality, 88, 131–133
realization, 3, 132, 246, 251
realm, 73, 142, 197, 237
recognition, 104, 127, 138, 148, 153, 204
recruitment, 17
redefinition, 27
reference, 31
reflection, 29
reform, 2–5, 7, 8, 17, 18, 22, 34, 37, 41, 50, 52, 54, 56, 59–61, 74, 80, 81, 88, 96, 104–109, 113, 115, 118, 119, 126–128, 132, 146, 202, 206–210, 217, 220, 231, 233, 237, 239, 240, 246–248
reformer, 54, 163, 202, 233
region, 162
relationship, 41, 93, 97, 118, 133, 168, 211, 213, 220, 248
release, 211
reliance, 163, 198
reminder, 14, 29, 37, 45, 56, 58, 60, 80, 87, 104, 126, 140, 207, 215, 220, 235, 248
renewable, 126, 162–165, 169, 170, 220–222, 224
renewal, 129, 250
report, 29, 31, 53, 56, 61, 120

reporting, 1, 4, 22, 24, 29–31, 33, 37, 46, 47, 50, 52, 53, 77, 78, 87, 125, 141, 169, 179, 195, 197–199, 202, 206
representation, 1–3, 7, 16, 34, 37, 39, 51, 106, 107, 141, 144, 177, 198, 207, 234, 235, 248
reputation, 19, 139, 169
requirement, 45
research, 18, 97, 138, 139, 214
resignation, 58, 95
resilience, 10, 23, 38, 49, 54, 56, 58, 61, 63, 80, 83–85, 113, 126, 139, 149, 173, 175, 180, 182, 184, 185, 188, 194, 200, 225, 227, 231–233, 241
resistance, 22, 41, 139, 174, 222
resolution, 18, 59
resolve, 2, 9, 21, 60, 62
resource, 155, 162
response, 14, 15, 41, 42, 55, 62, 77, 78, 88, 106, 114, 143, 207, 217, 222
responsibility, 2, 76, 95, 115, 138, 152, 162, 168, 170, 210, 217, 234, 243
responsiveness, 201
result, 31, 51, 53, 116, 161
retaliation, 78, 80
retribution, 94
return, 71
revelation, 4, 169
revenue, 22, 46, 198, 199
review, 86
revitalization, 197
revolution, 198
reward, 71

Richard Nixon, 58
right, 45, 63, 93, 138, 168, 183
rise, 3, 4, 30, 42, 87, 114, 115, 141, 158, 181, 198, 211, 216, 217, 224, 234, 246
risk, 30, 93
roadmap, 158, 233
Robert Bullard, 138
role, 1, 3, 4, 34, 47, 49, 56, 57, 60, 68, 73, 75, 77, 78, 87, 93, 96, 104, 115, 118, 120, 125, 126, 132, 142, 146, 147, 152, 153, 160, 161, 175, 177–181, 188, 195, 197–200, 202, 204, 207, 212, 213, 218, 224, 232, 233, 246, 249, 250
root, 194

s, 2–7, 12–16, 18–20, 22, 23, 28–31, 33–37, 39–42, 44, 45, 50–56, 58–63, 68–70, 72–78, 81, 83–88, 92–99, 103, 104, 106, 109, 111–114, 116, 118–129, 131, 132, 137–139, 143, 144, 146, 147, 149, 152, 153, 155–158, 160, 162, 163, 165, 167–170, 172, 174, 175, 177–185, 187, 188, 190–199, 201, 202, 204–207, 211–220, 222, 227–229, 231–235, 237, 239, 240, 243, 245–251
safeguard, 30, 86
safety, 54, 55, 97
Samarco, 161
Saudi Arabia, 174
scale, 25, 251

scandal, 30, 31, 53, 58, 72, 214
scenario, 30, 169
school, 1, 2, 115, 234
science, 175
scope, 181
score, 117
scrutiny, 33, 58, 96, 118, 169, 212
sea, 25, 131
secrecy, 93, 96, 211
section, 5, 17, 22, 31, 37, 40, 42, 47, 50, 54, 65, 73, 78, 81, 83, 86, 93, 99, 109, 112, 121, 124, 133, 137, 140, 147, 149, 152, 161, 168, 173, 178, 180, 190, 192, 200, 212, 218, 220, 227, 232, 233, 251
sector, 168, 169
security, 55
seeking, 18, 22, 37, 39, 63, 81, 147, 170, 199, 204
segment, 25, 41, 51
self, 53, 54, 63, 131, 213
sensationalism, 14, 22, 30, 87, 198, 199
sense, 17, 18, 22, 23, 41, 51, 63, 76, 77, 115, 131, 138, 233, 234, 243
sensitivity, 133
series, 2, 51, 53, 78, 92, 95, 169, 240
serve, 14, 58, 87, 93, 126, 143, 146, 149, 160, 170, 192, 202, 207, 231, 233
service, 29, 115
set, 4, 17, 24, 34, 41, 45, 132, 147, 206
setting, 2
shadow, 131
share, 23, 41, 52, 94, 141, 198, 212

sharing, 25, 125, 226
shield, 58
shift, 27, 29, 41, 86, 87, 114, 115, 118, 143, 181, 185, 188, 197, 200, 215, 239, 250
shooting, 115
show, 18, 19, 21–23, 51, 56, 141, 144
silence, 53, 55, 61, 81, 82, 125, 199
skepticism, 2, 12, 18, 19, 41, 75, 86
smear, 22, 53, 61, 82, 169
society, 5, 14, 29, 31, 34, 35, 37, 40, 45, 49, 51, 52, 54, 58, 62, 75, 80, 82, 88, 96, 111, 113, 118, 120, 124, 188, 194, 200, 202, 205, 207, 210, 212, 215, 217, 220, 225, 239, 243, 244, 246, 248, 251
socio, 5, 222, 225
sociology, 121
soil, 161
solace, 56
solidarity, 51, 54, 56, 58–60, 62, 82, 147–152, 155, 184, 252
solving, 18
sophomore, 131
soul, 109
source, 19, 30, 45, 50, 62, 82, 202
sovereignty, 148
space, 206
speaking, 55, 125, 191
speed, 30, 31
sphere, 195, 248
spill, 46
spirit, 22, 61, 109, 235, 241, 246
spotlight, 96
spread, 19, 30, 33, 41, 82, 206
Springfield, 72

sprint, 231
stability, 163
stage, 2, 24
stake, 76
stand, 63, 109
standard, 41, 45
state, 86
station, 4
status, 1, 4, 6, 16, 22, 35, 42, 49, 52, 53, 55, 60, 61, 79, 87, 98, 109, 125, 138, 139, 168, 183, 191, 215, 234, 235
step, 181
stewardship, 147, 240, 241, 243, 246
stone, 38
storm, 54
story, 25, 41, 58, 61, 63, 80, 85, 140, 233, 235
storytelling, 2, 22, 25, 141, 177
strategy, 22, 23, 33, 53, 147, 214, 225
streaming, 23
strength, 18, 82, 83
strengthen, 2, 119, 167
stress, 55, 83
strike, 171
structure, 125
struggle, 12, 56, 58, 60, 80, 87, 96, 98, 109, 120, 129, 169, 188, 199, 207, 231–233, 251
Stuart Hall, 2
study, 115
subject, 33
subscription, 197
subsection, 56, 68, 75, 116, 165, 188, 222, 243
substance, 14
success, 75, 101, 114, 125, 180, 224

summary, 2, 118, 147, 170, 175, 177, 184, 192, 235
supply, 162
support, 51, 54, 56, 58, 60–63, 75, 76, 78, 80, 82, 85, 98, 99, 149, 152, 184, 199, 205, 227, 251
surge, 4, 86, 181
survival, 22, 133
susceptibility, 225
sustainability, 156, 158, 160, 161, 163, 169, 170, 174, 182, 184, 185, 192, 222, 224, 225, 227, 229, 243
sword, 177
symbol, 63, 233
synergy, 145
synthesis, 7
system, 87, 108, 129, 215, 225, 248

tactic, 53
take, 62, 113, 126, 158, 181, 191, 192, 217, 231
tale, 56
talent, 17
tandem, 149
tapestry, 3, 19
target, 54, 61
teaching, 239
team, 2, 17–20, 23, 30–32, 42, 51, 53, 61, 65, 206, 214
tech, 23, 33
technology, 4, 22, 33, 34, 157, 198, 216, 241, 243, 244, 246, 247
telling, 29, 87
temperature, 174
tenacity, 22, 73
tenet, 93

tension, 41
term, 50, 86, 87, 118–120, 126, 146, 161, 185, 219, 222, 224, 231, 234
testament, 14, 54, 60, 61, 75, 87, 126, 139, 144, 168, 182, 192, 231, 233, 240
The City of New York's, 211
the City of San Francisco, 183
the Doce River, 161
the United States, 114, 174
theory, 2, 29, 45, 51, 53, 61, 63, 114, 118, 121, 138, 163, 168, 179, 198, 213, 217, 218, 225, 249
thinking, 1, 38, 115, 126, 139, 191, 234, 235, 237–239, 243
thought, 198
threat, 19, 30, 31, 40, 45, 53, 55, 56, 60–62, 133, 171
time, 4, 23, 33, 50, 114, 117, 126, 135, 141, 229, 237, 241
today, 52, 83, 111, 135, 229
toll, 55
tomorrow, 31, 40, 111, 246
tool, 2, 33, 54, 60, 77, 140, 146, 152, 177
topic, 107
torch, 140, 241
town, 1, 170
traction, 18, 61, 234
tragedy, 83
training, 30
trait, 84, 85
trajectory, 116, 124, 126, 190
transaction, 71
transformation, 170, 197, 248–250
transition, 163, 165, 185, 188, 220–222

transparency, 4, 23, 27, 29, 31, 33,
    41–45, 49, 50, 53, 56, 58,
    68, 70, 72, 73, 75, 76, 78,
    83, 86, 87, 92, 93, 96–99,
    102, 104, 106, 109, 113,
    114, 116–120, 127, 128,
    141, 158, 160, 168, 169,
    182, 185, 195, 198, 199,
    202, 207, 210–213,
    215–218, 220, 240, 243,
    248, 251
transportation, 185
trauma, 83, 148
trend, 76, 88, 185, 197, 222
trespassing, 172
trip, 131
triumph, 61
trust, 18, 23, 30, 31, 41, 42, 45, 50,
    68, 71, 72, 75–78, 86, 88,
    96, 102, 195, 200, 202,
    206, 210, 211, 213, 216,
    248
trustworthiness, 200
truth, 14, 29, 31, 37, 39, 47, 50–52,
    54, 56, 58, 62, 63, 68, 71,
    73–75, 81–83, 85, 87,
    118, 121, 124, 207, 234
truthfulness, 201
turn, 146
turning, 40, 61, 132
type, 67

underpinning, 73, 109, 152, 180,
    222
underrepresentation, 51
understanding, 3, 5, 35, 47, 51, 60,
    121, 131–133, 140, 155,
    227, 251
unity, 147, 149

university, 38
unrest, 162
up, 1, 3, 40, 42, 62, 63, 76, 131, 138,
    191, 207
urgency, 47, 131–133, 135, 138,
    140, 152, 163, 165, 235
use, 9, 54, 120, 161, 204, 235, 241
utilitarianism, 29

value, 71
variety, 105, 146, 198
verification, 30, 33, 50
viability, 48
victory, 139
video, 14
view, 53, 61, 172, 181
viewer, 23
vigilance, 34, 68, 80, 98, 118, 215
village, 131
violence, 55, 115
visibility, 23, 51, 95, 152, 181, 234
vision, 5, 14, 15, 17, 18, 21–23, 28,
    31, 34, 39, 40, 63, 129,
    155–158, 165, 184,
    192–194, 207, 220,
    227–229, 239, 243, 245,
    246
voice, 3, 4, 31, 40, 81, 82, 111, 124,
    126, 135, 143, 144, 169,
    194, 202, 232, 235, 246
voter, 109–111, 218
vulnerability, 199, 225

wake, 51, 78, 88, 104, 112, 113, 119,
    121, 171, 195, 197, 210,
    215, 248
warfare, 55
warming, 174, 184
warning, 62

waste, 25, 138, 139, 161
watchdog, 87, 118, 120, 202
water, 149, 161, 162
wave, 104, 248
way, 14, 31, 42, 87, 96, 168, 184, 194, 210, 222, 225, 248
wealth, 109, 162, 211
weapon, 81
web, 68, 71, 81
well, 30, 76, 83, 86, 152, 158, 174, 184, 215
whistleblower, 94–96
whistleblowing, 95, 96
whole, 29, 215
wildfire, 82
will, 5, 30, 49, 58, 75, 85, 99, 107, 109, 119, 120, 124, 126, 129, 133, 155, 161, 179, 182, 190, 192, 194, 197, 199, 202, 204, 212, 218, 231, 233, 243, 251
willingness, 61, 210
wind, 164, 170, 224
woman, 2, 234

work, 2, 7, 42, 45, 50, 52, 53, 55, 56, 58, 61, 63, 68, 69, 73, 75, 78, 81, 86, 87, 103, 113, 116, 118, 119, 122, 125, 126, 133, 138, 140, 141, 152, 158, 168–170, 181, 184, 185, 187, 200, 218, 219, 231, 246
working, 47, 55
workshop, 38
world, 1, 3, 5, 7, 37, 45, 49, 52, 56, 62, 63, 73, 85, 109, 112, 115, 116, 121, 131, 135, 144, 149, 150, 155, 158, 165, 170, 173, 192, 194, 212, 220, 227, 229, 231, 233, 235, 241, 243, 246, 252
worldview, 1, 131

year, 131
youth, 115, 144, 149, 152–155, 158, 168, 174, 181, 182, 188, 190, 191, 217, 234, 235